Eighties Spotting Days
Back to the Ashes

Strathwood

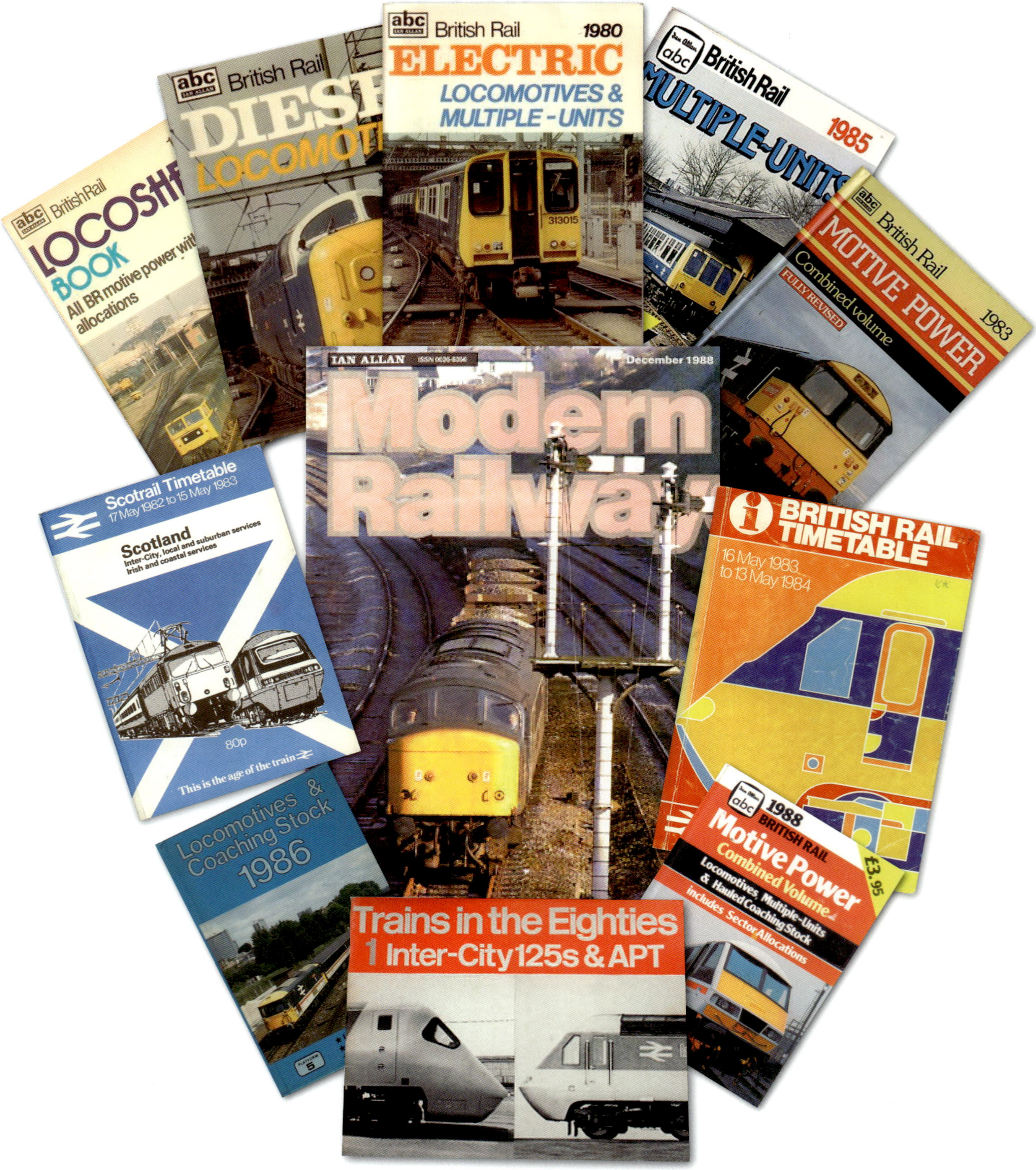
abc British Rail
LOCOSHED BOOK
All BR motive power with allocations
abc Ian Allan British Rail
DIESEL LOCOMOTIVES
abc Ian Allan British Rail 1980
ELECTRIC
LOCOMOTIVES & MULTIPLE-UNITS
313015
Ian Allan abc British Rail
MULTIPLE-UNITS
1985
abc British Rail
MOTIVE POWER
Combined volume
FULLY REVISED
1983
IAN ALLAN ISSN 0026-8356
December 1988
Modern Railways
Scotrail Timetable
17 May 1982 to 15 May 1983
Scotland
Inter-City, local and suburban services
Irish and coastal services
80p
This is the age of the train
BRITISH RAIL TIMETABLE
16 May 1983 to 13 May 1984
Locomotives & Coaching Stock 1986
Ian Allan abc 1988 BRITISH RAIL
Motive Power
Combined Volume
Locomotives, Multiple-Units & Hauled Coaching Stock
includes Sector Allocations
£3.95
Trains in the Eighties
1 Inter-City 125s & APT

Eighties Spotting Days
Back to the Ashes

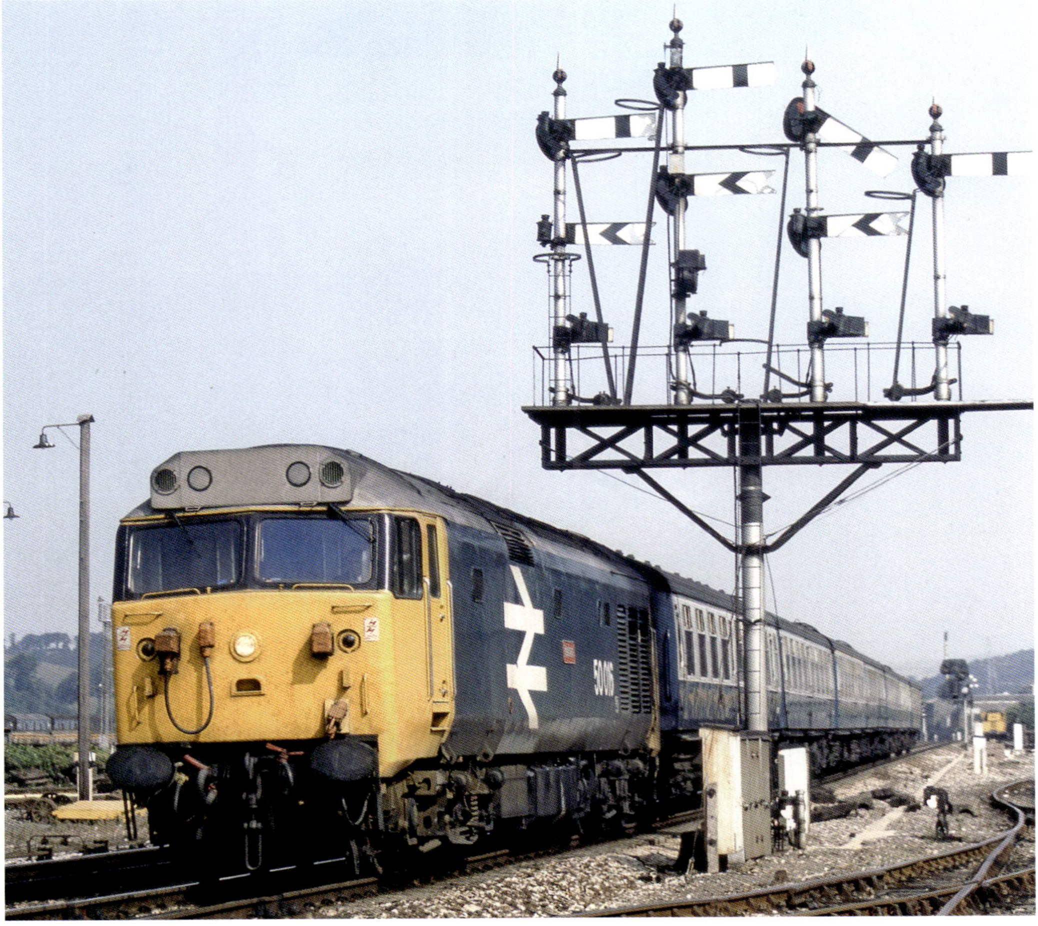

Cover: A splendid array of signals greet the arrival of 50016 Barham in Exeter St. Davids with a Cardiff to Paignton service on 18 August 1984. ***Rail Photoprints/John Chalcroft***

Kevin Derrick

Strathwood

Eighties Spotting Days
Back to the Ashes

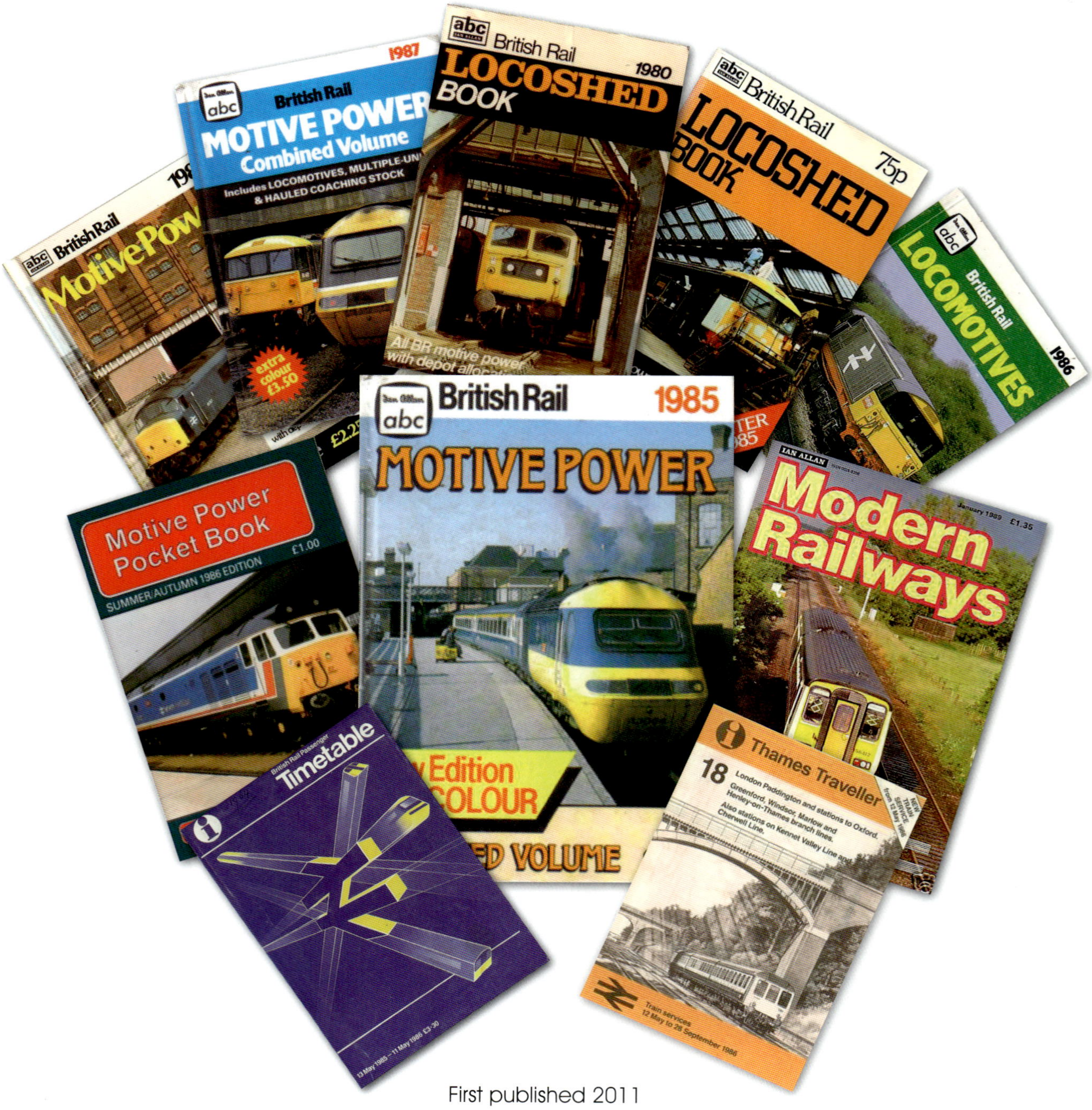

First published 2011

ISBN 1-905276-54-0
ISBN 978-1-905276-54-7

Published by Strathwood Ltd, Glenavon House, Kinchurdy Road, Boat of Garten, Inverness-shire, PH24 3BP. Tel 01479 831139

Proudly printed with the United Kingdom

Contents **Page**

Introduction

The first of the Eighties Spotting Days books entitled Out of the Ashes was more put together as a suitable platform to exhibit some of the wonderful colour images that had been kindly submitted to Strathwood for possible publication. Its release coincided with the television success of the series Ashes to Ashes and seems to have struck a chord with many who were lineside throughout the 1980s.

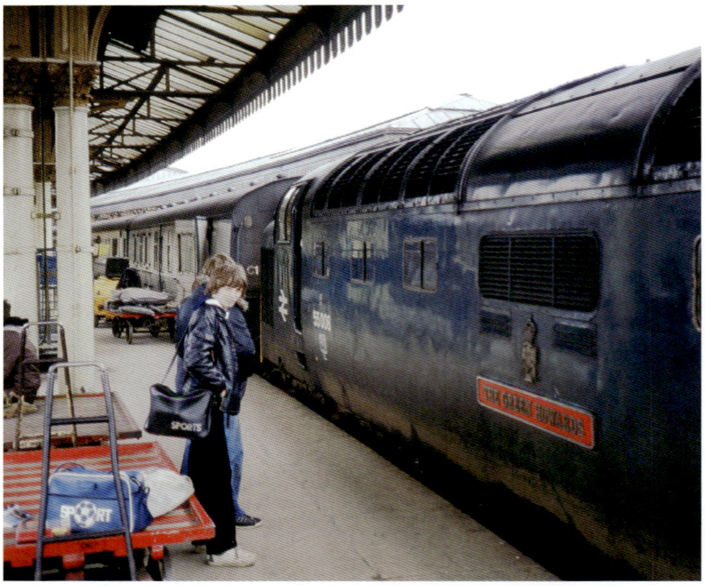

These young lads from 11 April 1980 at York seen watching 55008 The Green Howards would be into their forties now as they read this. ***Ken Gambles***

That success of the first volume which had almost sold out at the time I was drafted this volume which is what has prompted this further selection of images entitled Back to the Ashes, perhaps as the with those Back to the Future films starring Michael J. Fox from the eighties which went on to become a trilogy, then so might the Eighties Spotting Days as well.

One of the fortunate aspects of more recent times is the larger number of photographic collections from which to trawl and the improved quality of filmstocks, cameras and through the magazines a greater awareness of composition.

I have attempted to include shots that portray people and places to bring life to views that in so many cases are today unrecognisable were one to go back to the present and visit them once again. I make no excuse for including another selection of Deltics as whilst they are among my favourites, I know that many of my readers likewise have a soft spot for them too.

So lets imagine our time machine and drift back once more to the 1980s for another wallow in railways and nostalgia of the time.

Kevin Derrick
Boat of Garten 2011

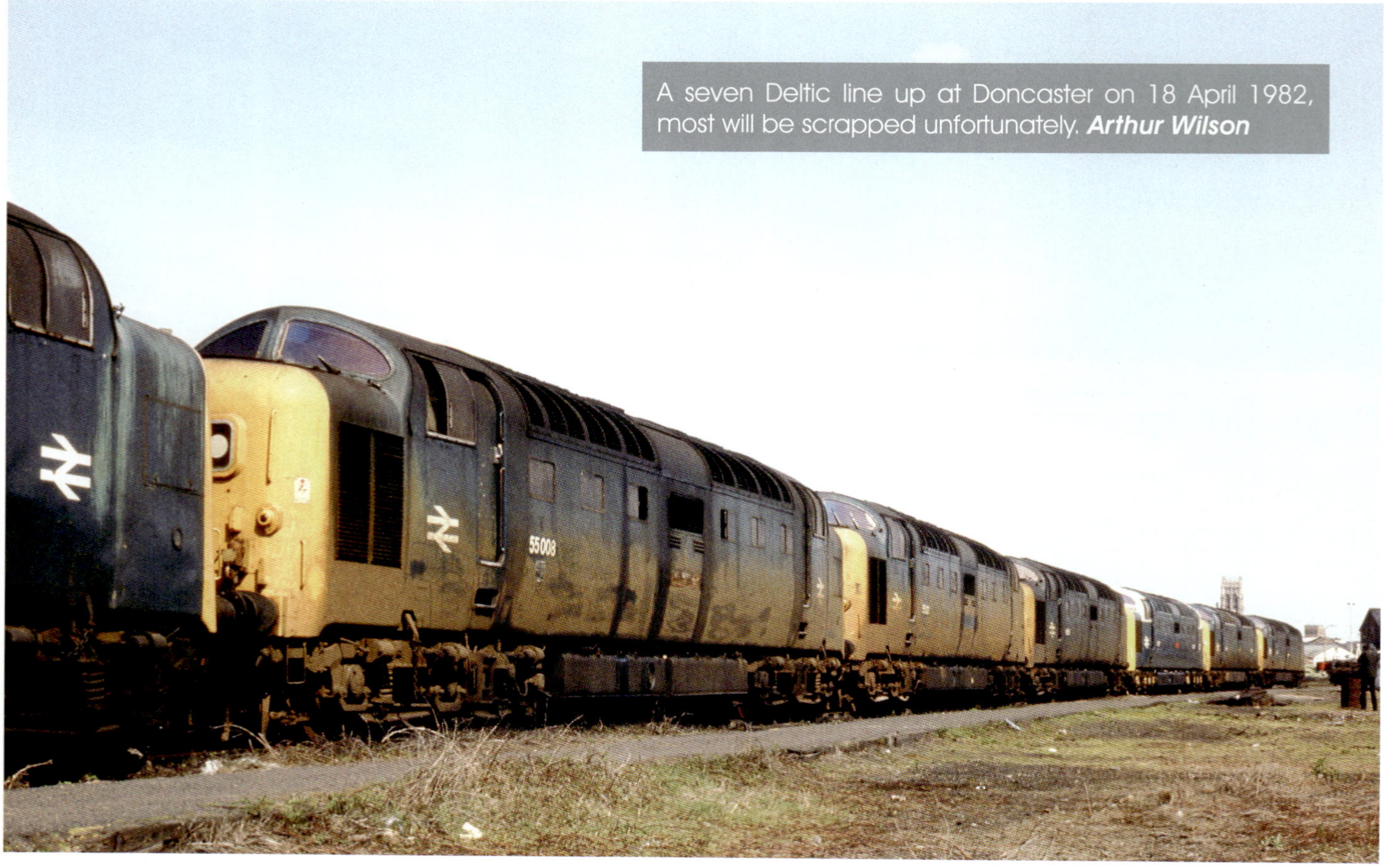

A seven Deltic line up at Doncaster on 18 April 1982, most will be scrapped unfortunately. ***Arthur Wilson***

Signalling the Lines

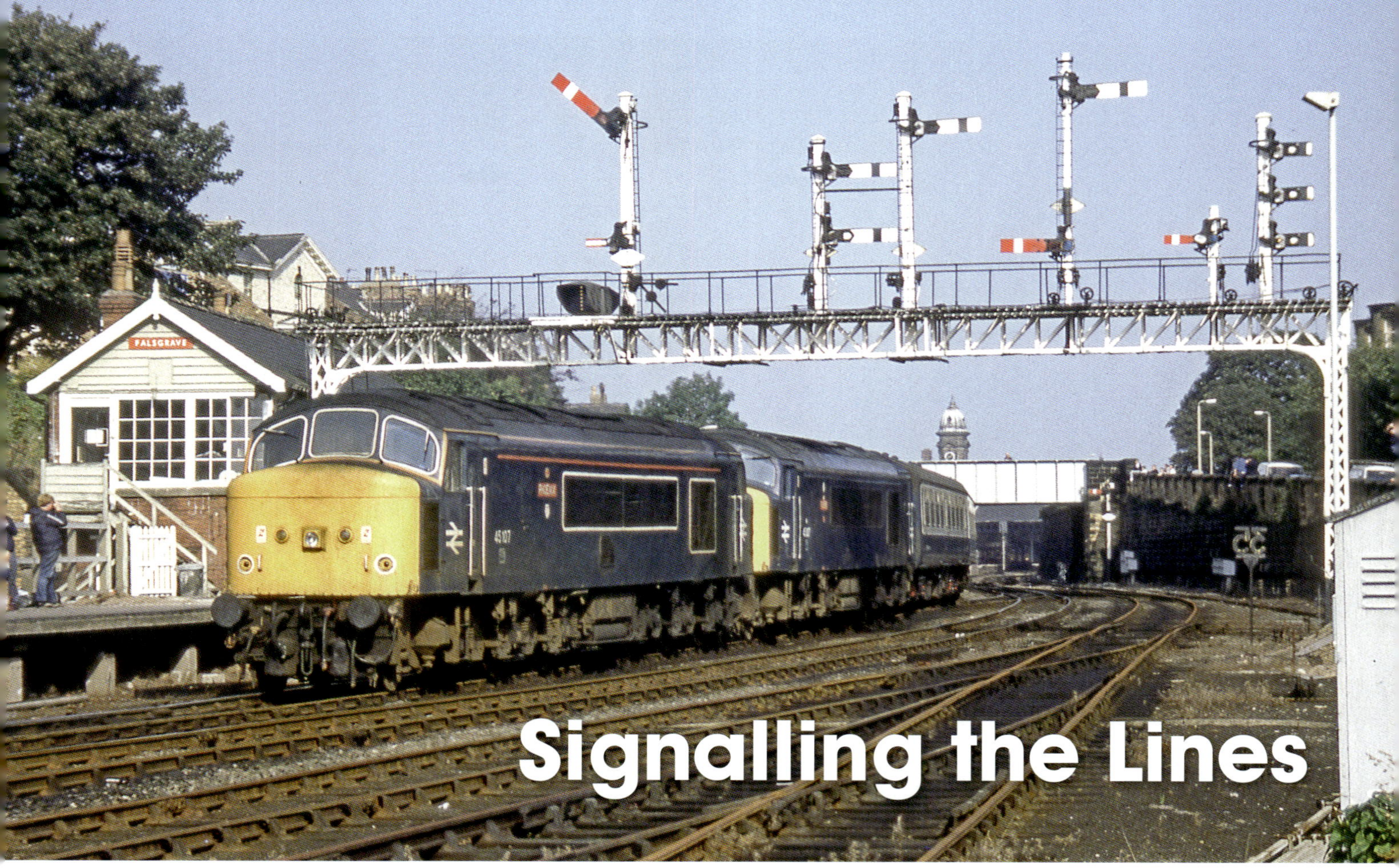

Pathfinder's Class 45 Finale tour waits outside Falsgrave Signal Box at Scarborough with twin Peaks 45007 Taliesen and 45107 Pheonix in charge on 3 October 1987. ***Rail Photoprints/John Chalcroft***

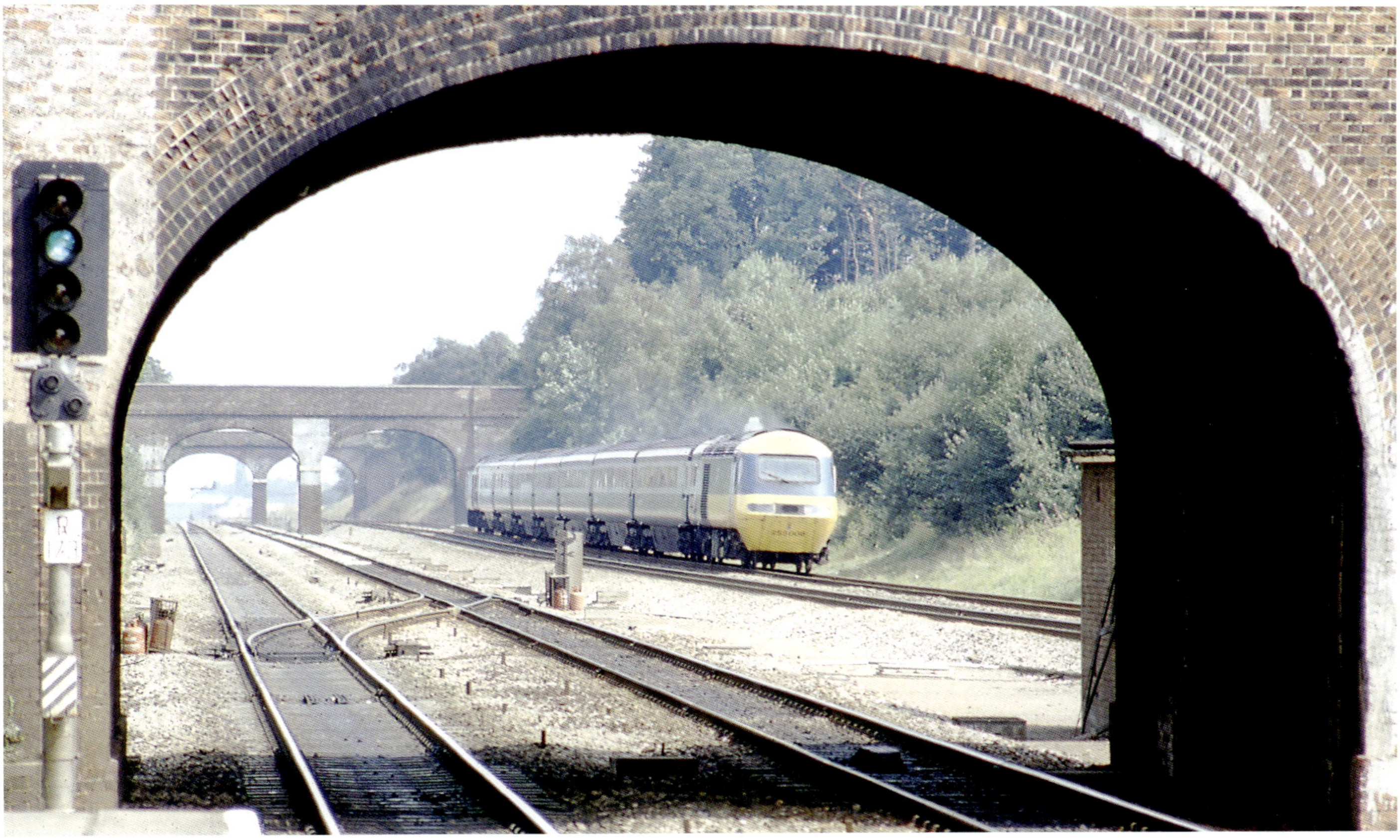

Running fast under clear signals with a down HST service for Bristol on 21 August 1981 through Twyford was 253009. Making a much longer journey was the spacecraft Voyager 2 launched on 20 August four years earlier was now making its closest approach to Saturn, passing within 41,000 kilometers of the ringed planet. Voyager 2 had reached Jupiter during 1979, and would go on to pass by Uranus in 1986 and as far as Neptune by 1989. ***John Arthur Bennett/Strathwood Library Collection***

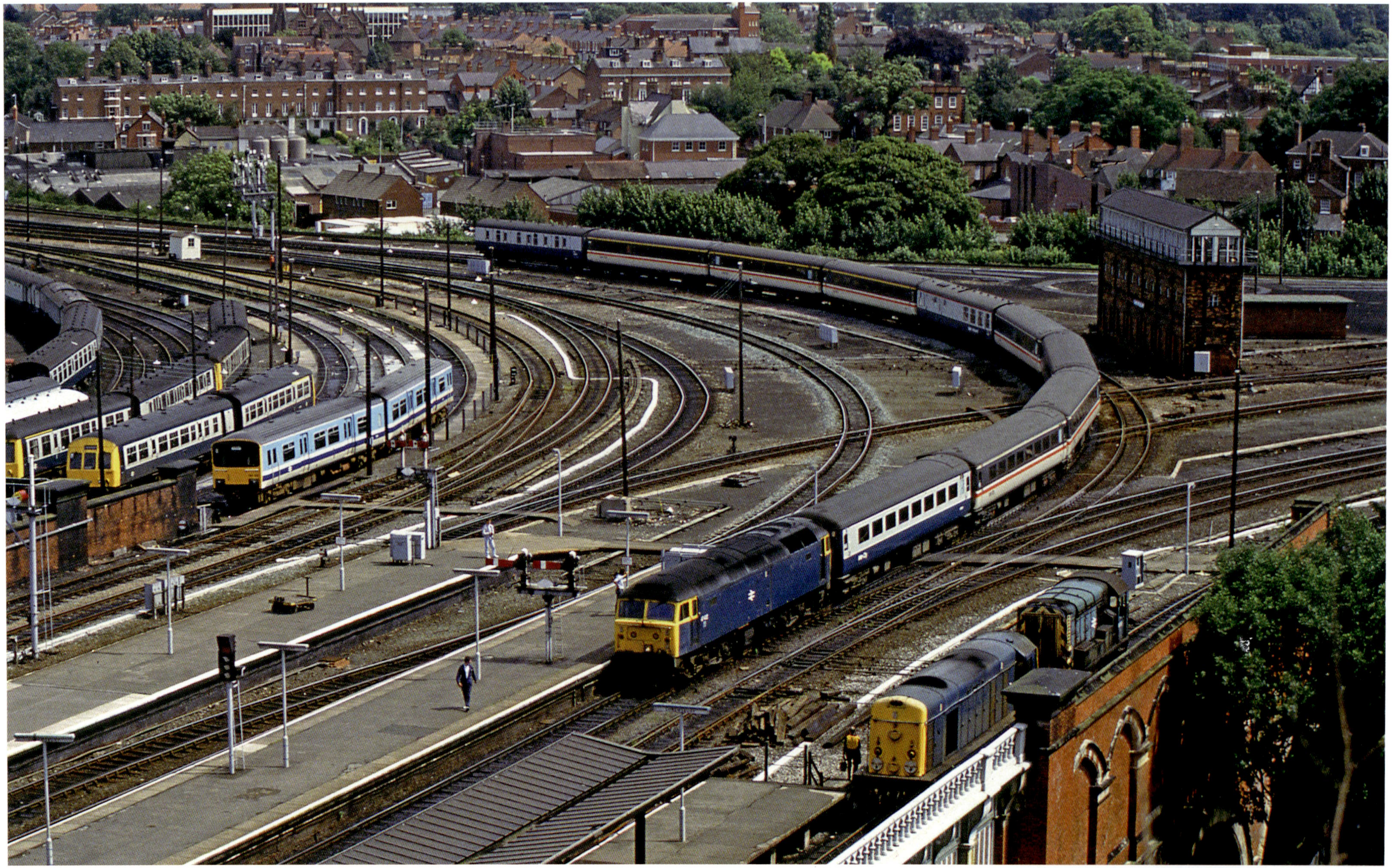

On 11 July 1987 47432 drifted around the curves into Shrewsbury station with the stock for a service to Euston, in the bay 20026 keeps company with an 08 shunter. Also on this day for the first time in history the world's population exceeded 5 billion when the UN Secretary General proclaimed the infant Matej Gasper born today as the 5 billionth person on earth. Ironically perhaps but the top grossing film of the year was Three Men and a Baby! ***Rail Photoprints/John Chalcroft***

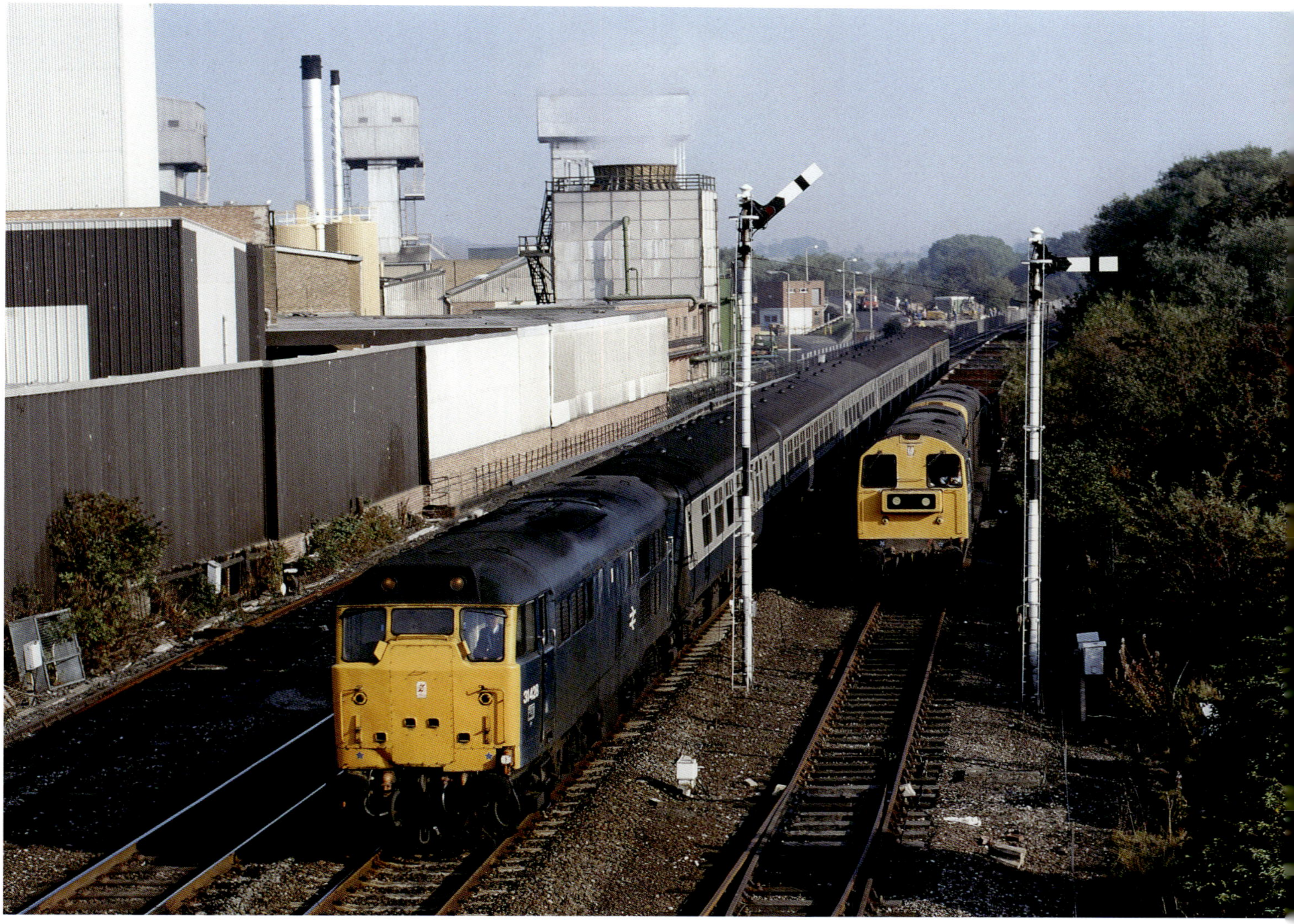

Class 20s 20165 and 20167 wait patiently at the signal in the loop at Melton Mowbray for 31428 to pass with a Norwich to Birmingham service on 25 October 1985. ***Rail Photoprints/John Chalcroft***

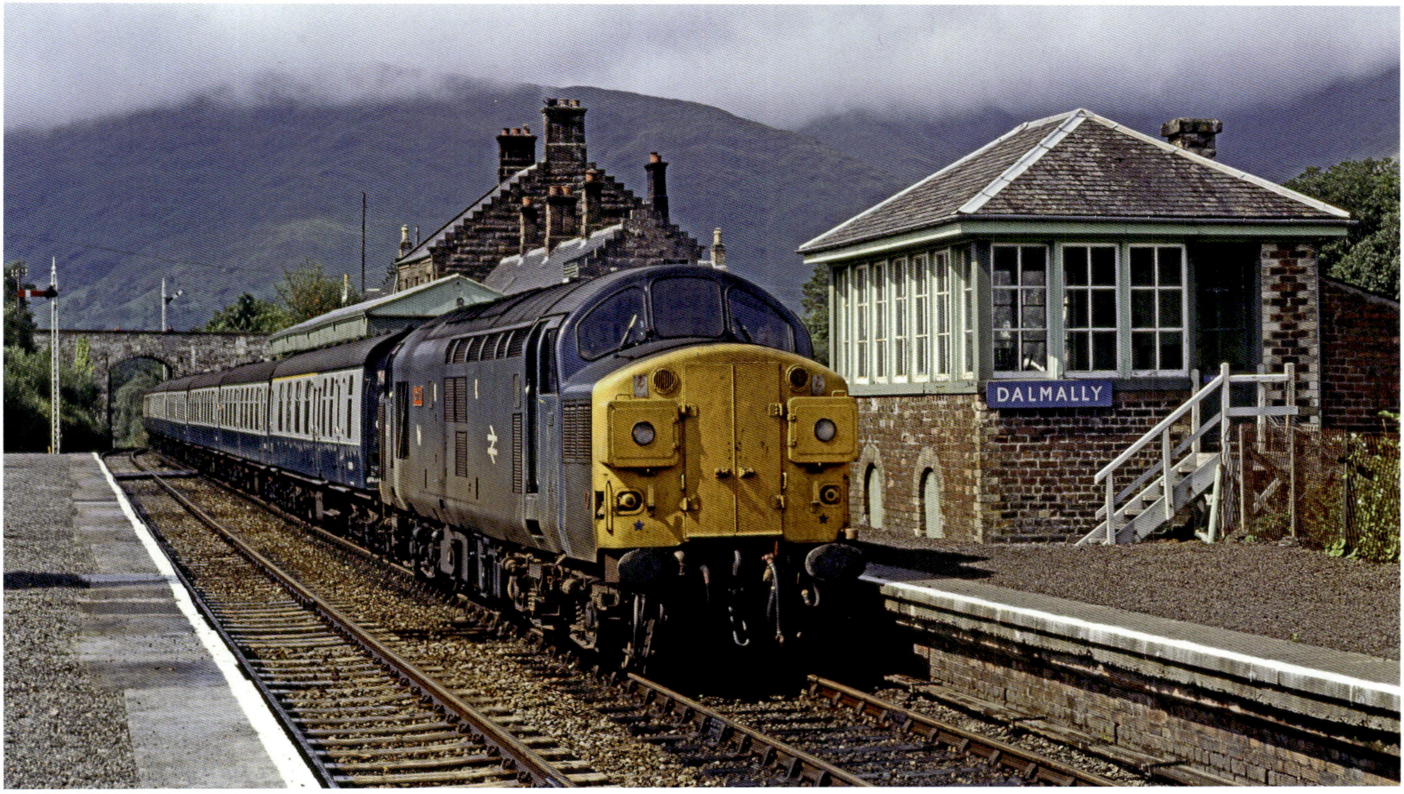

No radio signalling just yet, only the semaphores at Dalmally on 12 August 1982 as 37027 arrives with the 12.25 Oban to Glasgow Queen Street service. ***Rail Photoprints/John Chalcroft***

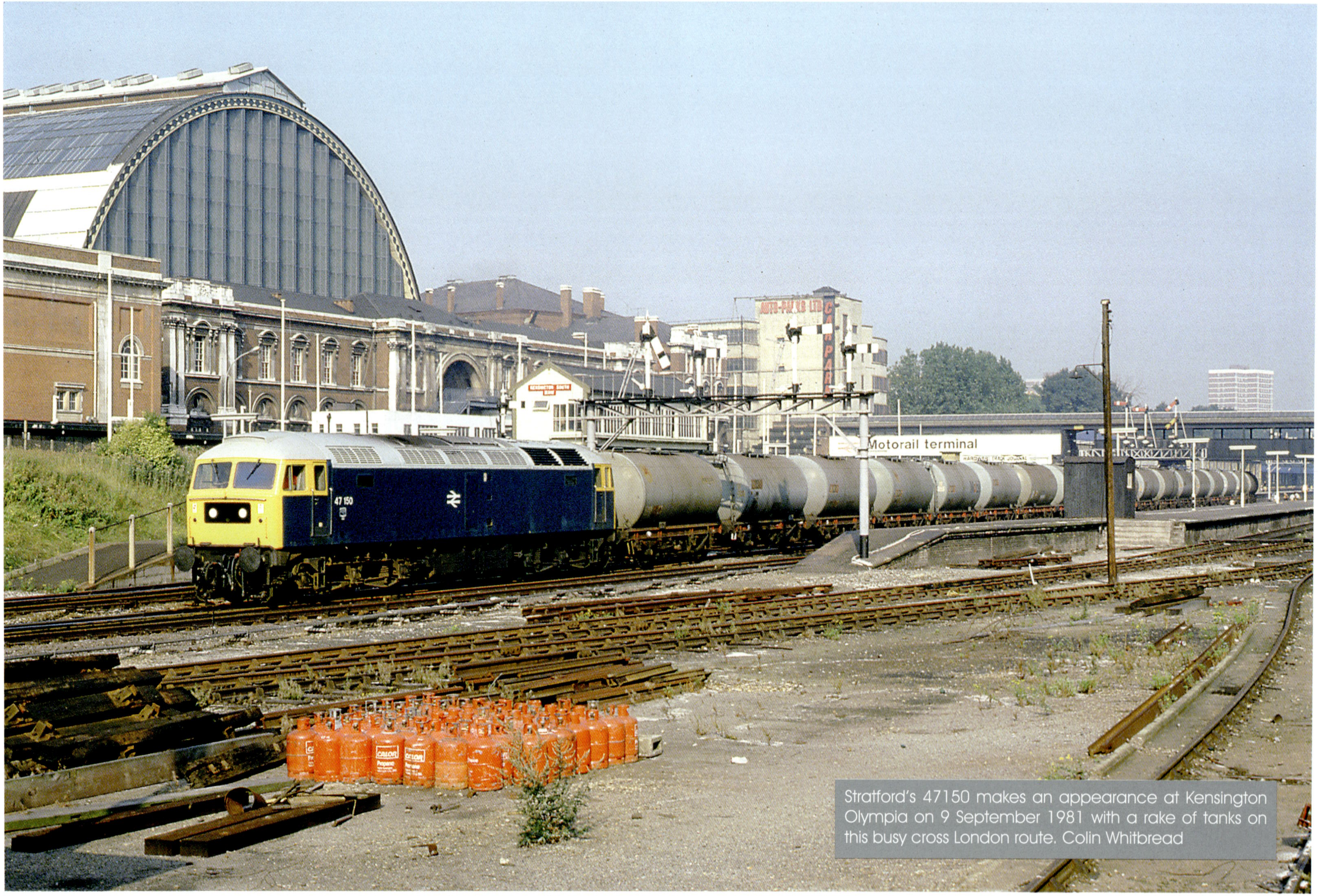

Stratford's 47150 makes an appearance at Kensington Olympia on 9 September 1981 with a rake of tanks on this busy cross London route. Colin Whitbread

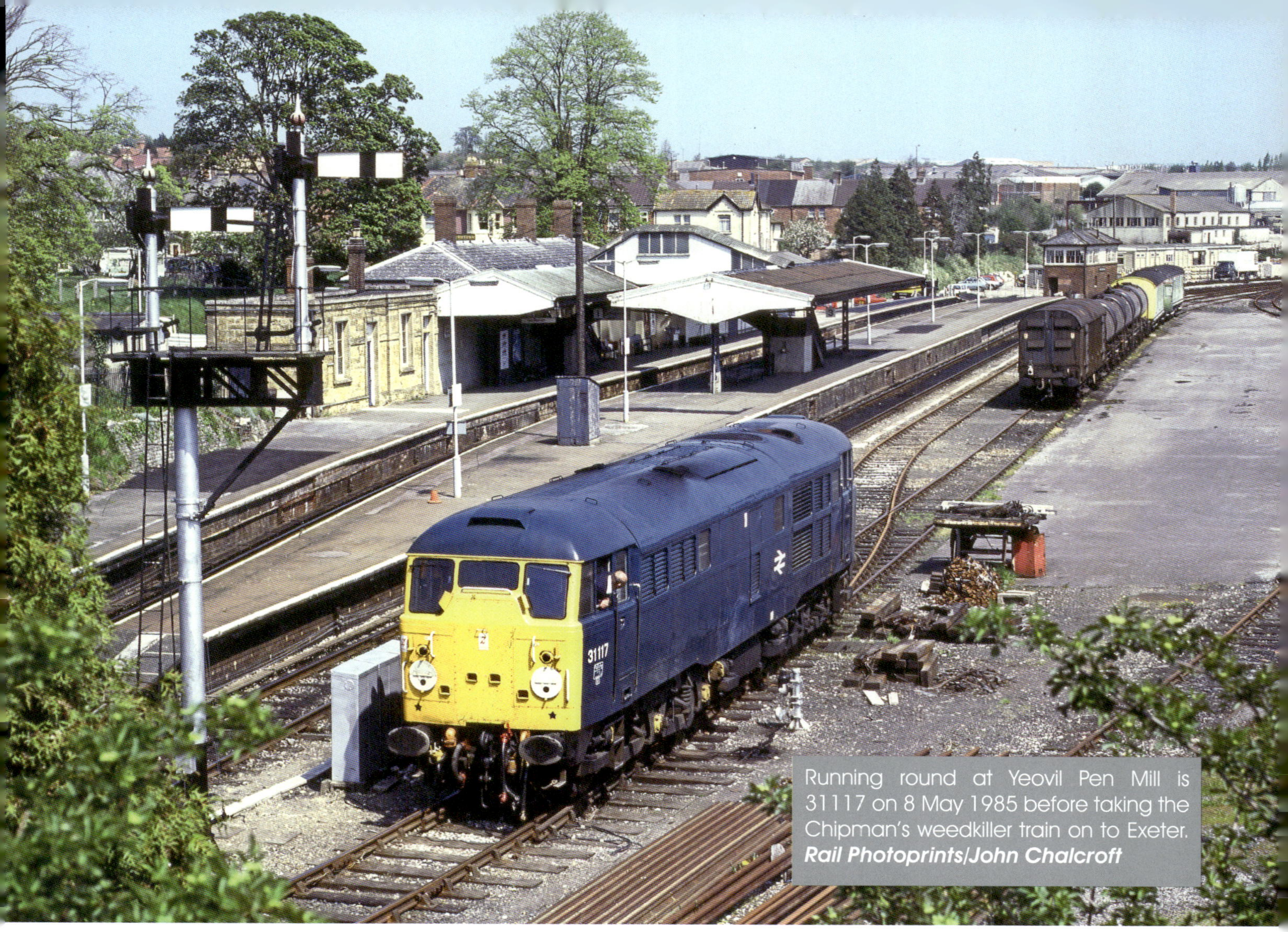

Running round at Yeovil Pen Mill is 31117 on 8 May 1985 before taking the Chipman's weedkiller train on to Exeter. ***Rail Photoprints/John Chalcroft***

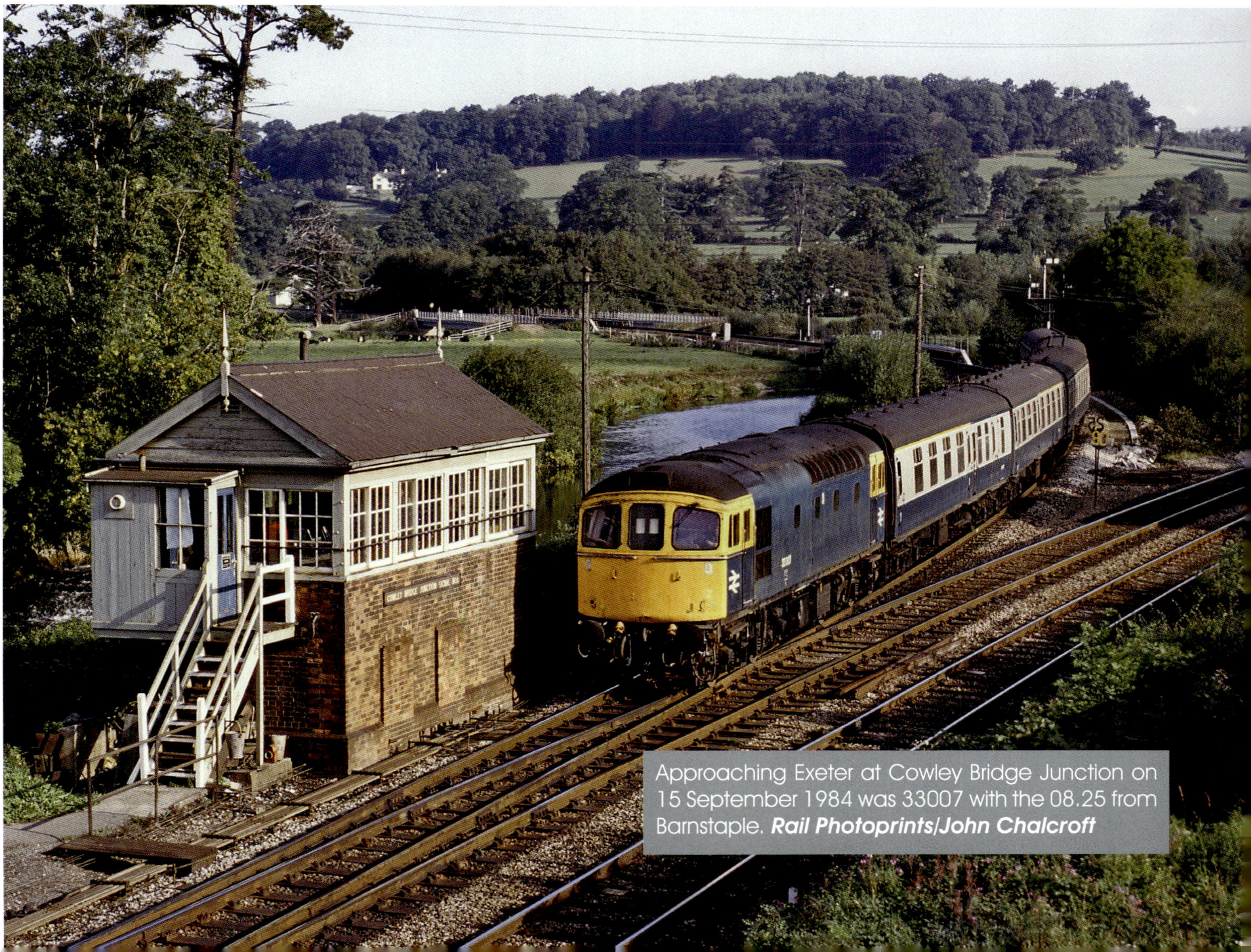

Approaching Exeter at Cowley Bridge Junction on 15 September 1984 was 33007 with the 08.25 from Barnstaple. ***Rail Photoprints/John Chalcroft***

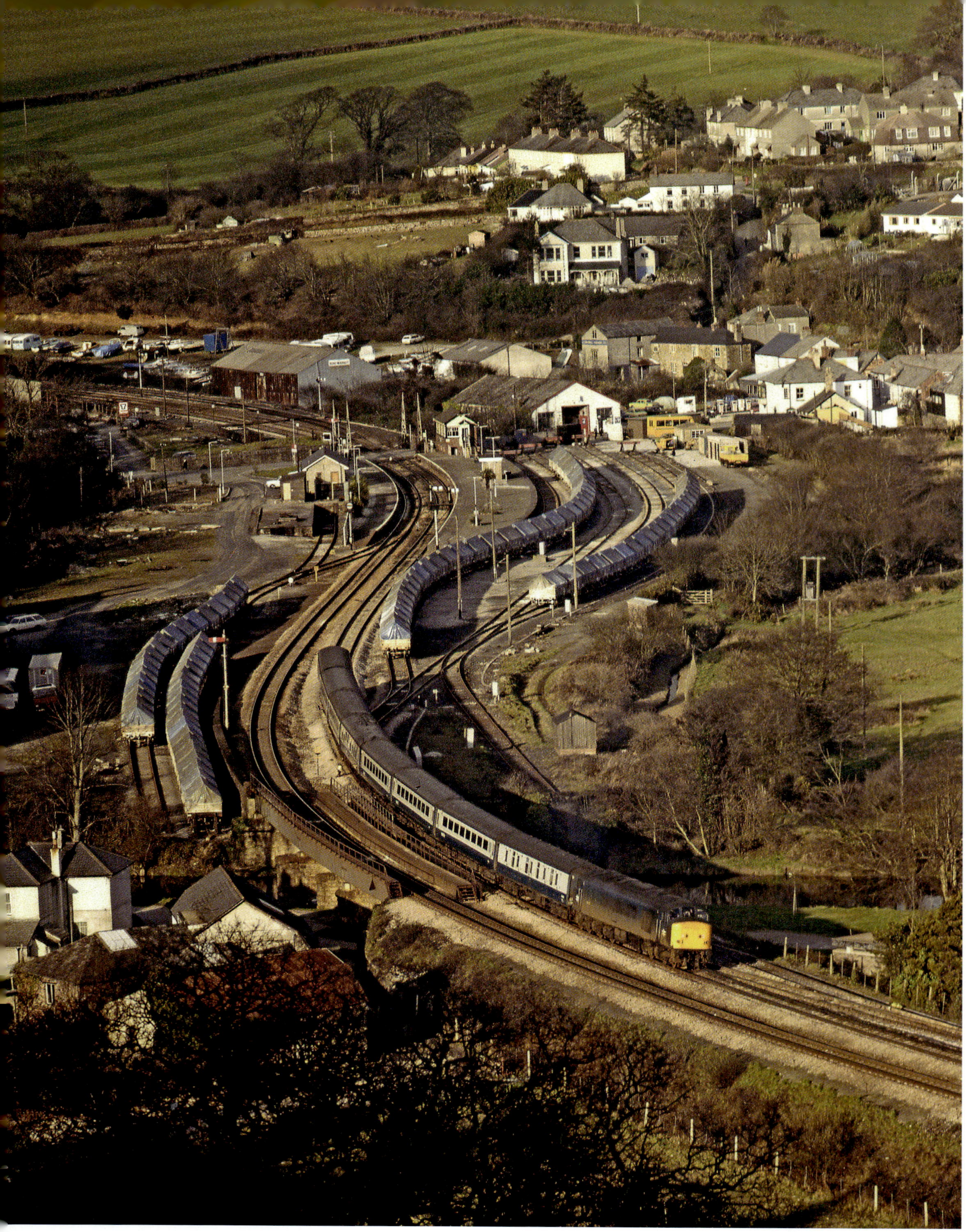

A delightful sweep across Lostwithiel on 1 March 1984 shows the extensive layout controlled from the signal box at the far end of the down platform as a Class 45/1 Peak heads the 09.20 Liverpool to Penzance westwards. A fortnight previously we had all seen Jayne Torvill and her partner Christopher Dean crowned as the Olympic ice skating champions after scooping gold in Sarajevo, Yugoslavia. More than 24 million of us watched the couple score maximum points for their slow, sensuous free dance performance of Ravel's Bolero. ***Rail Photoprints/John Chalcroft***

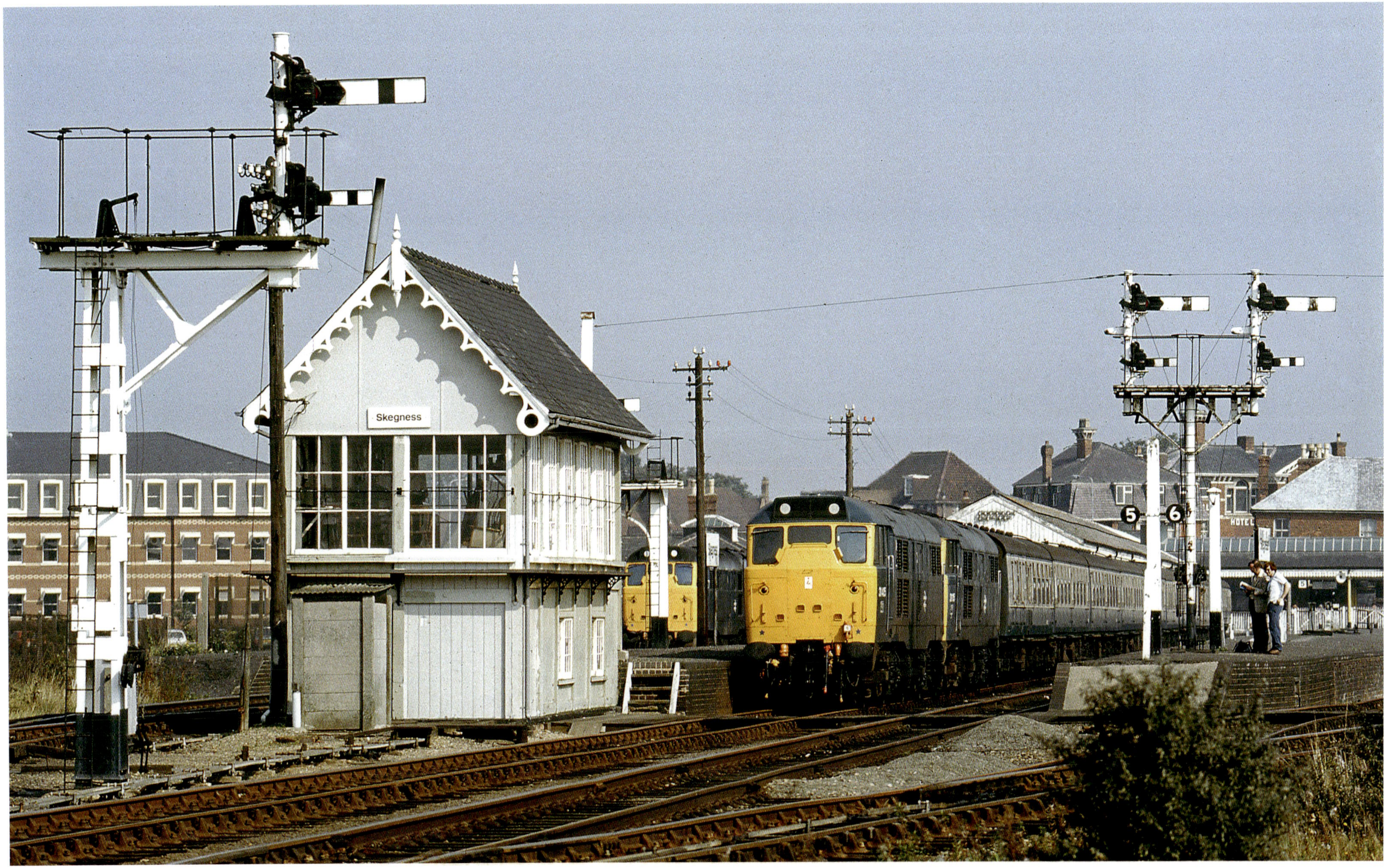

Famous through the years for being ever so bracing is Skegness, and during this decade among railway enthusiasts for its locomotive hauled holidaymaker trains as well. Typified here with 31415 leading 31115 as they await the signal in the sunshine to head off with a summer saturdays only service to Derby on 18 September 1982. ***Rail Photoprints/John Chalcroft***

Snow Worries

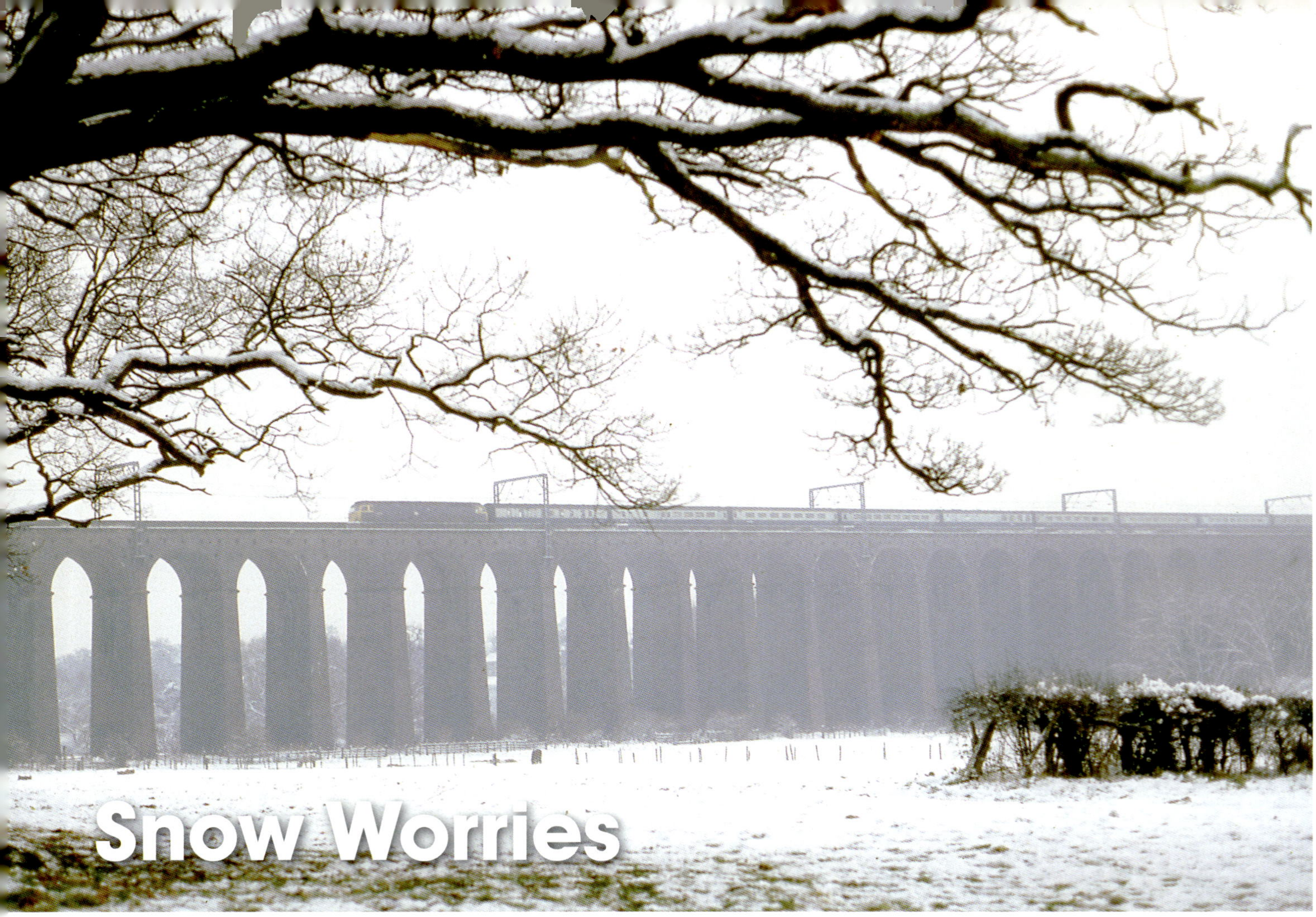

A Class 47 takes the 14.03 Kings Cross to York across Welwyn's viaduct on 9 December 1981. ***Colin Whitbread***

Three days later and the snow still lays on the ground at Gloucester as 50017 Royal Oak makes its stop for at least one freezing passenger. ***Gilroy A. Kerr***

Opposite: Kicking up large quantities of powdery snow on 10 February 1985 was 31305 as the Class 31 stormed out of Box Tunnel with the Birmingham to Bristol empty vans. ***Rail Photoprints/John Chalcroft***

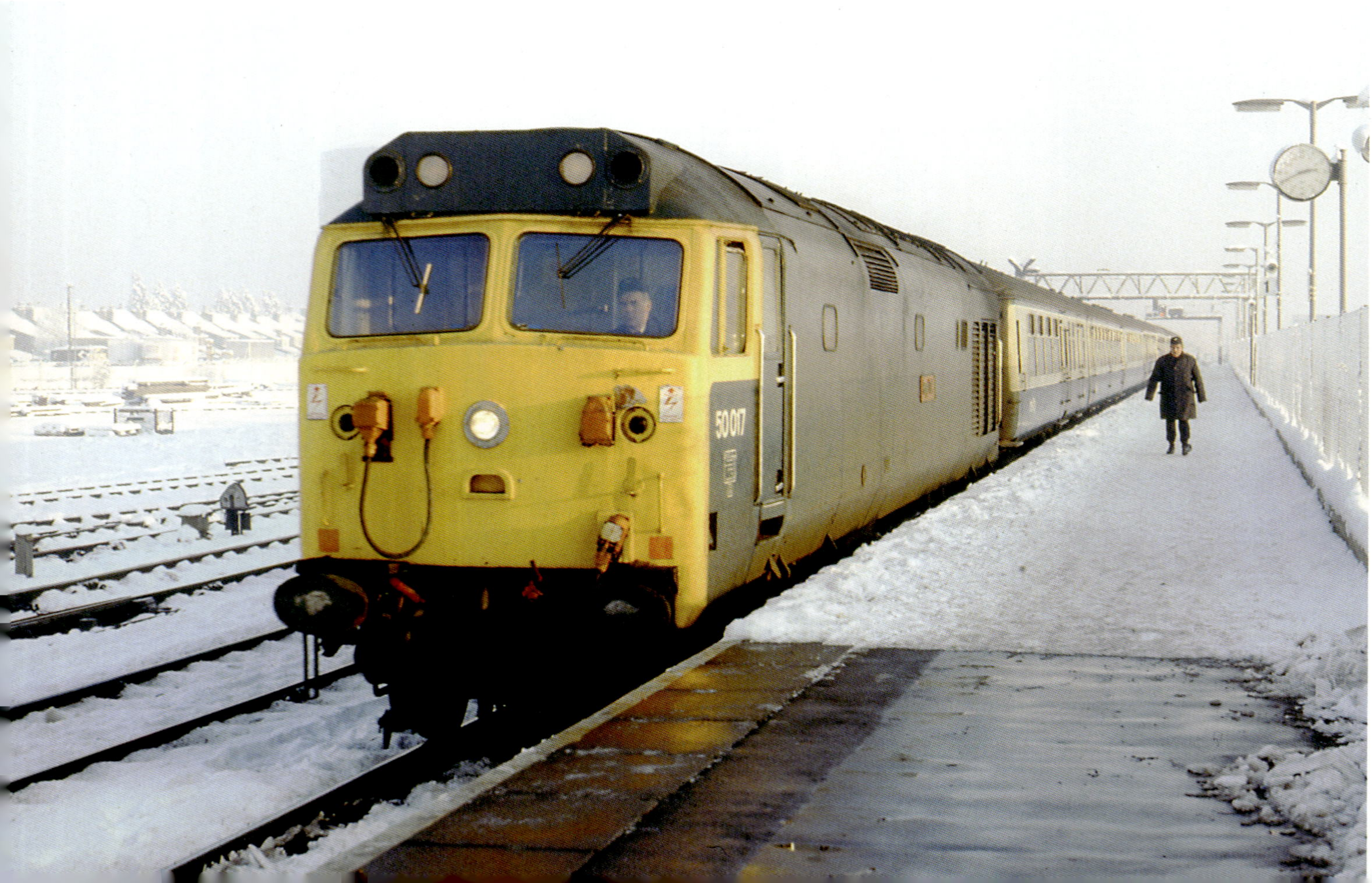

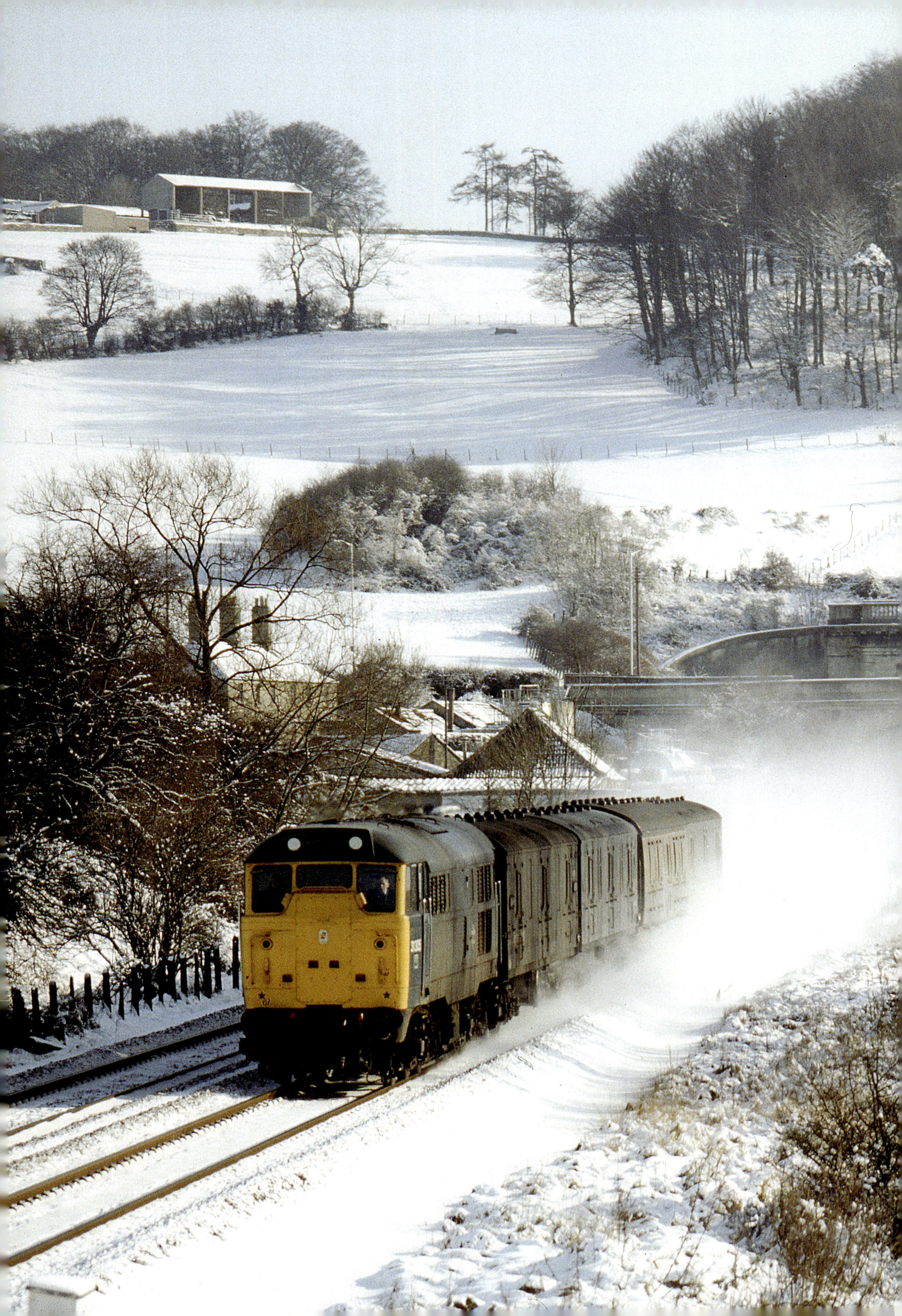

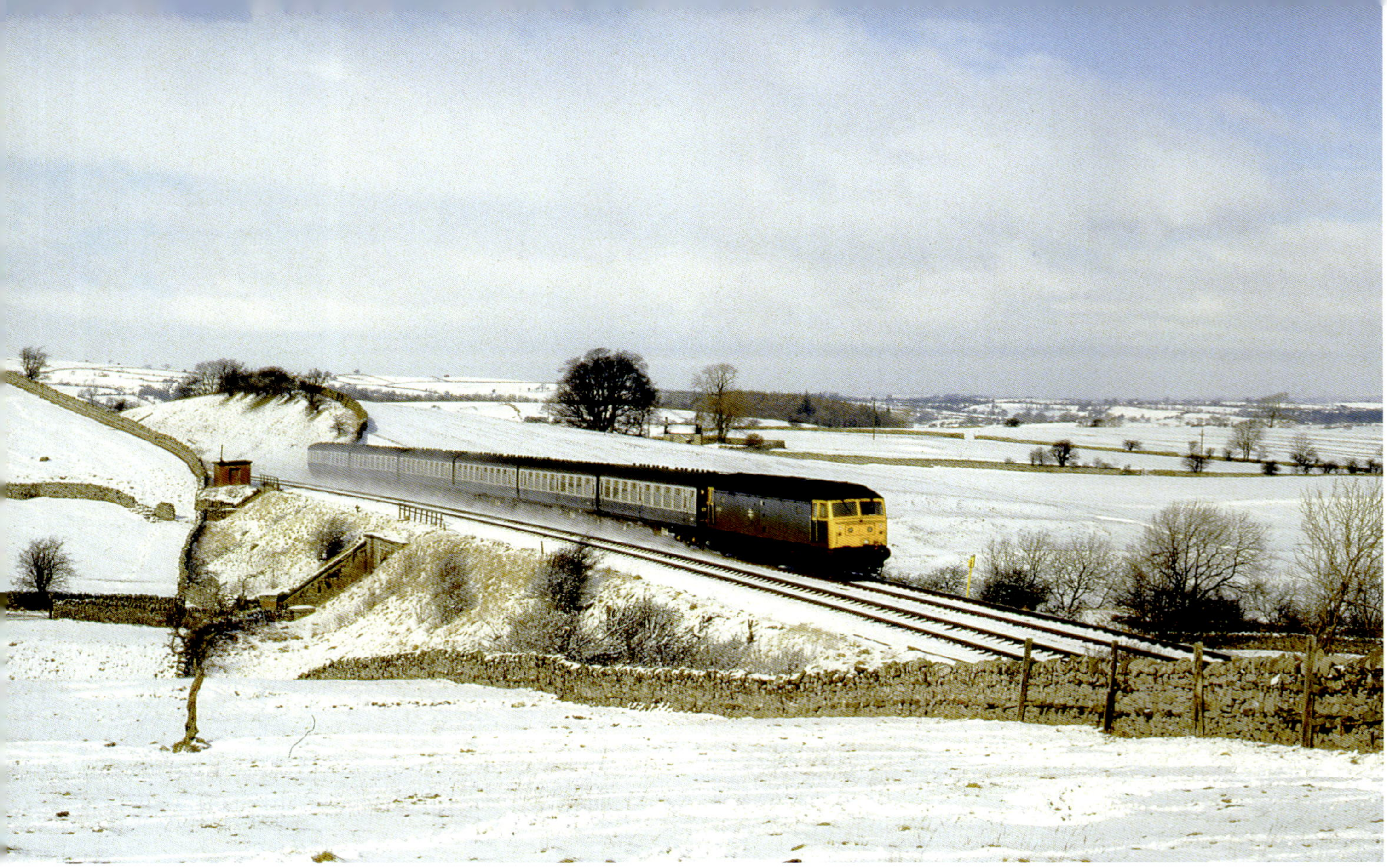

Snow lays across the fells on the Settle & Carlisle route on 16 March 1985 as 47463 makes its way through the cold between Kirkby Stephen and Smardale southbound with a stopping service. ***Late Pete Walton/Sid Steadman***

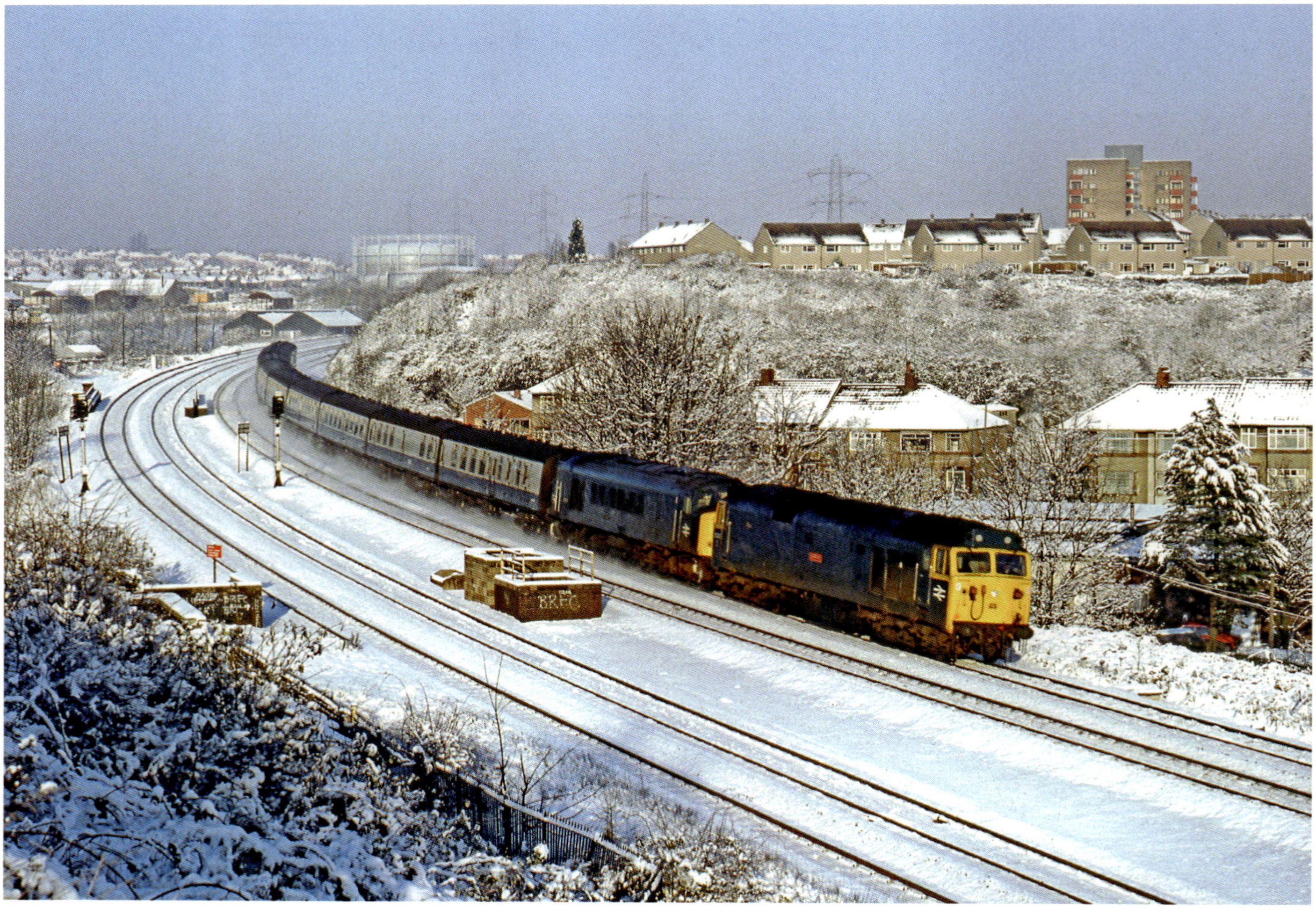

An early winter snowfall caught out 45051 as it struggled with a Manchester to Plymouth service on 12 December 1981. The refurbished 50047 Swiftsure has been put on to provide assistance as the pair approach the site of Ashley Down station in Bristol. The christmas number one that year would be Don't You Want Me by the Human League, as ever Cliff Richard would be thereabouts with Daddys Home at number two. ***Rail Photoprints/John Chalcroft***

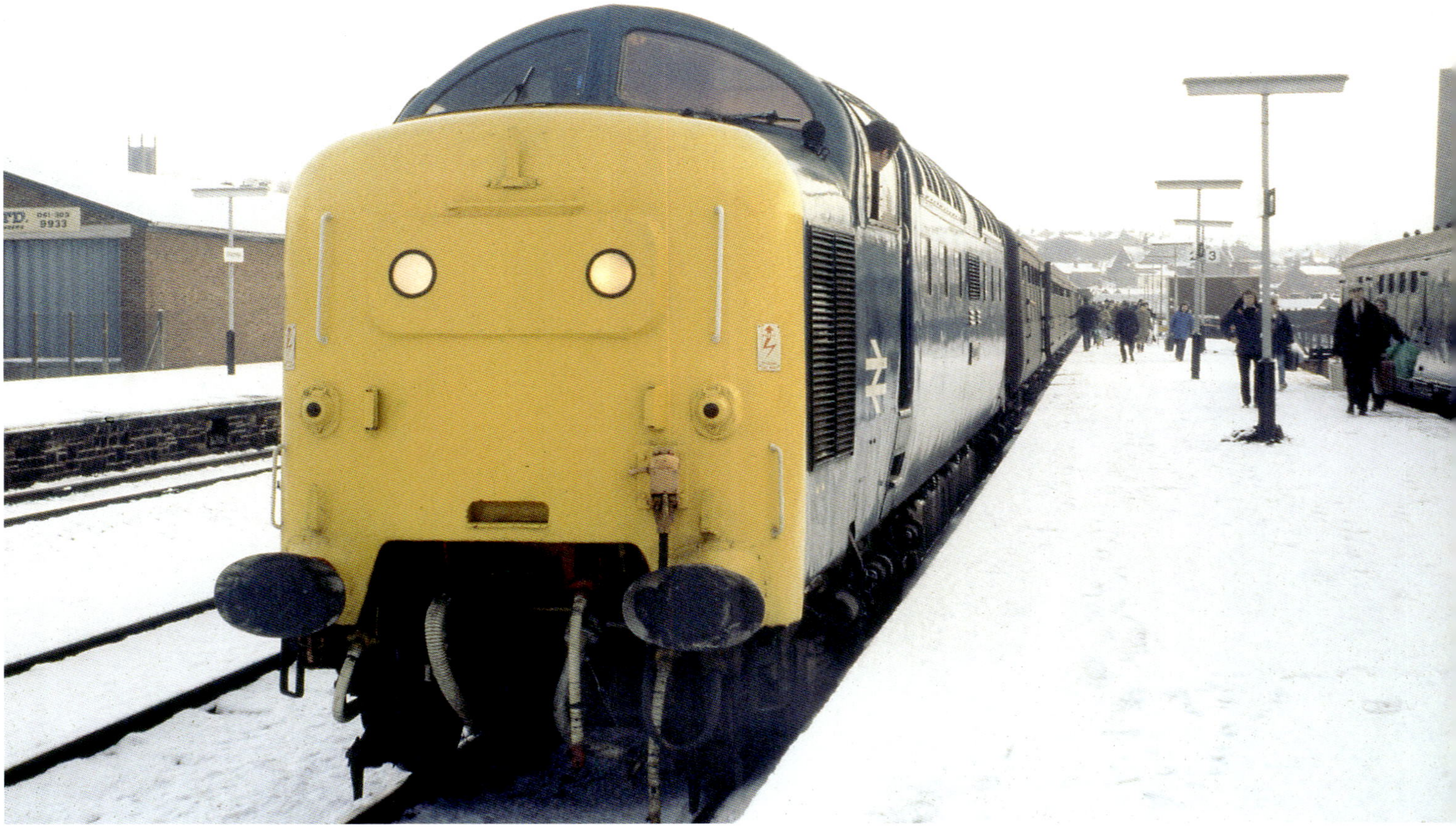

More snow again in December 1981 for 55009 Alycidon making the stop at Stalybridge whilst on a York to Liverpool service on Christmas Eve. ***Matthew Hall***

Clambering towards the summit at Upton Scudamore on 13 February 1985 was 33027 Earl Mountbatten of Burma heading south with the 11.10 Bristol to Portsmouth train. ***Rail Photoprints/John Chalcroft***

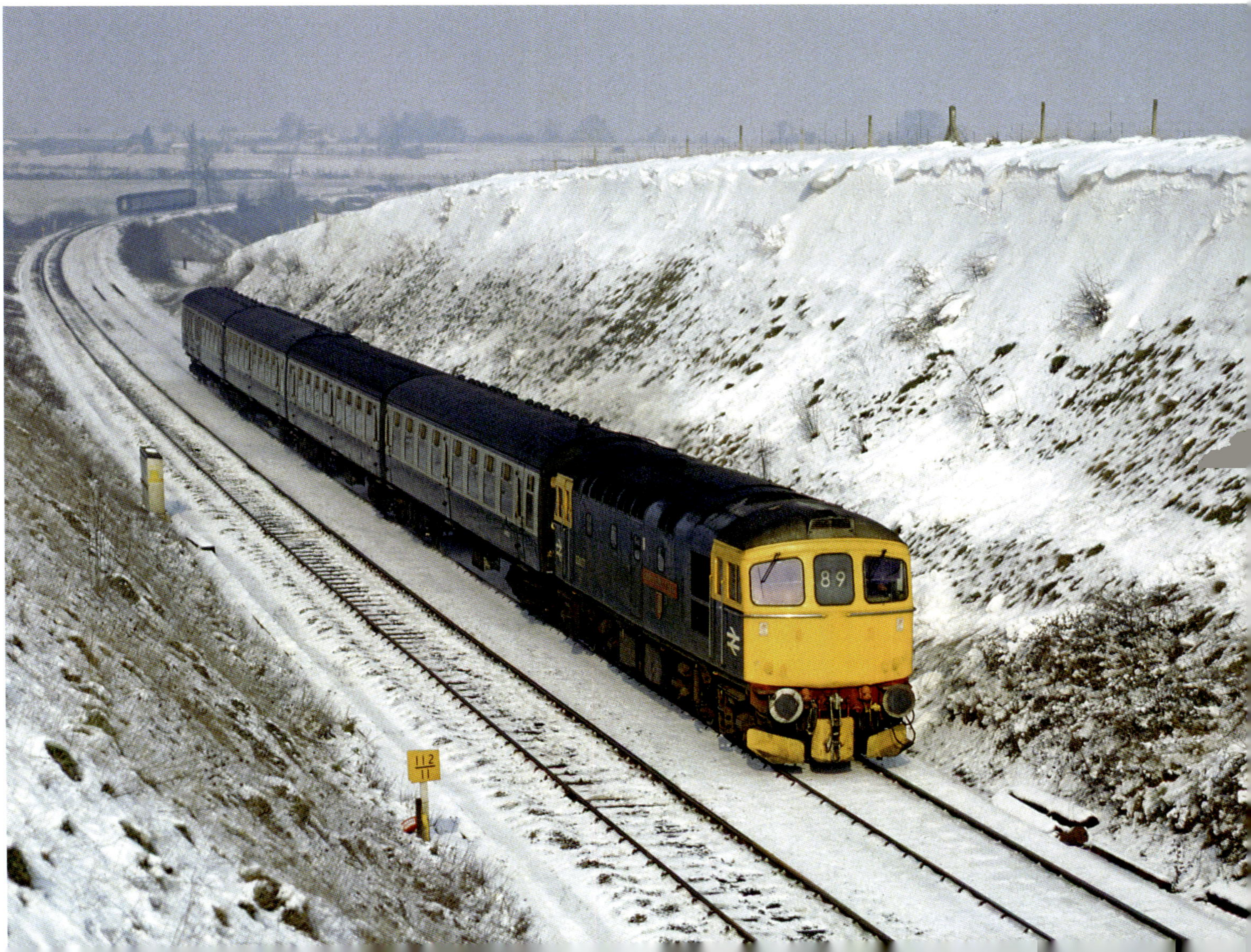

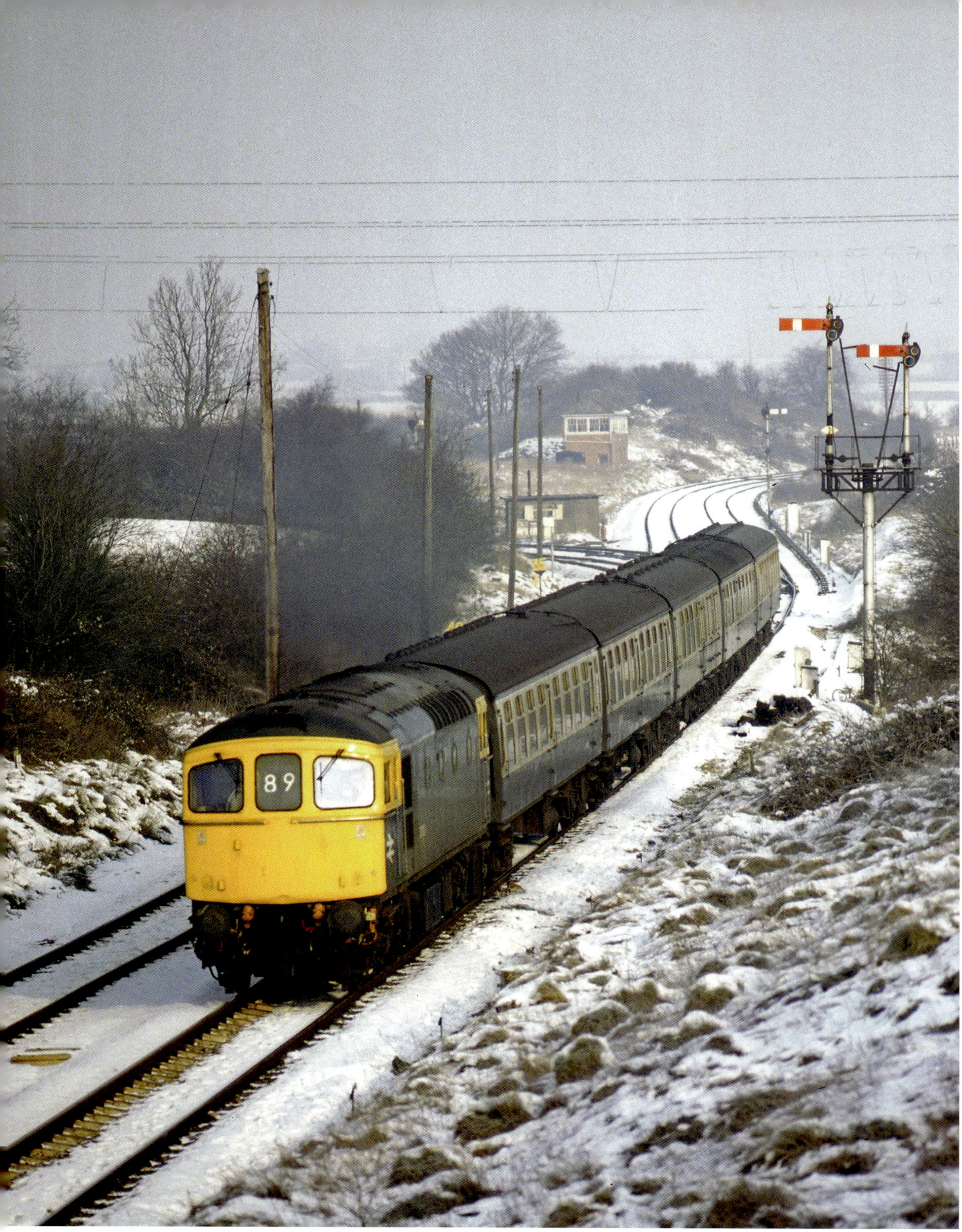

Glints of sunshine to warm the photographer's frozen feet as we capture 33023 seen here passing Bradford Junction in charge of the 09.10 Bristol to Portsmouth again on 13 February 1985. This would be the last year for Roger Moore to play James Bond in A View to a Kill which was poorly received by the critics. Timothy Dalton would take over the mantle for the next two films until 1989 and a six year gap until Pierce Brosnan appeared in Golden Eye in 1995. ***Rail Photoprints/John Chalcroft***

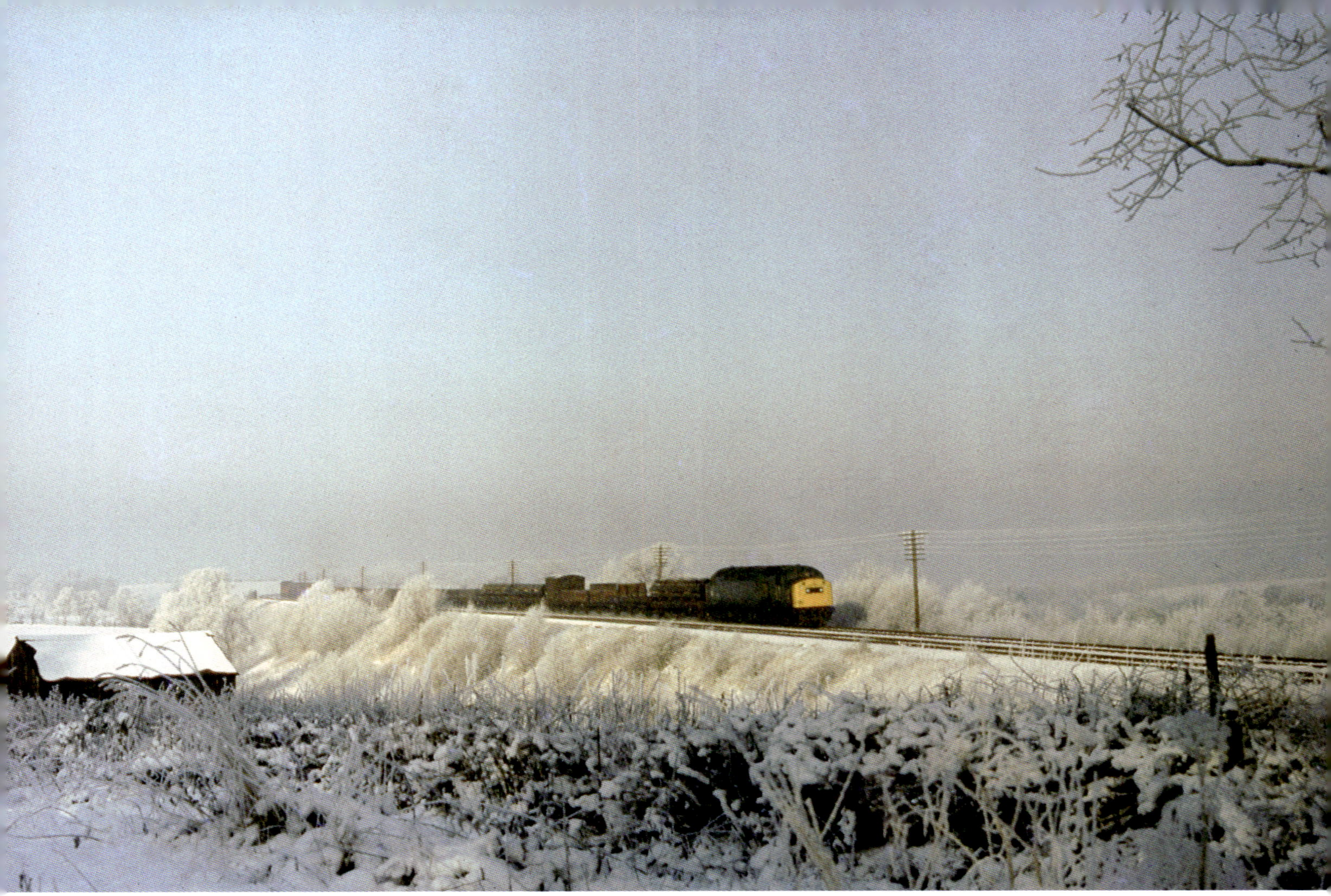

Back to the harsh winter of 1981 as 40187 battles along at Helm with an up goods on 17 December after a dreadful hoarfrost took hold after the previous day's snowfalls. ***Late Pete Walton/Sid Steadman***

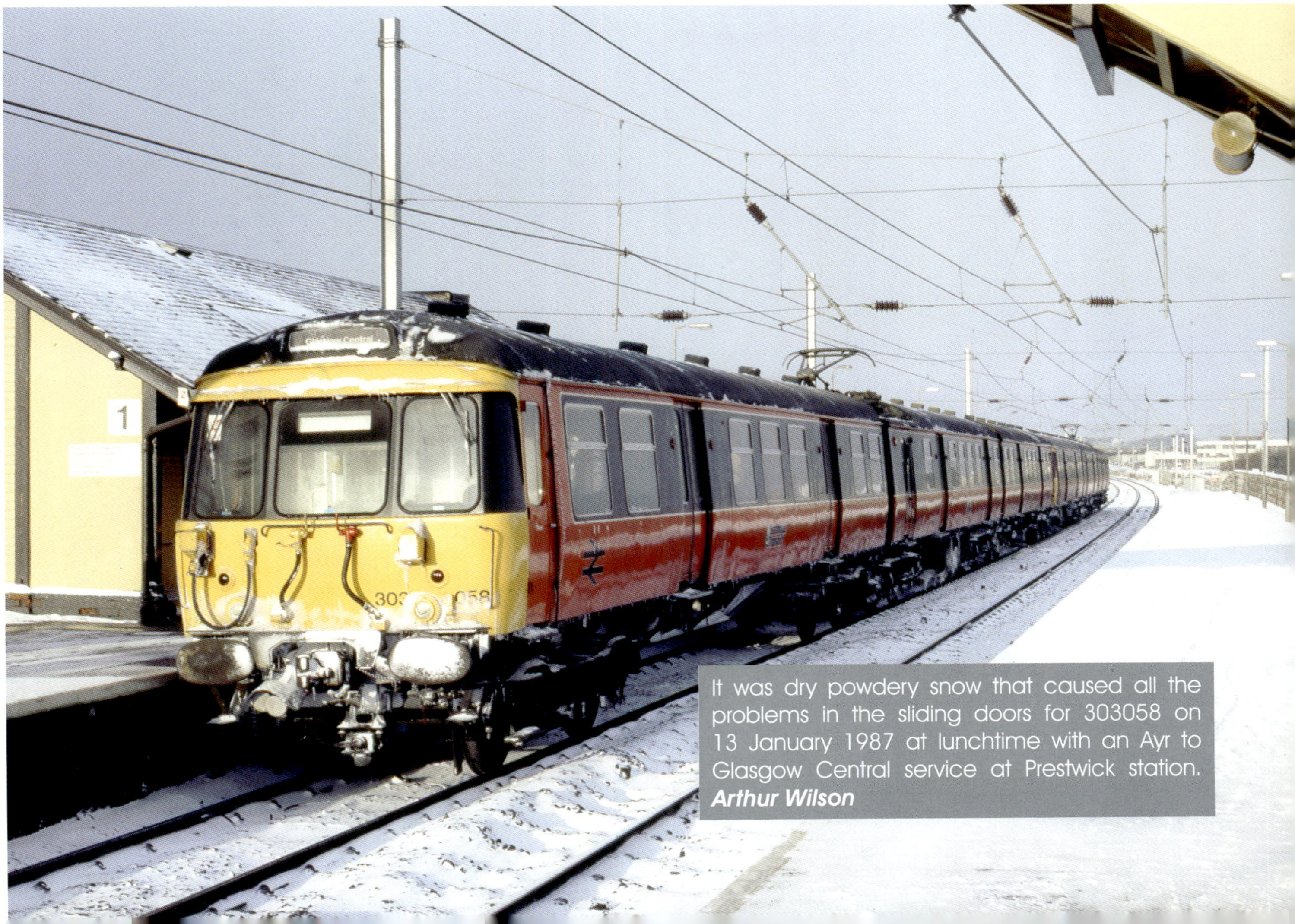

It was dry powdery snow that caused all the problems in the sliding doors for 303058 on 13 January 1987 at lunchtime with an Ayr to Glasgow Central service at Prestwick station. ***Arthur Wilson***

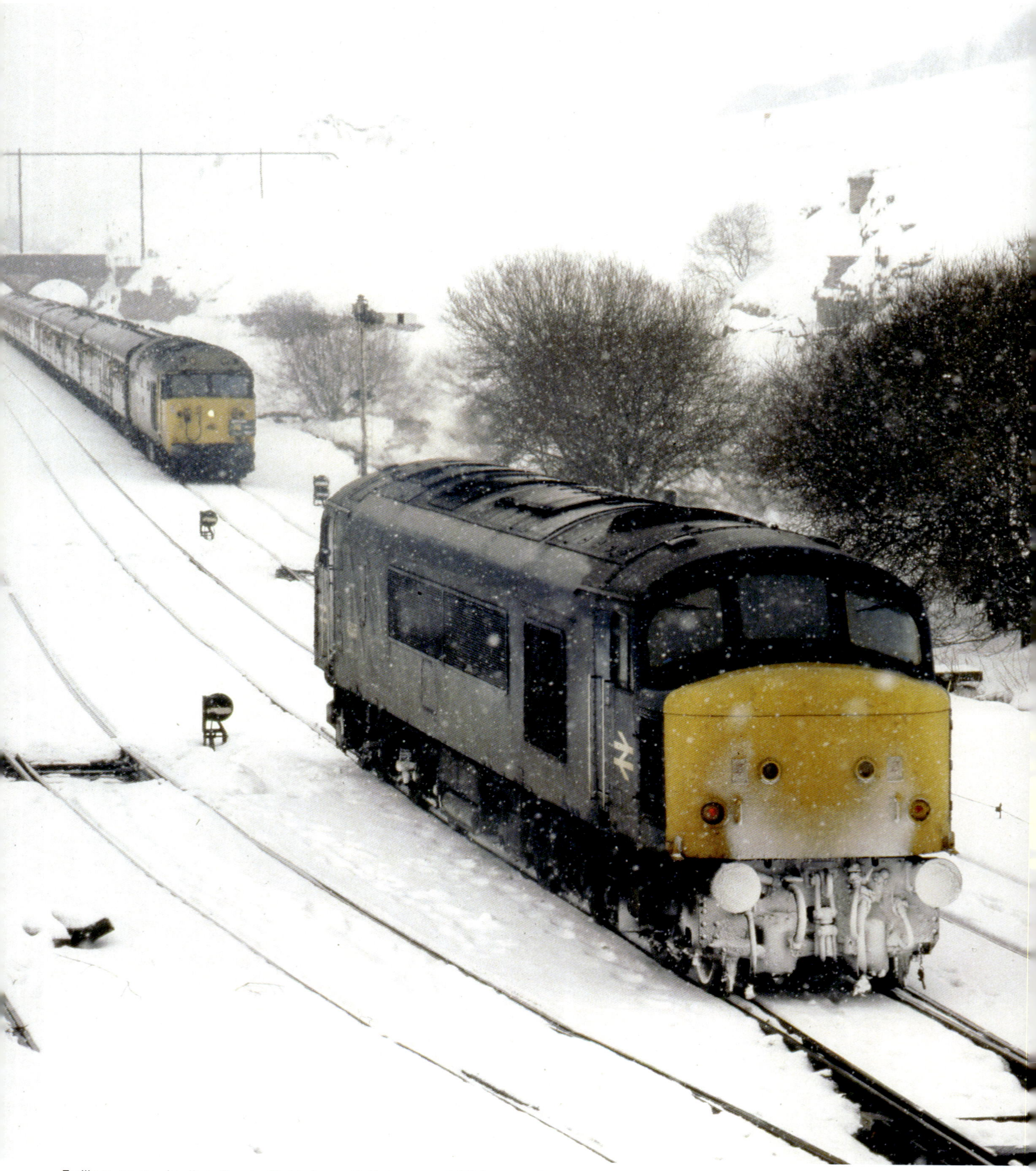

Falling snow in the Peak District on 8 February 1986 as 45037 makes its way light engine past Great Rocks and the passengers onboard 50012 Benbow as it stands with the Hertfordshire Railtours Derbyshire Dingle tour from Paddington and bound for Manchester Piccadilly. ***M Szczeblewski***

Opposite: What a contrast for enthusiasts at Leeds City in 1984 in the days when we were all relaxed about platform safety and security as we went about our hobby. Oh how things would change in later years! ***Ken Gambles***

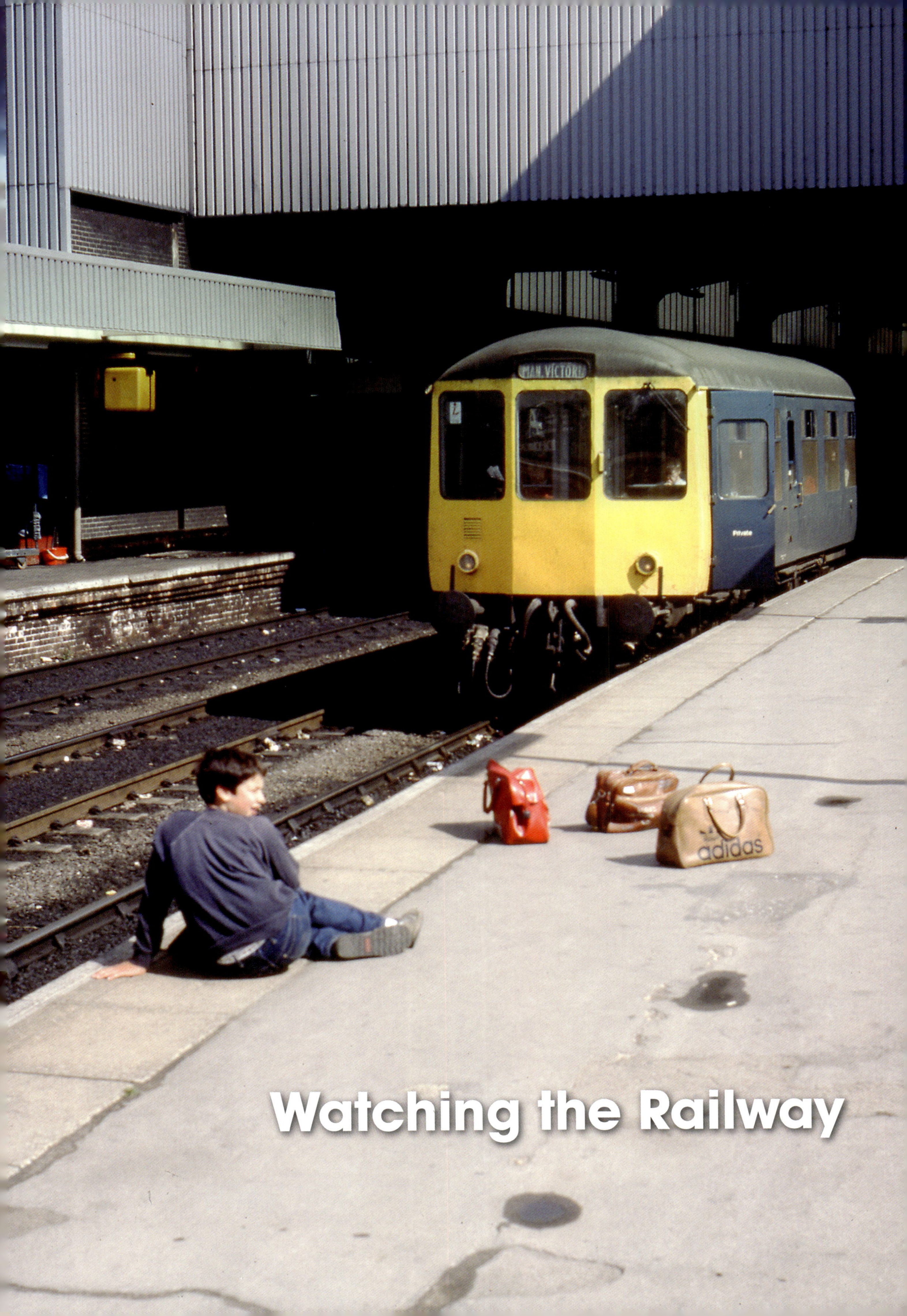

Watching the Railway

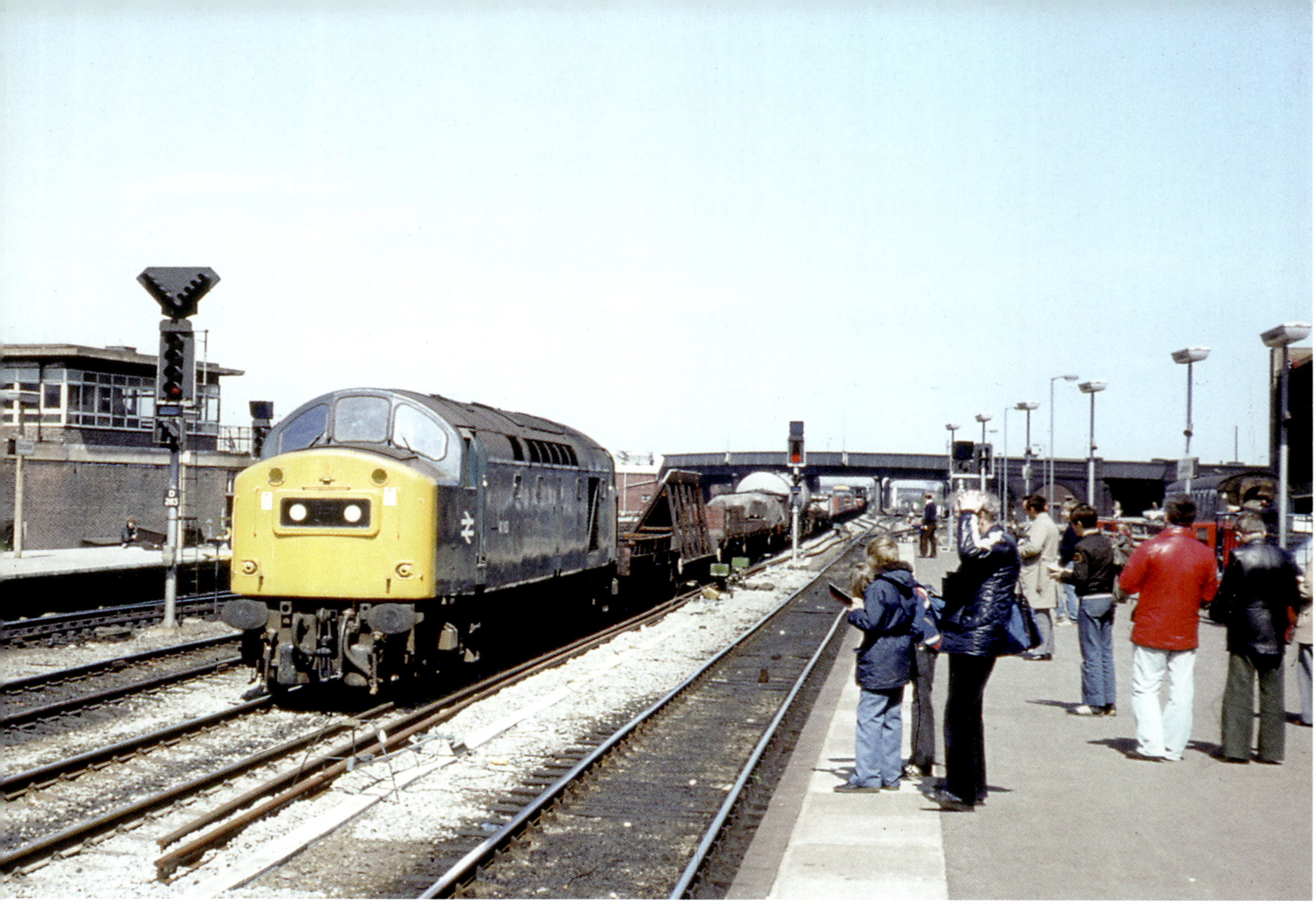

A typical saturday gathering at Doncaster to greet 40163 on 3 May 1980. ***Ken Gambles***

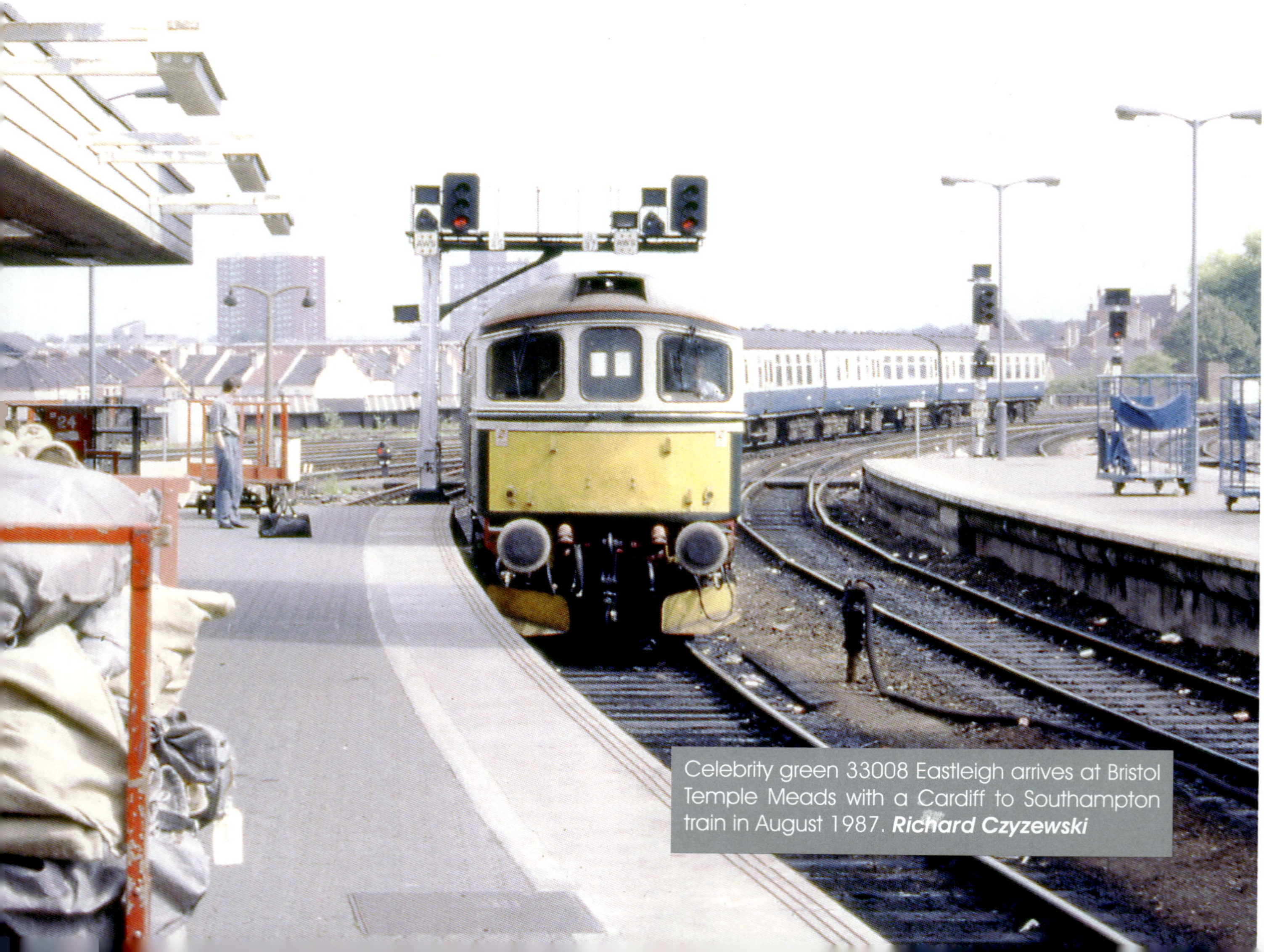

Celebrity green 33008 Eastleigh arrives at Bristol Temple Meads with a Cardiff to Southampton train in August 1987. ***Richard Czyzewski***

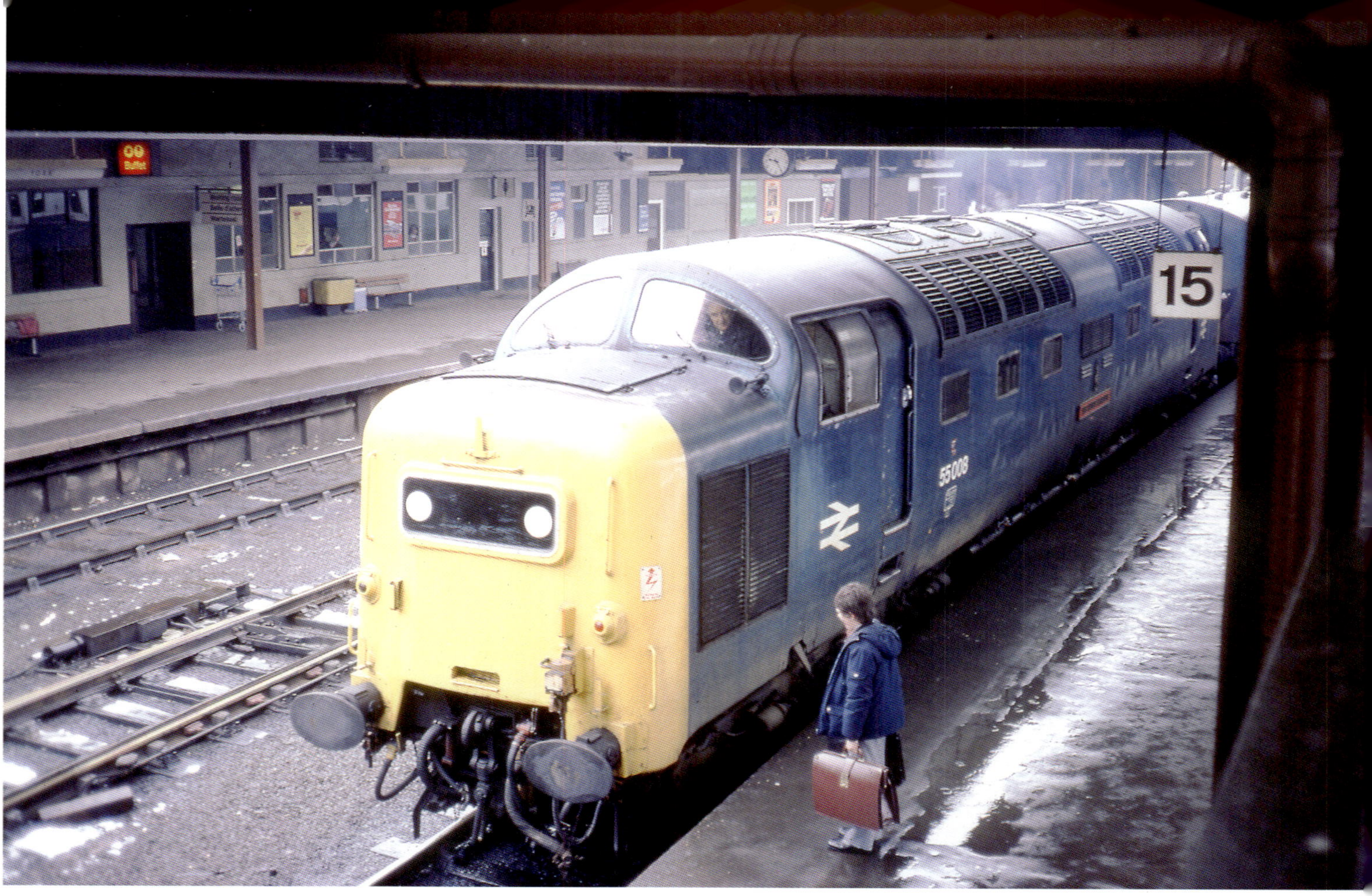

Things would be changing soon forever at York on the East Coast Main Line, but on 25 April 1981, 55008 The Green Howards was still on home turf. ***Ken Gambles***

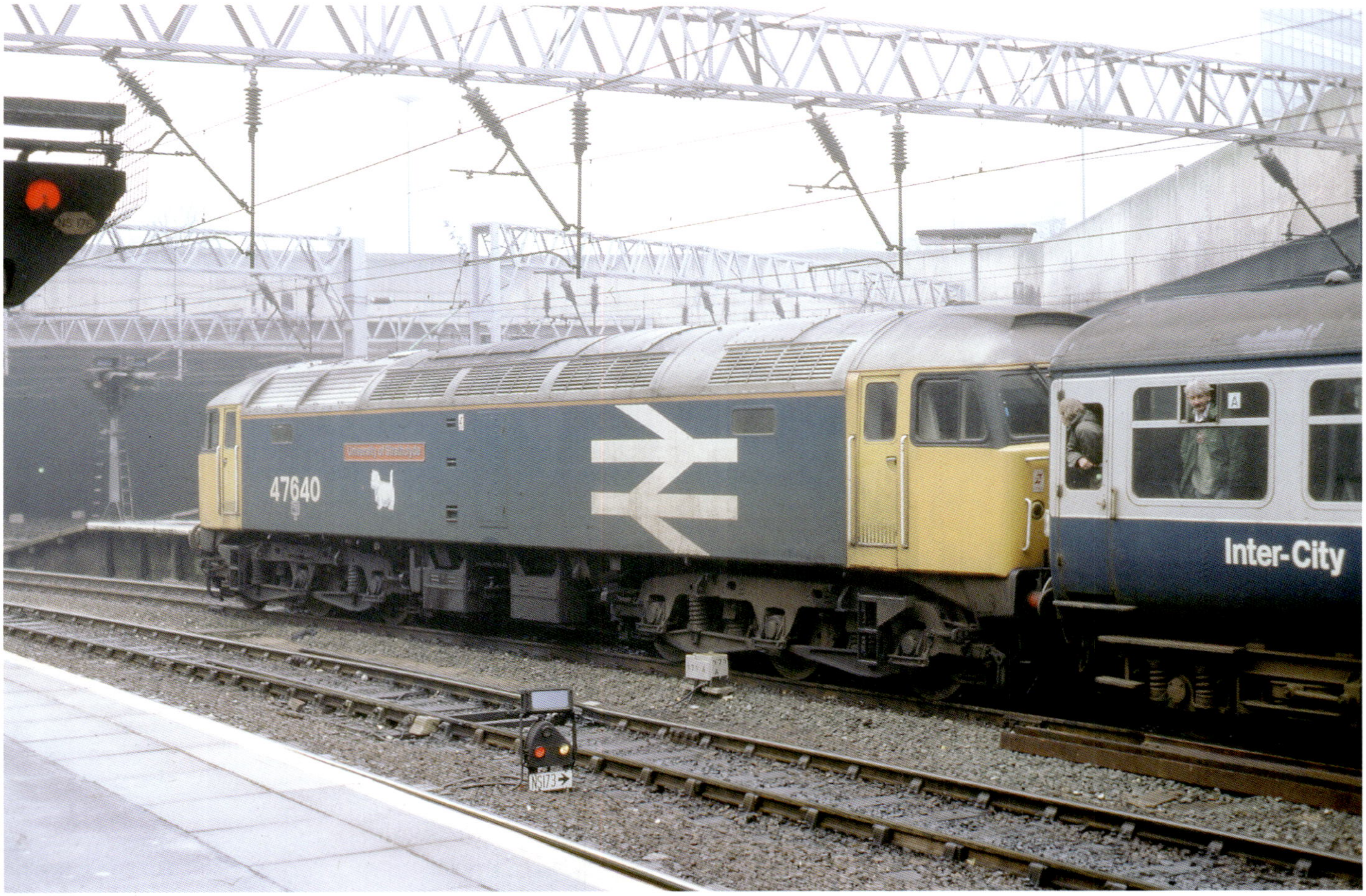

Eager enthusiasts await the off from Birmingham's New Street station behind 47640 University of Strathclyde on 24 March 1987. Large logo livery and the use of mascots such as the Scottie Dog motif along with mass namings of locomotives brought about renewed interest for many in the eighties. ***Strathwood Library Collection***

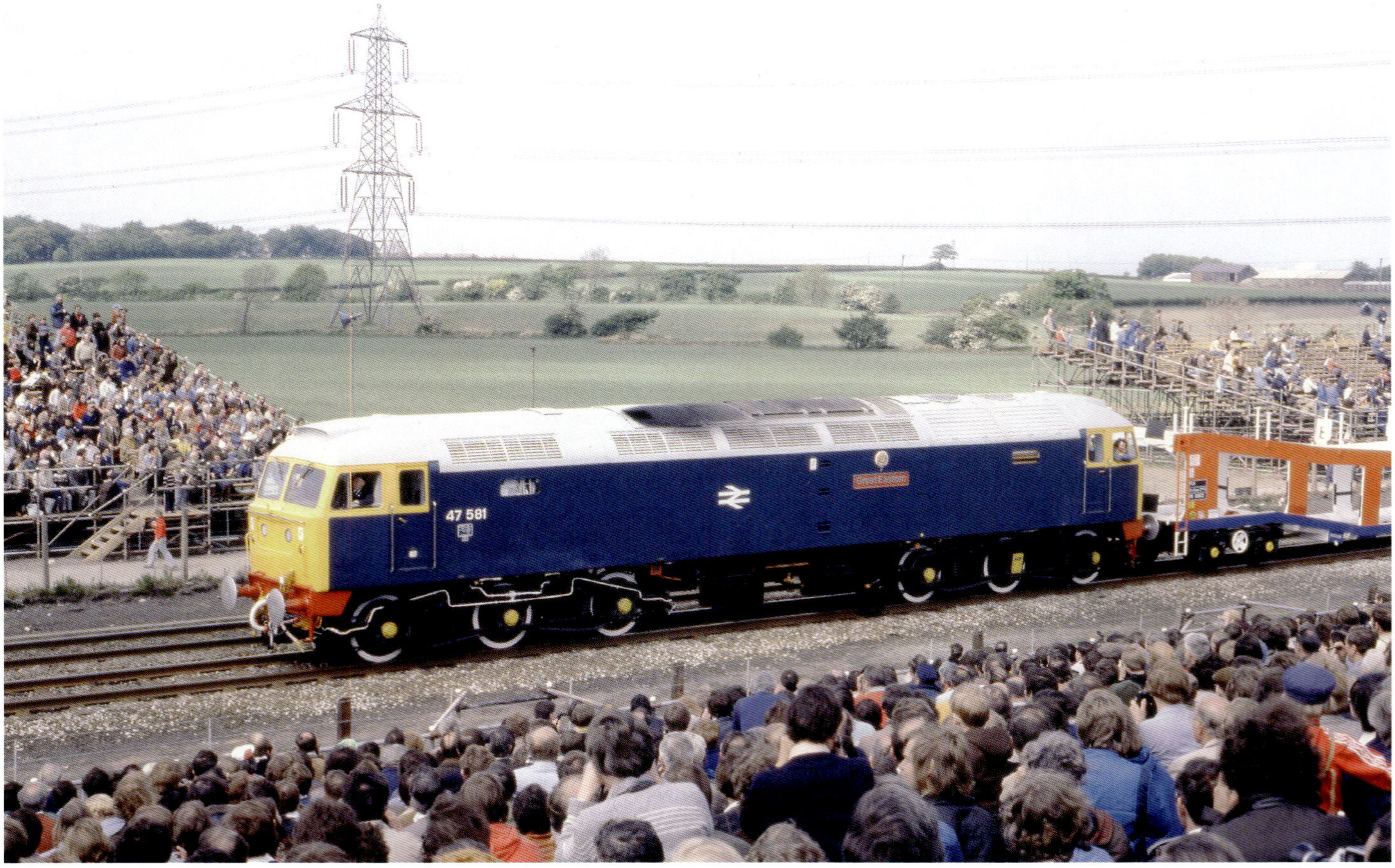

Straford's trade mark roof on 47581 Great Eastern suggests why other depots thought better of this embellishment as the crowds enjoy the Rainhill 150 parade on 24 May 1982. ***Ian James***

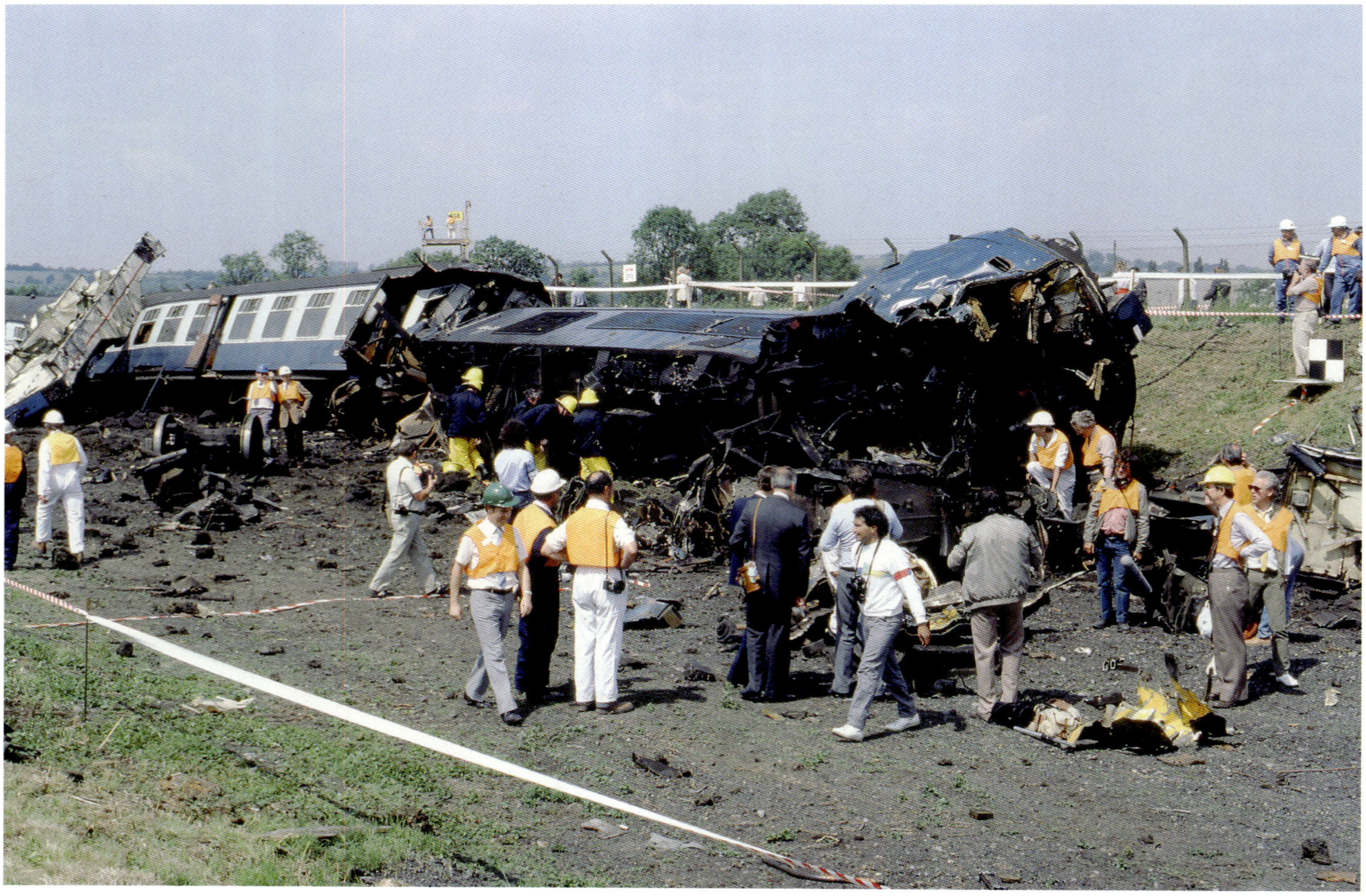

On 17 July 1984 we all watched the news coverage as 46009 was sacrificed at 100mph into a nuclear flask at the Old Dalby test centre. This was the scene after the stunt, as the press and officials were allowed to pick over the wreckage. The battered remains of the Peak were cut up on site. ***Bruce Smetham***

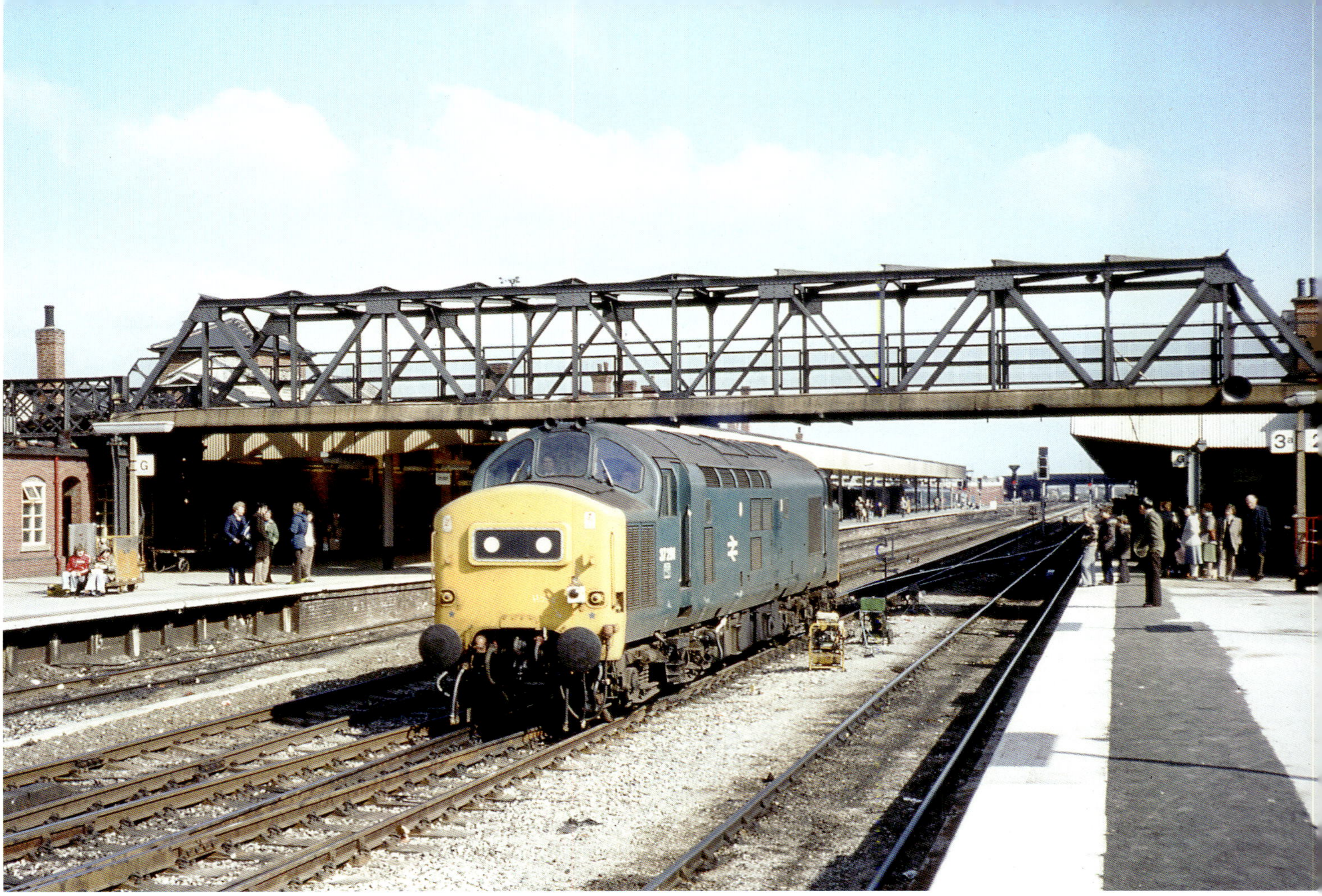

Back to Doncaster on 3 May 1980 as 37291 passes light engine through the centre roads of the station complex under the gaze of the ever present spotters. ***Ken Gambles***

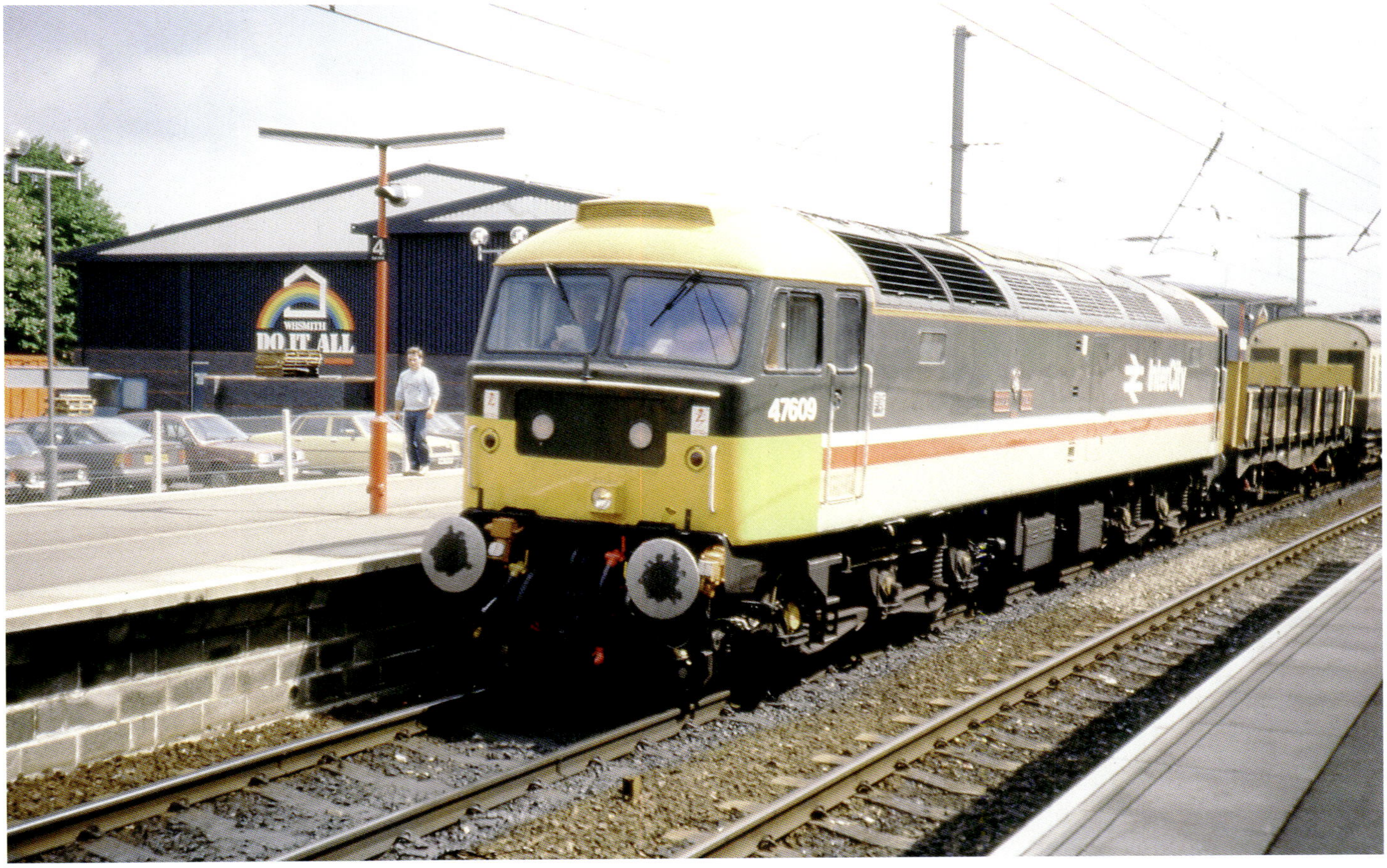

The rainbow inspired logo of the home improvements store built in the former goods yard at Bedford would be able match the paintwork of the large number of new paint schemes appearing by May 1987 as 47609 Fire Fly drew into the station. ***Strathwood Library Collection***

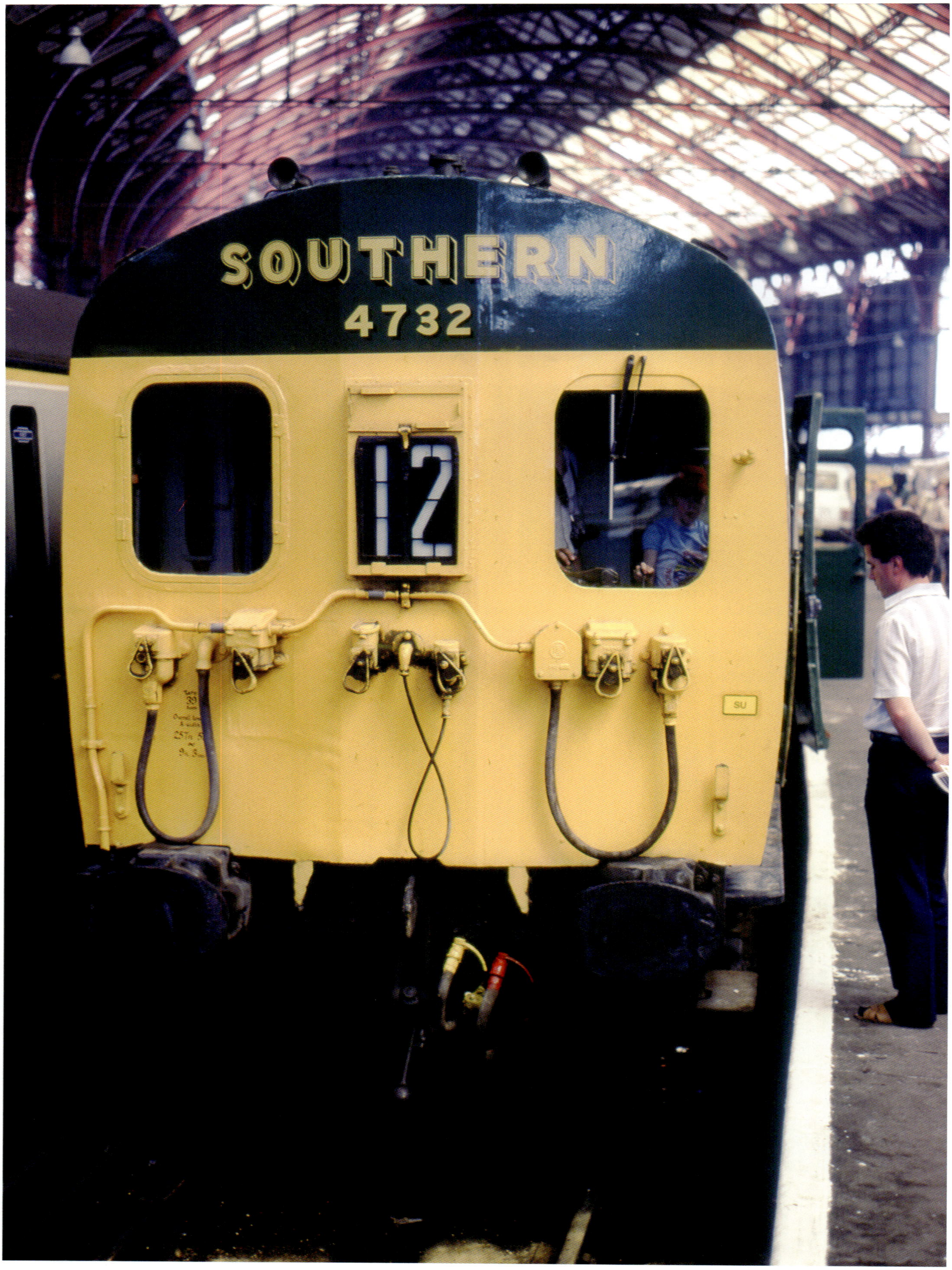

Adaptions of old heritage paint schemes were being allowed once again as here on the 4-SUB chosen for preservation and displayed to the public as part of the Brighton Station Open Day on 16 July 1983. ***Tom Bigley/Strathwood Library Collection***

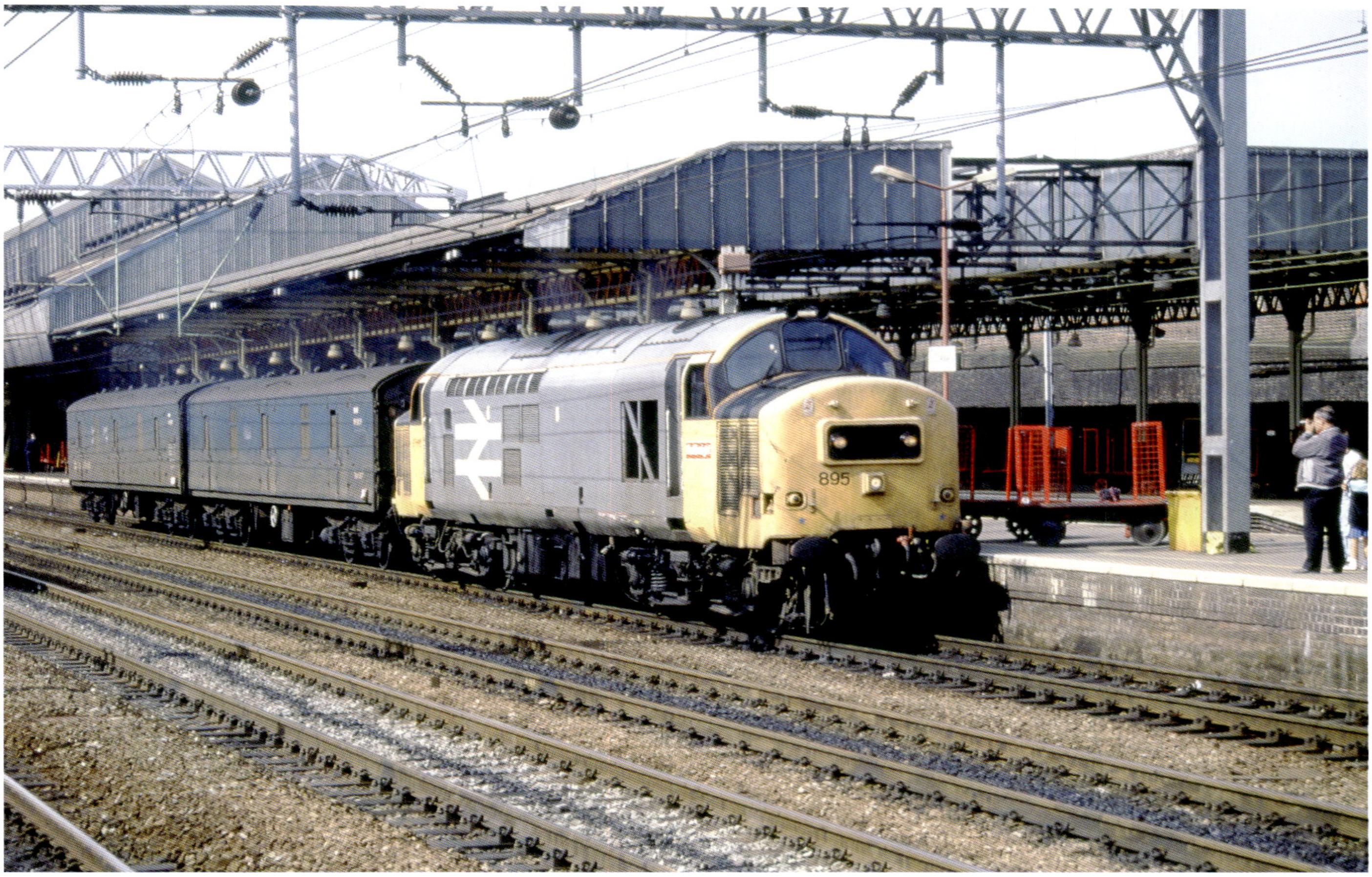

Not all of the new liveries would be in bright and vibrant colours as modelled by 37895 on 3 August 1989 shuffling around Crewe station with a couple of parcels vans. ***Gilroy A. Kerr***

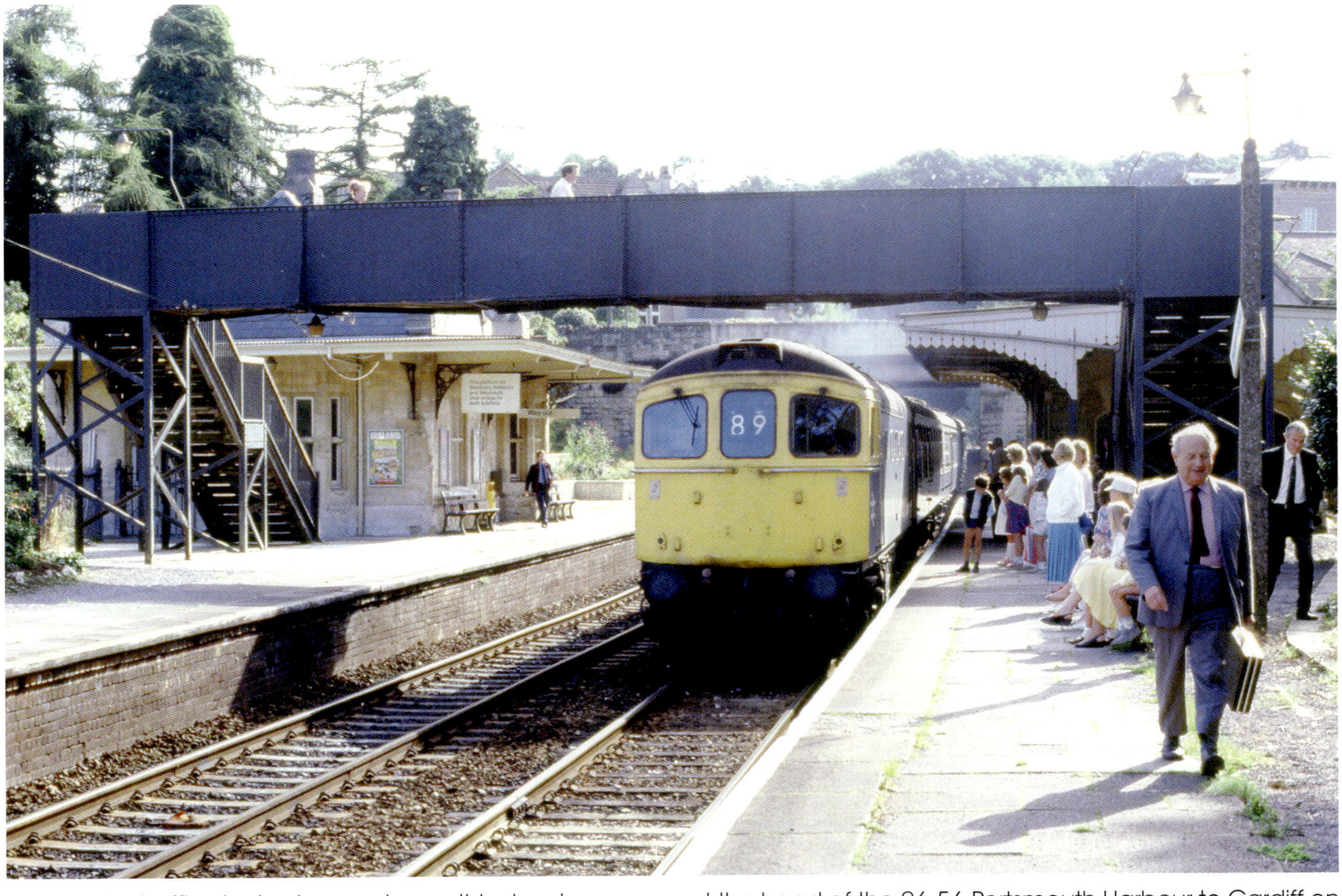

Passenger traffic looks bouyant on this lovely warm summer morning as 33021 draws into Bradford-on-Avon at the head of the 06.56 Portsmouth Harbour to Cardiff on 5 August 1987. ***Gilroy A. Kerr***

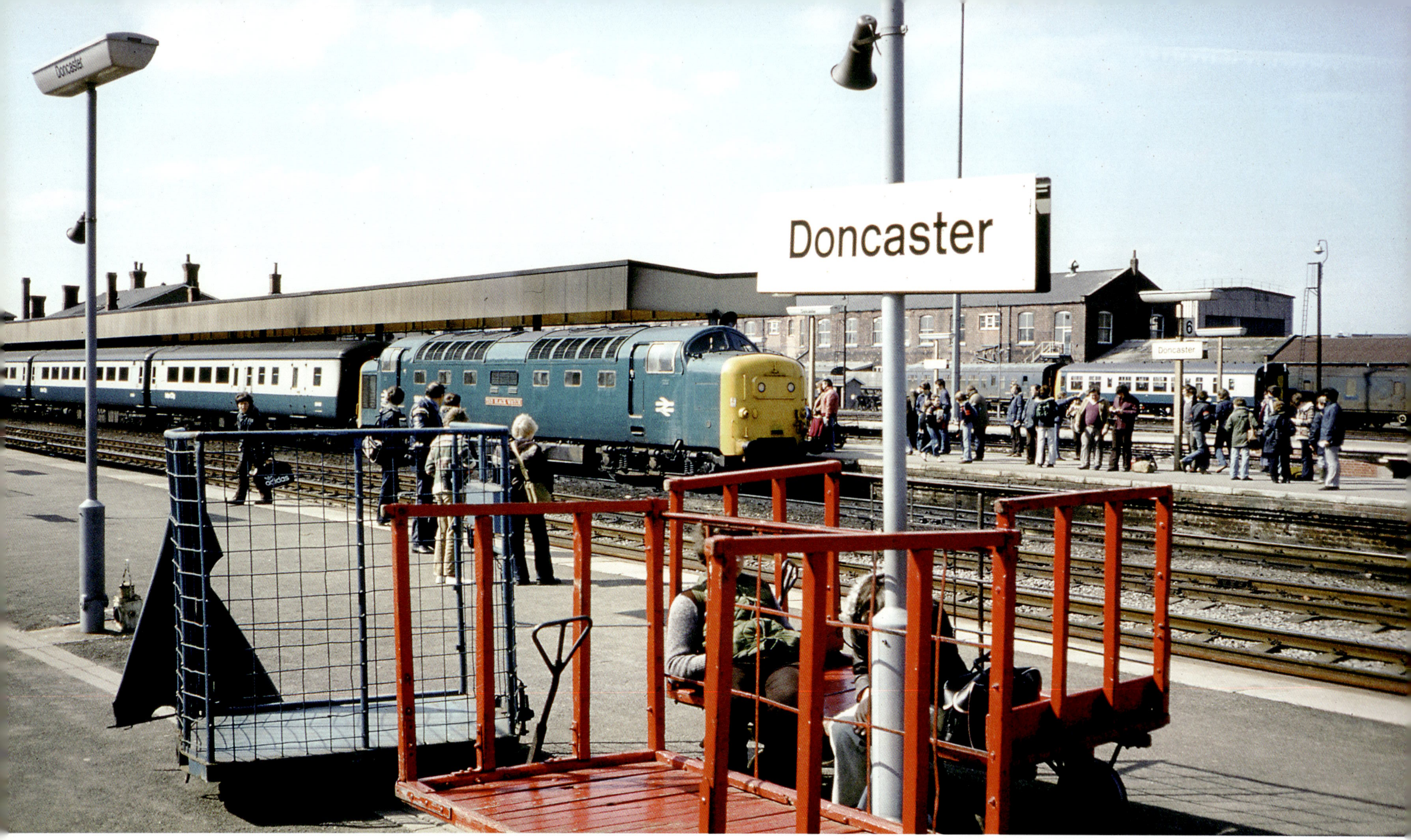

The numbers of spotters on the platforms at Doncaster on 3 May 1980 has strengthened as 55013 The Black Watch awaits the departure northwards with a service from Kings Cross to Hull. For at least a few of those gathered here the arrival of this Deltic is no special thing worthy of their glances upwards as they lounge on the platform trolleys. You will think otherwise in a couple of years and they have all gone... ***Ken Gambles***

A sure favourite spot for enthusiasts to wait and watch train movements was the footbridge that leads to Canton depot in Cardiff as this pair of lads await their next sighting. Meanwhile our cameraman has gone around the shed and recorded 47317 stabled in the lines outside in the sunshine on 21 June 1980. ***Arthur Wilson***

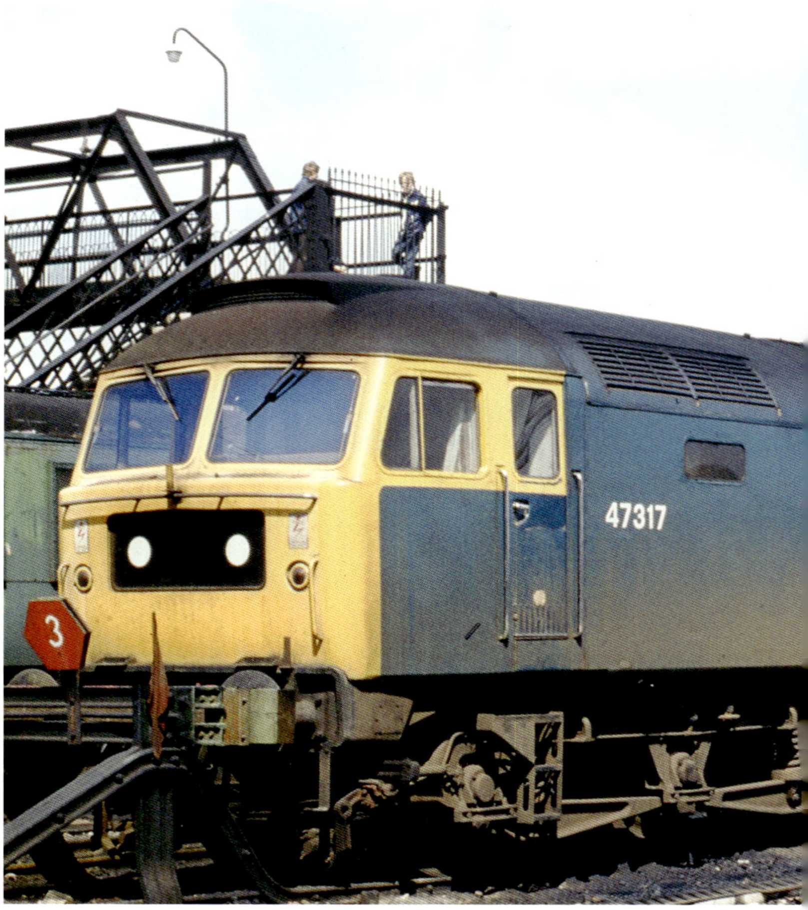

Another Class 47 is seen at Doncaster inside the shed on 29 March 1981, is that the foreman approaching in the distance? Best note down 47376 quick and make yourself scarce if you don't have permission. ***Colin Whitbread***

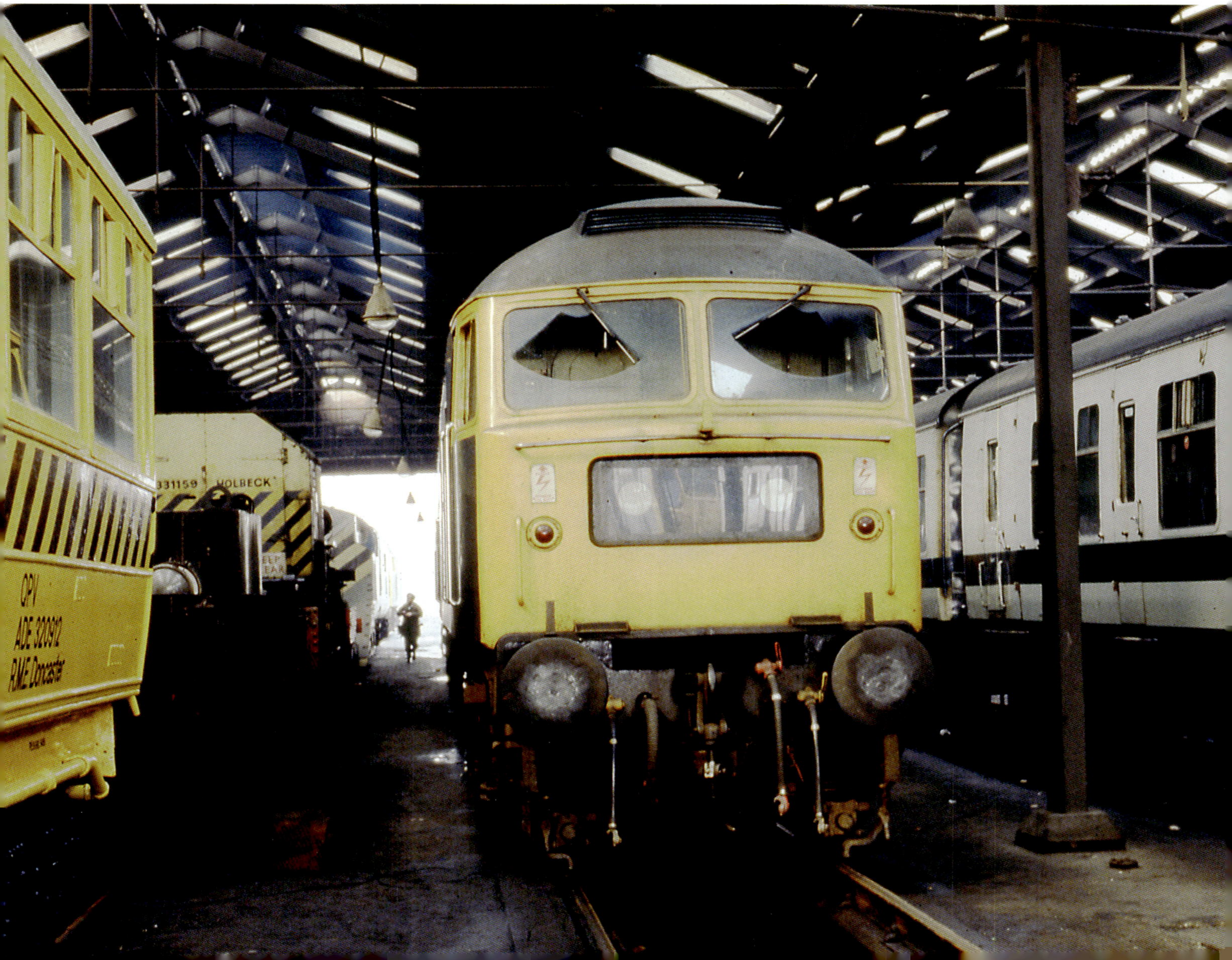

Down by the Waterside

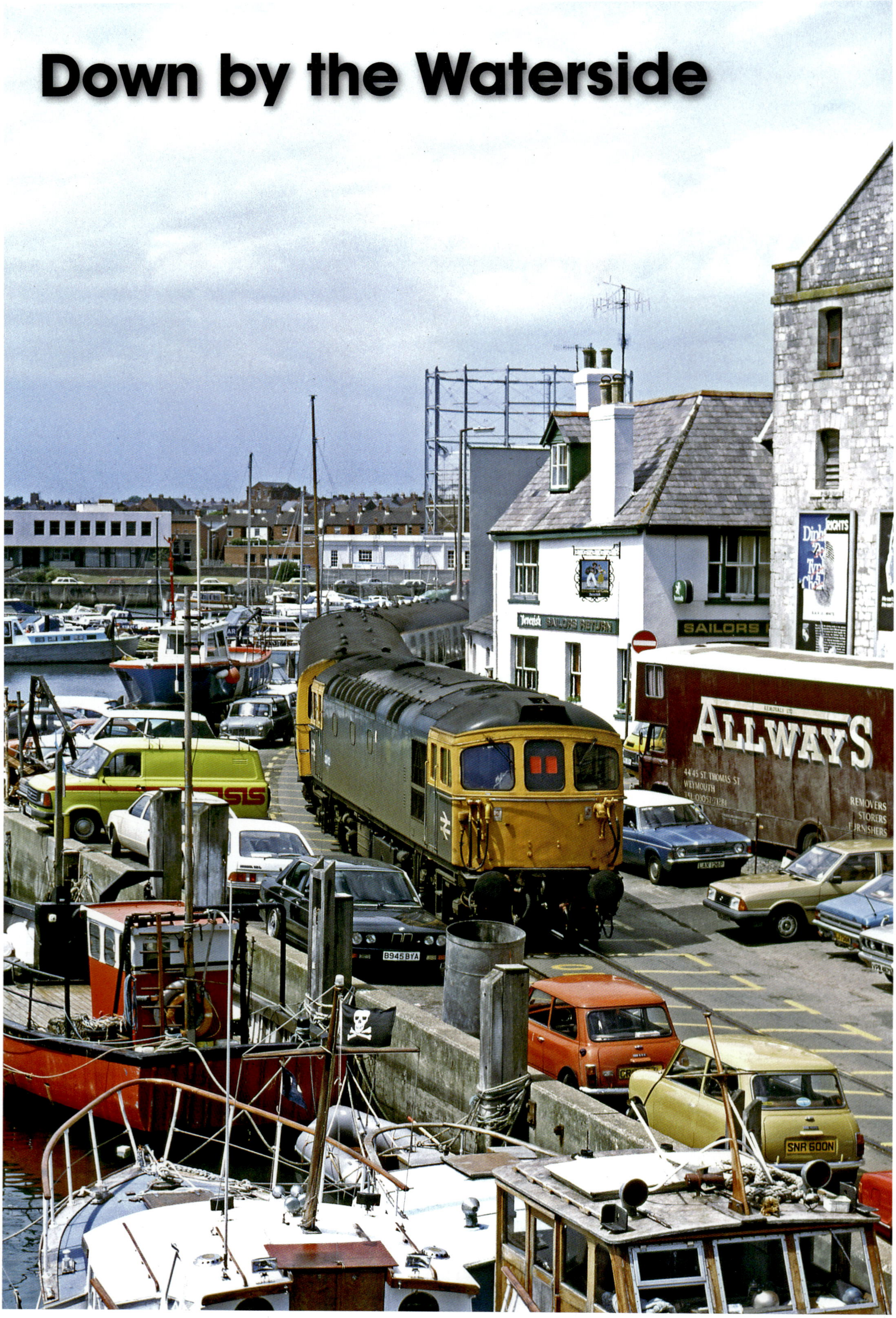

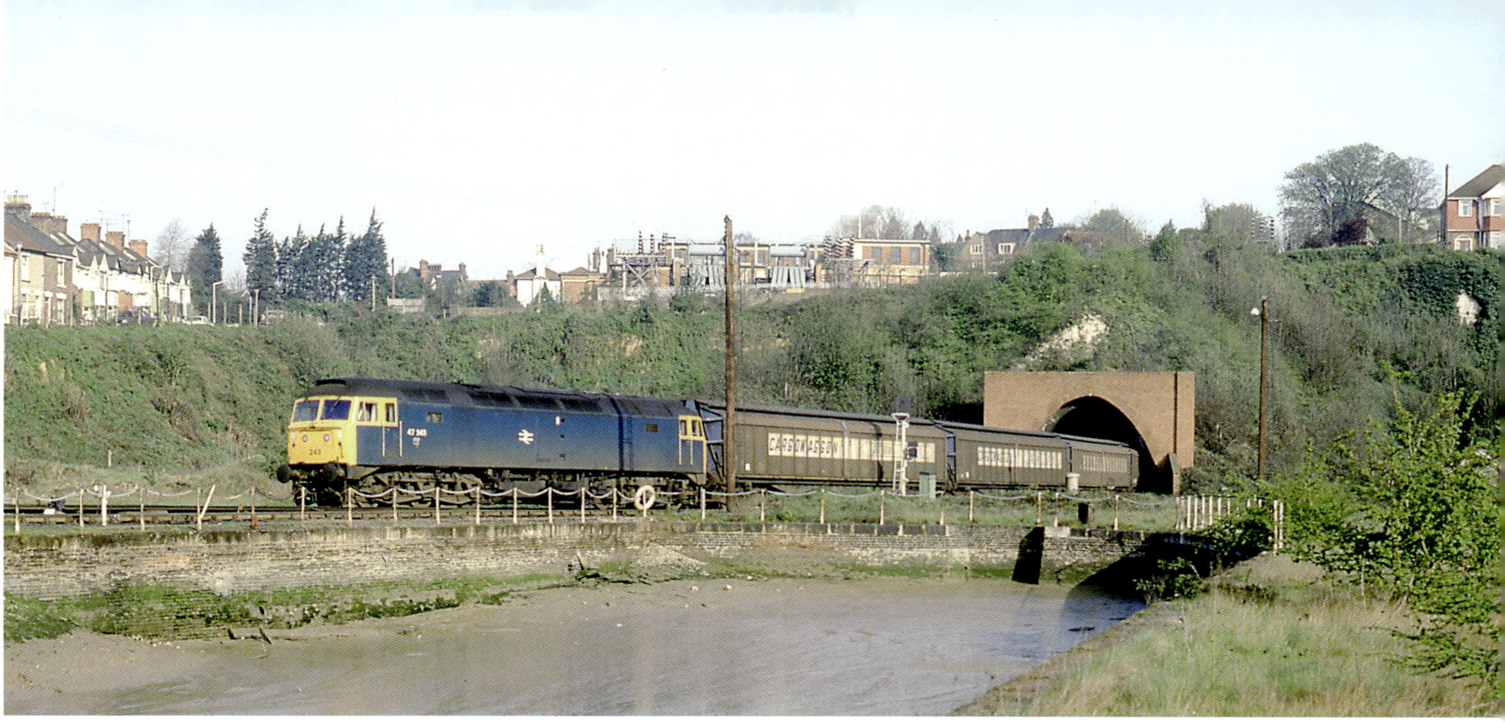

Strood lies on the River Medway in Kent and once relied for its prosperity on freight traffic both off the water and the railways. The river traffic has dried up in this basin as 47243 passes with the 01.50 Severn Tunnel Junction to Dover Town Yard on 28 April 1983. ***Colin Whitbread***

Below: Brimscombe on the Thames and Severn Canal once also enjoyed importance during the Industrial Revolution, but by 2 May 1987 when 50018 Resolution rolled by with a Cheltenham to Paddington express it was just a pleasant backwater. ***Gilroy A. Kerr***

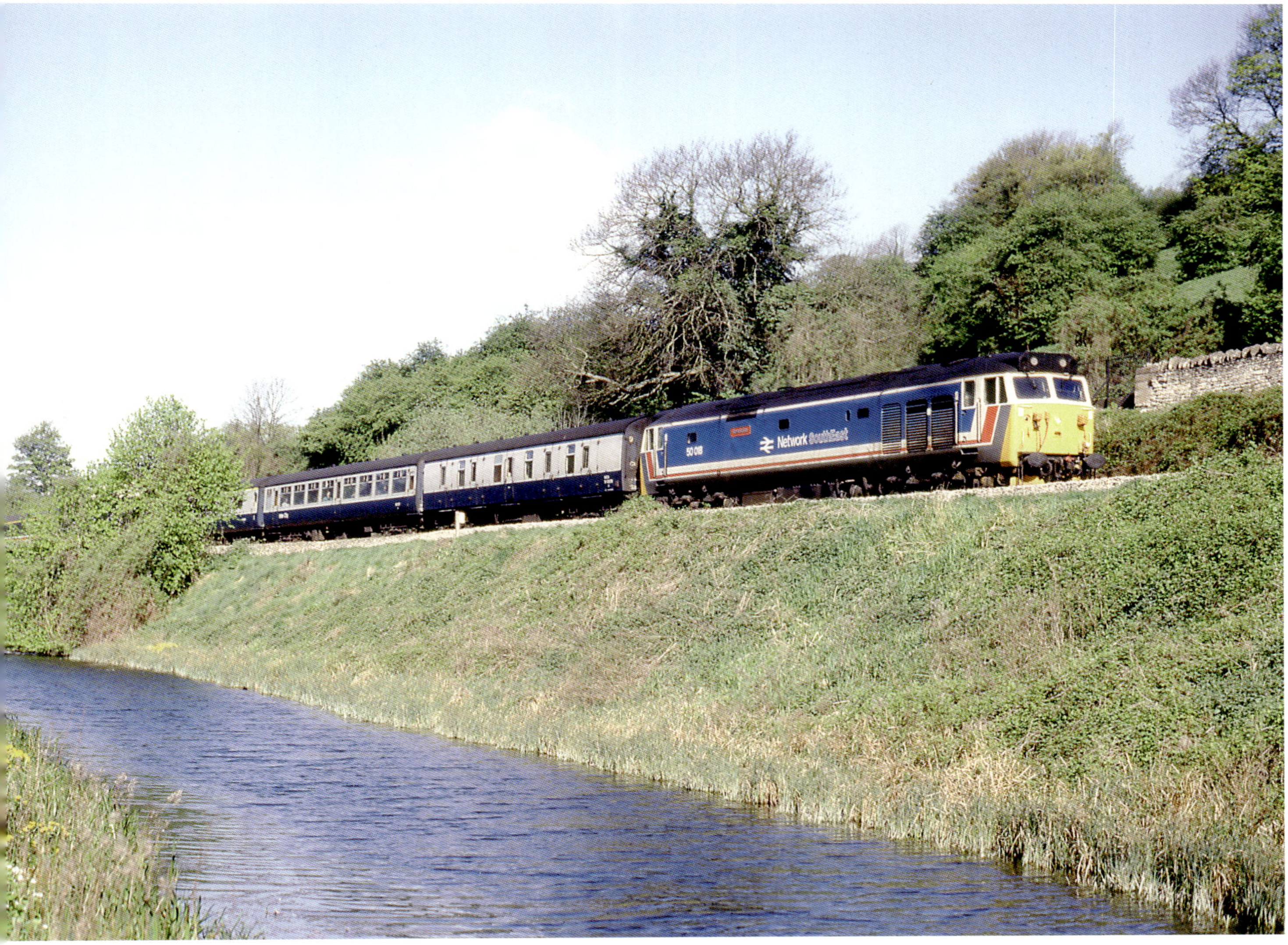

Page left: Tailing the 15.00 Weymouth Quay to Waterloo boat train through the streets of Weymouth on 8 June 1985 was 33102 past the rows of contemporary parked cars. ***Rail Photoprints/John Chalcroft***

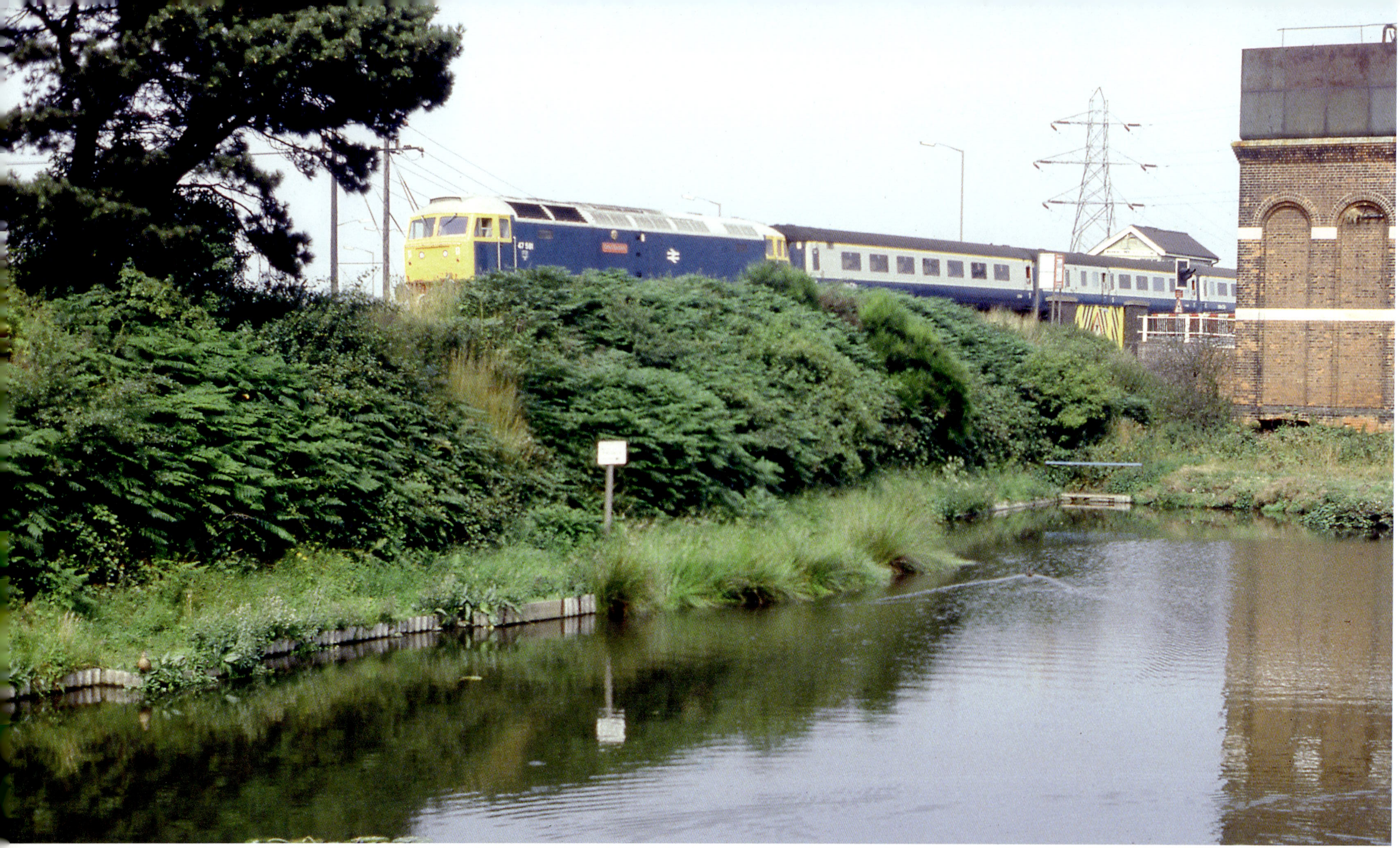

Putting in another appearance is Stratford's 47581 Great Eastern this time with the 14.28 Norwich to Liverpool Street at Manningtree on 4 August 1981, the town is on Holbrook Bay, part of the River Stour in the north of Essex once famous for witches. ***Colin Whitbread***

Opposite: The hydraulic era has long gone on 26 June 1984 as an HST 125 sweeps westwards with a down Penzance service at Dawlish Warren and out onto the famous seawall section of Brunel's mainline. ***Strathwood Library Collection***

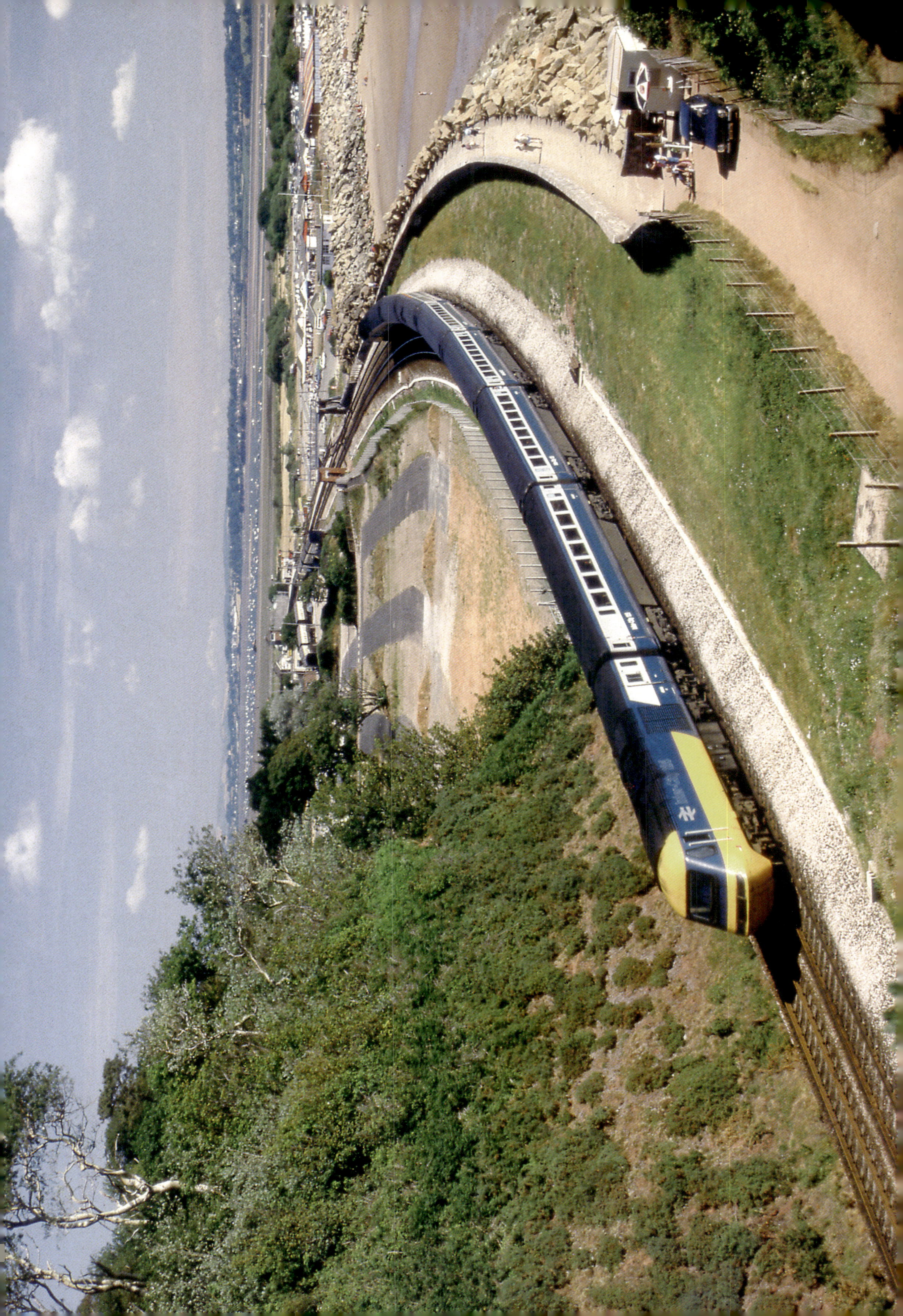

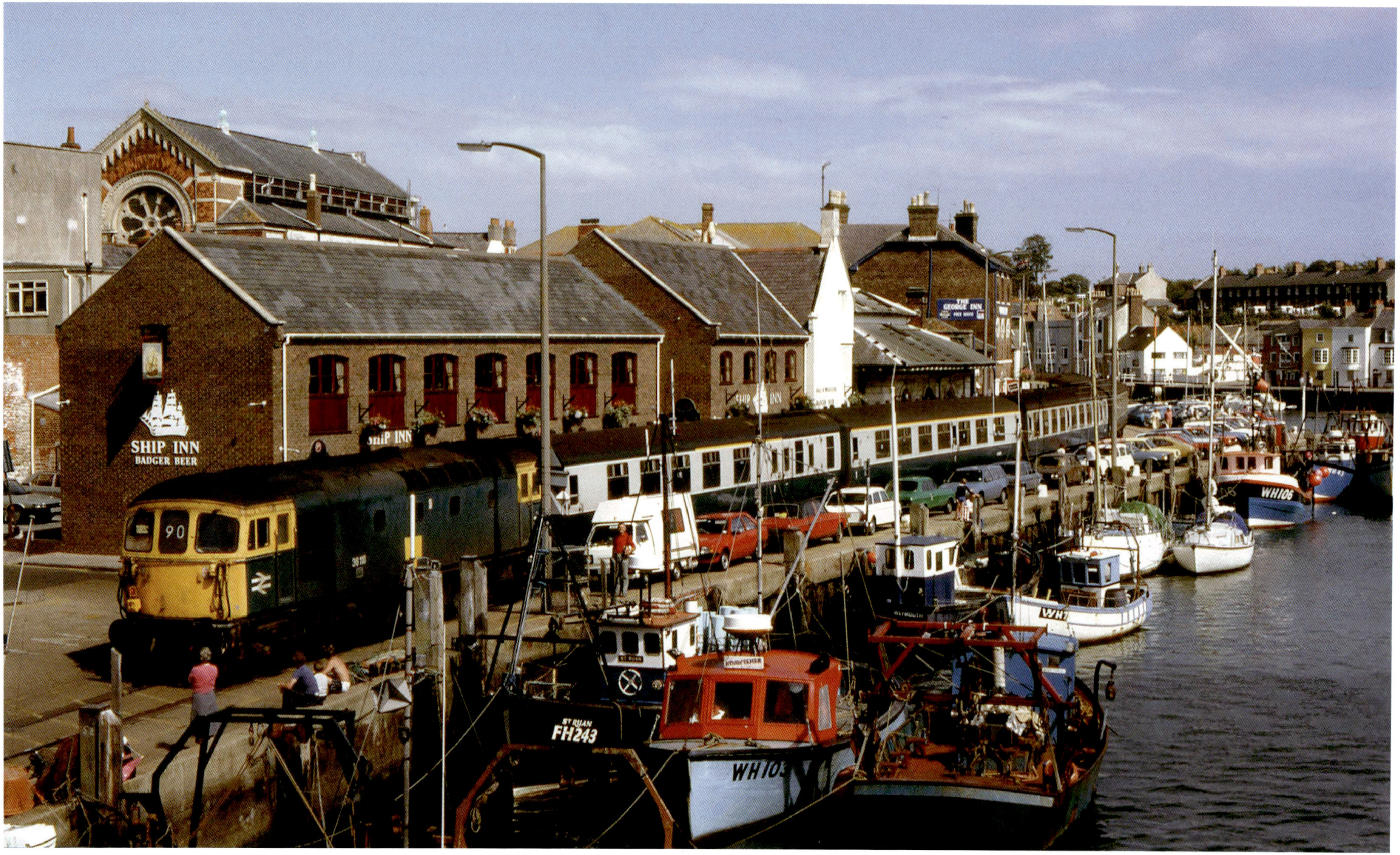

Tiptoeing carefully past The Ship Inn on the tramway section from Weymouth station down to the quayside where the Channel Island ferries landed we find 33113 with another boat train for Waterloo. This tramway section opened in 1889 after investment by the Great Western Railway and operated until 25 July 1940. After hostilities ceased it reopened for traffic in 1946 once again, goods traffic came to an end in 1972 and the regular use of passenger trains on the branch would cease on 26 September 1987. ***Rail Photoprints/John Chalcroft***

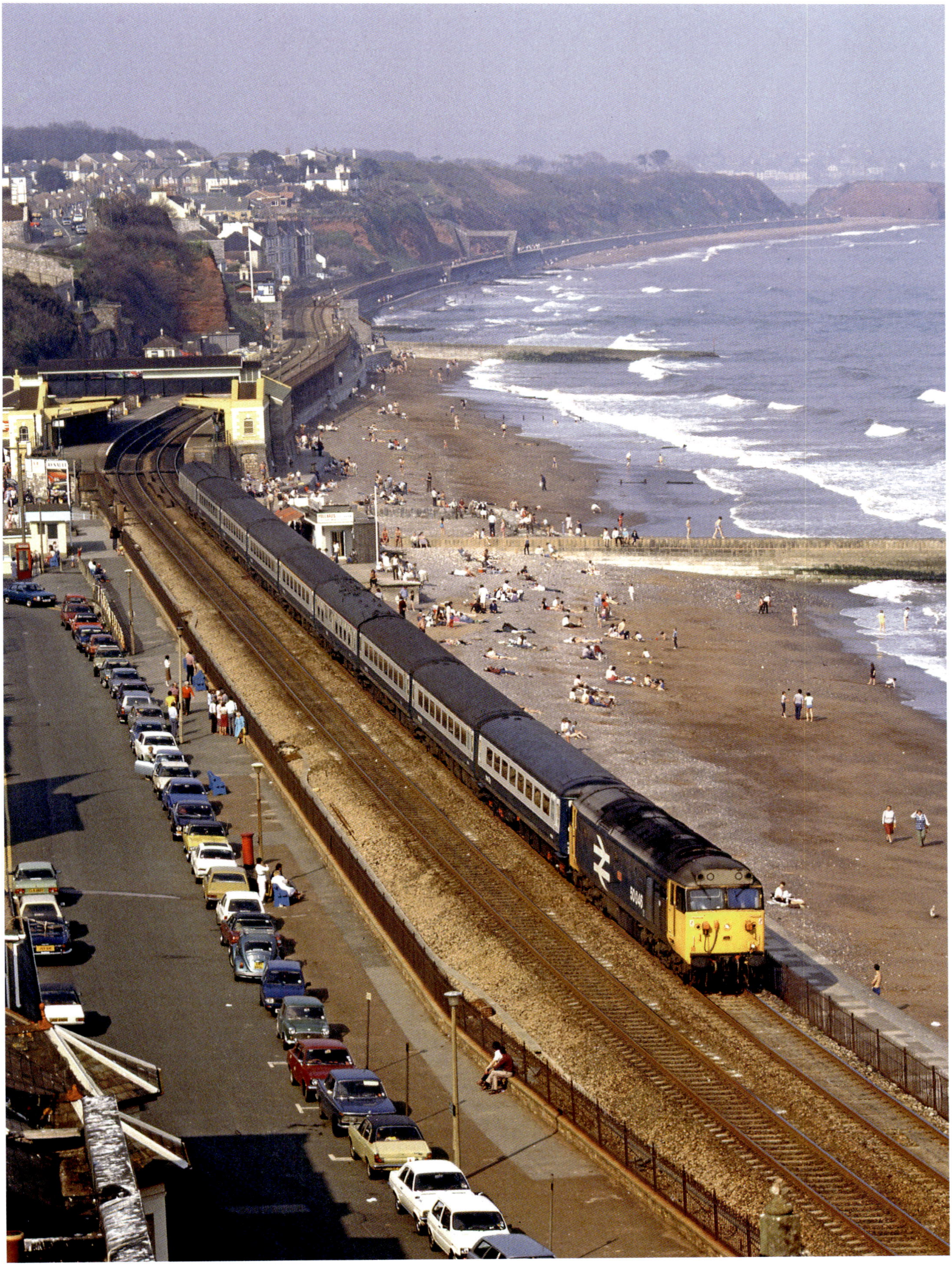

On a sunny 23 April 1984 it would be mostlyß daytrippers on the sandy beaches at Dawlish as 50046 Ajax made its way past on a Manchester to Plymouth service. The four year refurbishment programme for all fifty the Class 50s had been completed a few months beforehand with the release of 50014 Warspite in December 1983. ***Rail Photoprints/John Chalcroft***

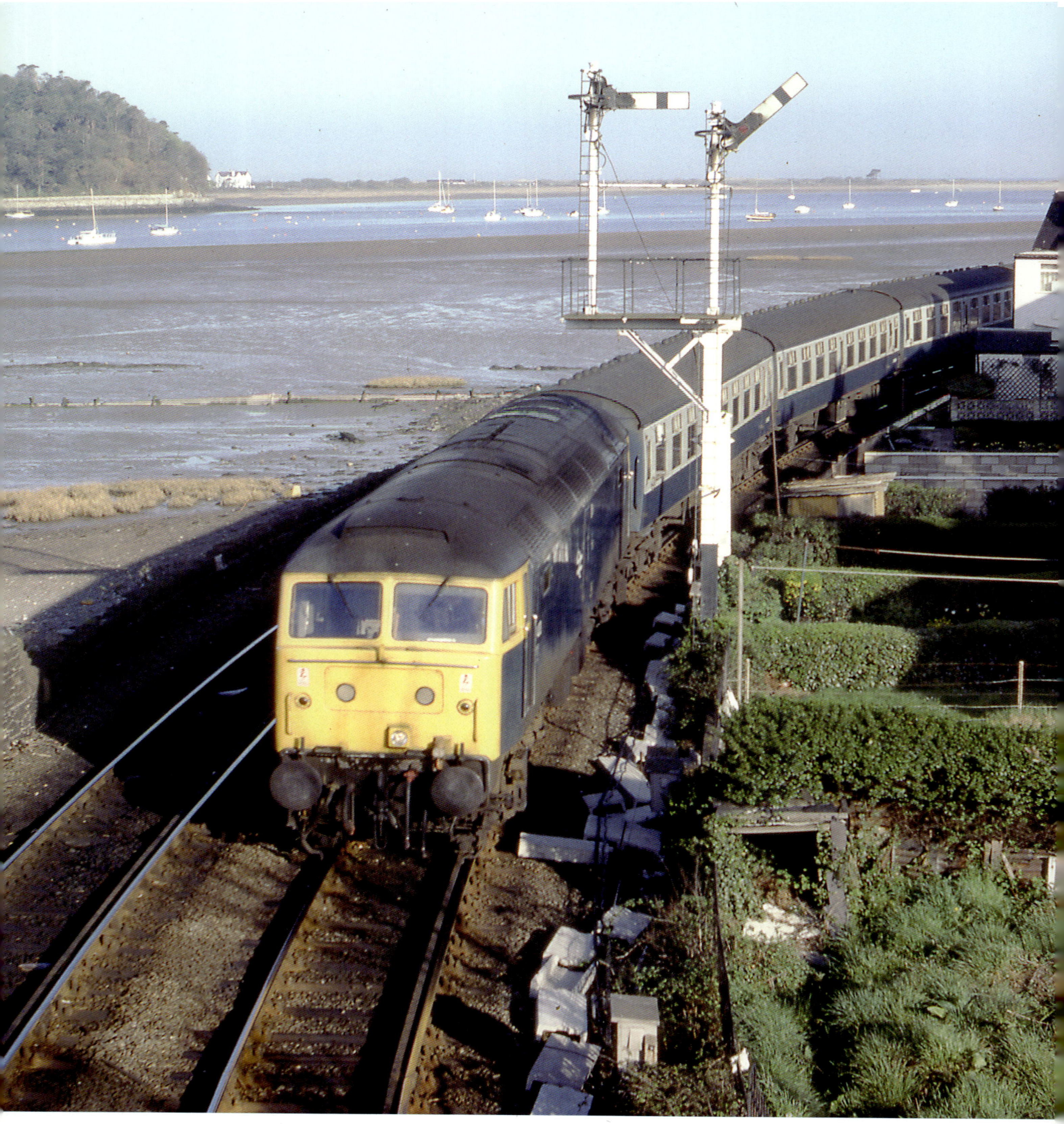

Its a cracking start to the day on the Conwy estuary at around 07.45 on 28 April 1984 as 47433 has been rostered to work from Llandudno Junction with an excursion to Worcester this morning. ***Ken Gambles***

Opposite: Another lovely early summer's morning setting at Claverton Weir in the Avon Valley near Bath sees 33044 taking the 05.50 Portsmouth to Cardiff past on 4 July 1987. At Claverton, the Kennet and Avon Canal is cut into the side of the valley 48 feet above the River Avon. The pumping station is located in a pump house built of Bath Stone, located at river level and separated from the canal by the railway line. It pumps water from the River Avon into the Kennet and Avon Canal using power from the flow of the River Avon, and was built by John Rennie between 1809 and 1813 to overcome water supply problems on the canal. ***Rail Photoprints/John Chalcroft***

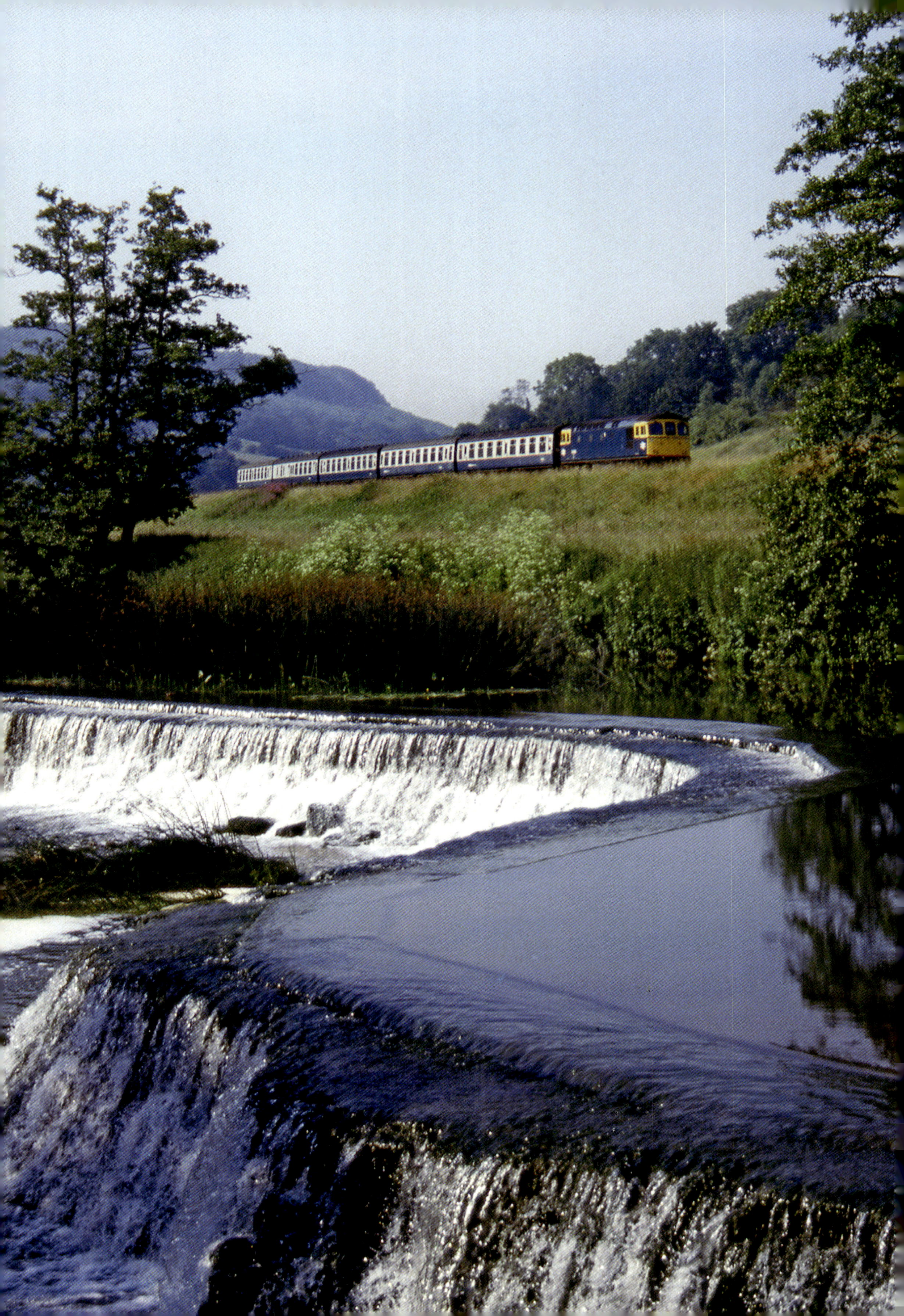

Places of Worship

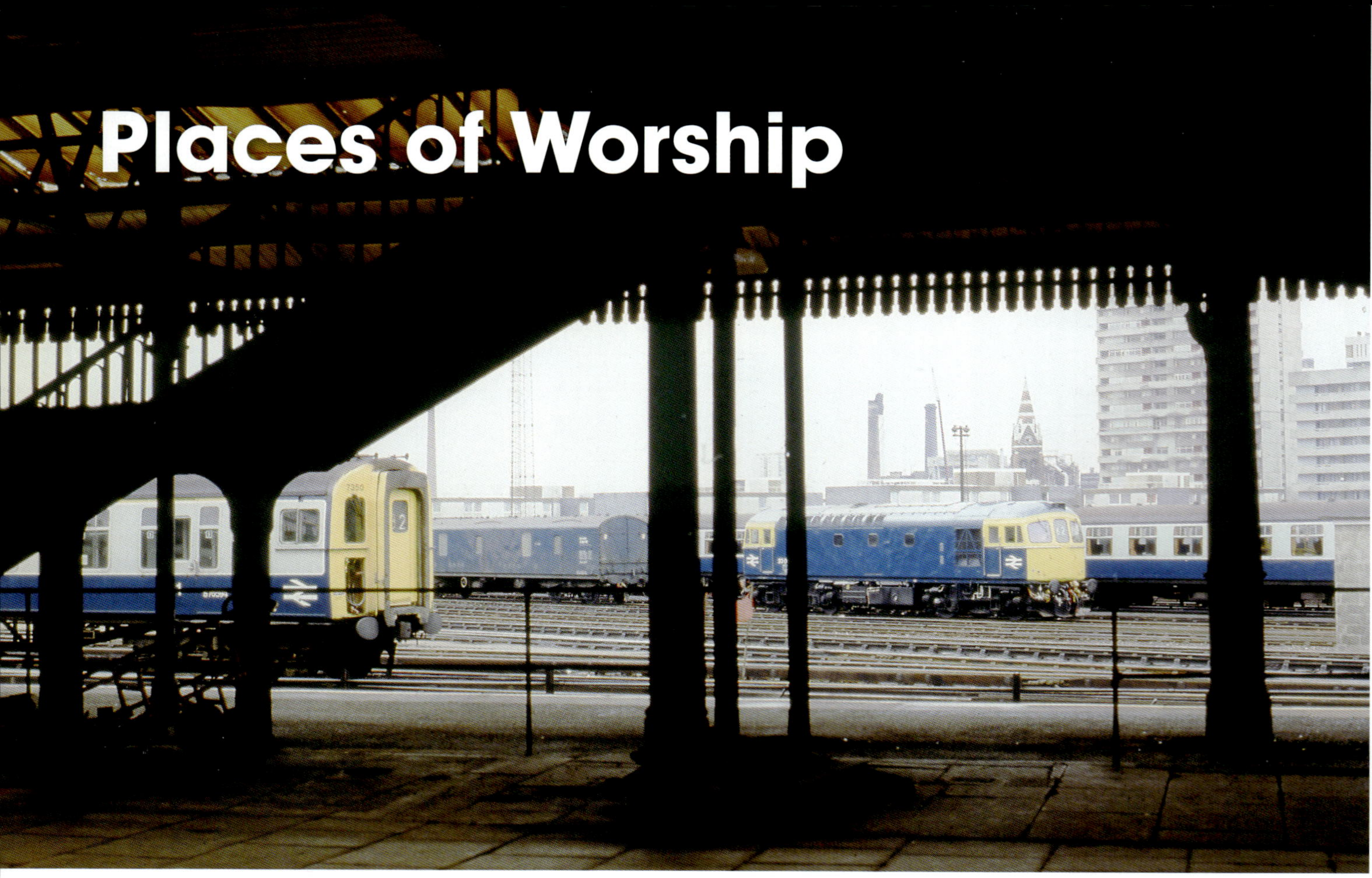

The Church of the Nazarene can be glimpsed in the background to 33001 stabled at Clapham Junction on 17 March 1981. ***Colin Whitbread***

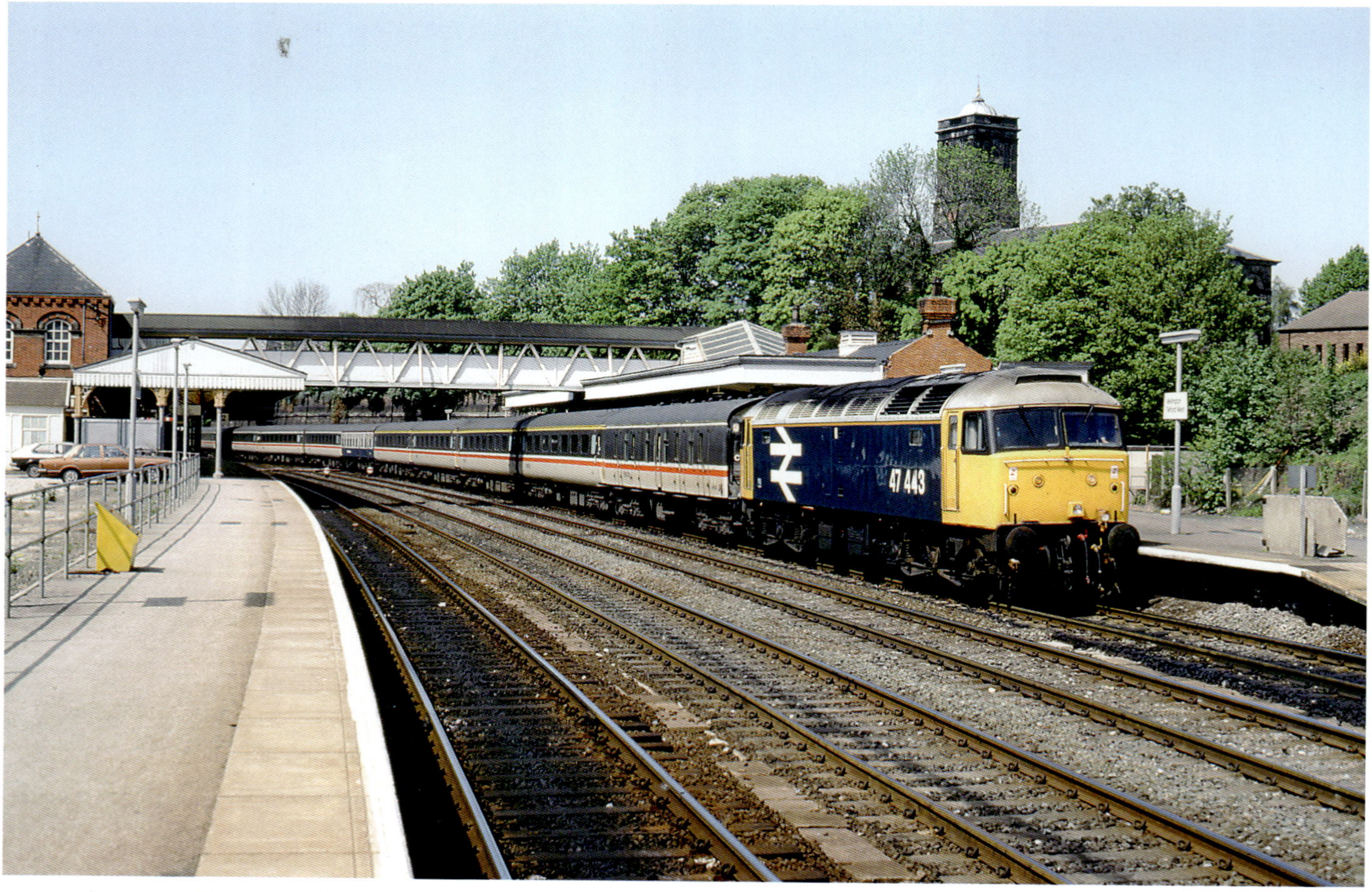

Overlooking the station at Wellington in Shropshire is the bell tower of All Saints Church as 47443 arrives in May 1987. Closer to the other Wellington in the southern hemisphere the same month the first ever Rugby World Cup kicked off with New Zealcnd playing Italy at Eden Park, Auckland. ***David T. Williams***

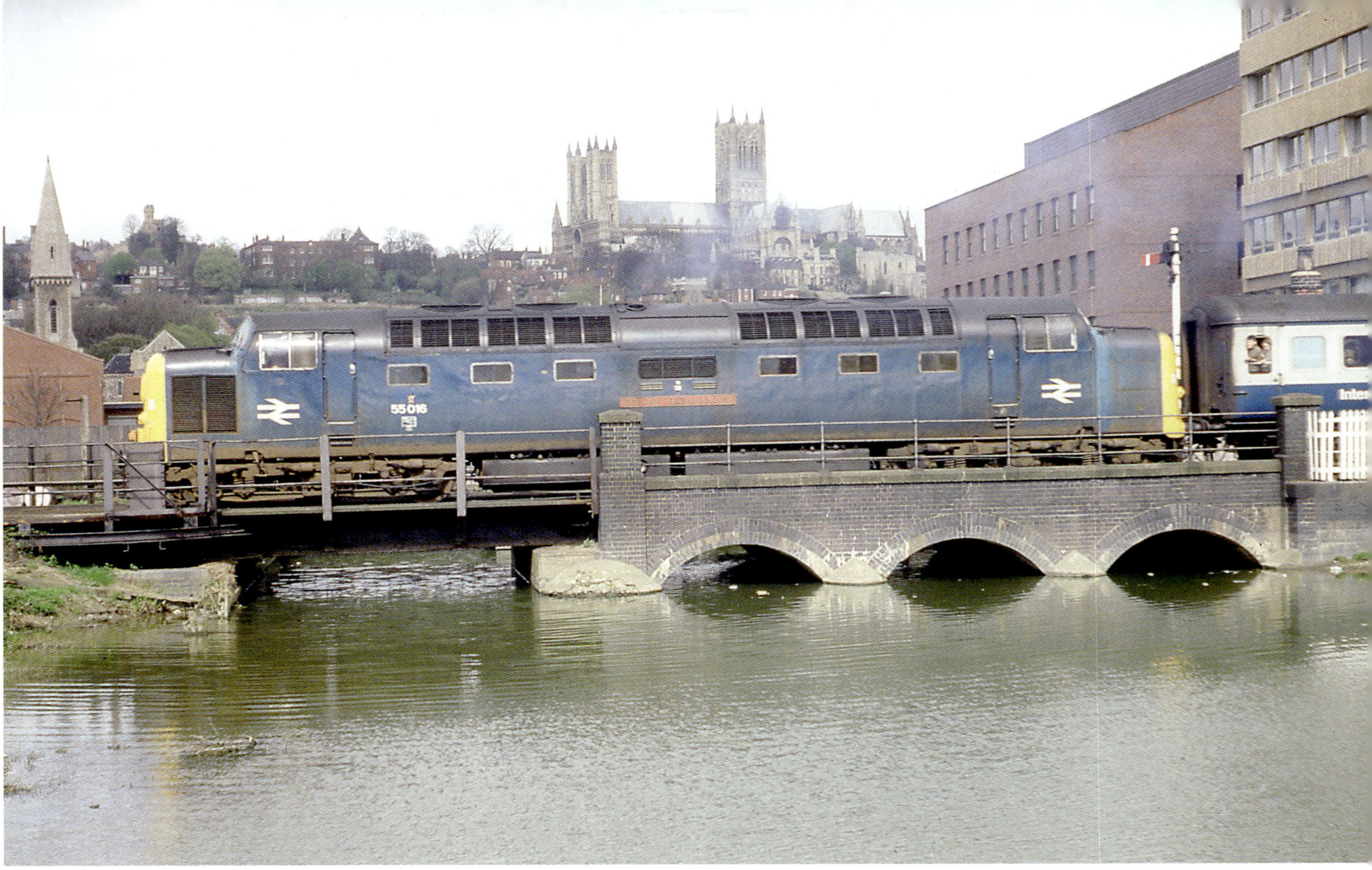

It is The Cathedral Church of the Blessed Virgin Mary of Lincoln that dominates the high ground above the city as 55016 Gordon Highlander finds itself re-routed through Lincoln on Easter Sunday in 1981. ***Strathwood Library Collection***

Another Class 47 runs nearby to a hallowed church ground as 47351 passes through Sutton Bridge Junction on 9 April 1983 in Shrewsbury. The town is also the birthplace of the biologist Charles Darwin whose evolution theories threw the church into chaos in the nineteenth century. ***John Arthur Bennett/Strathwood Library Collection***

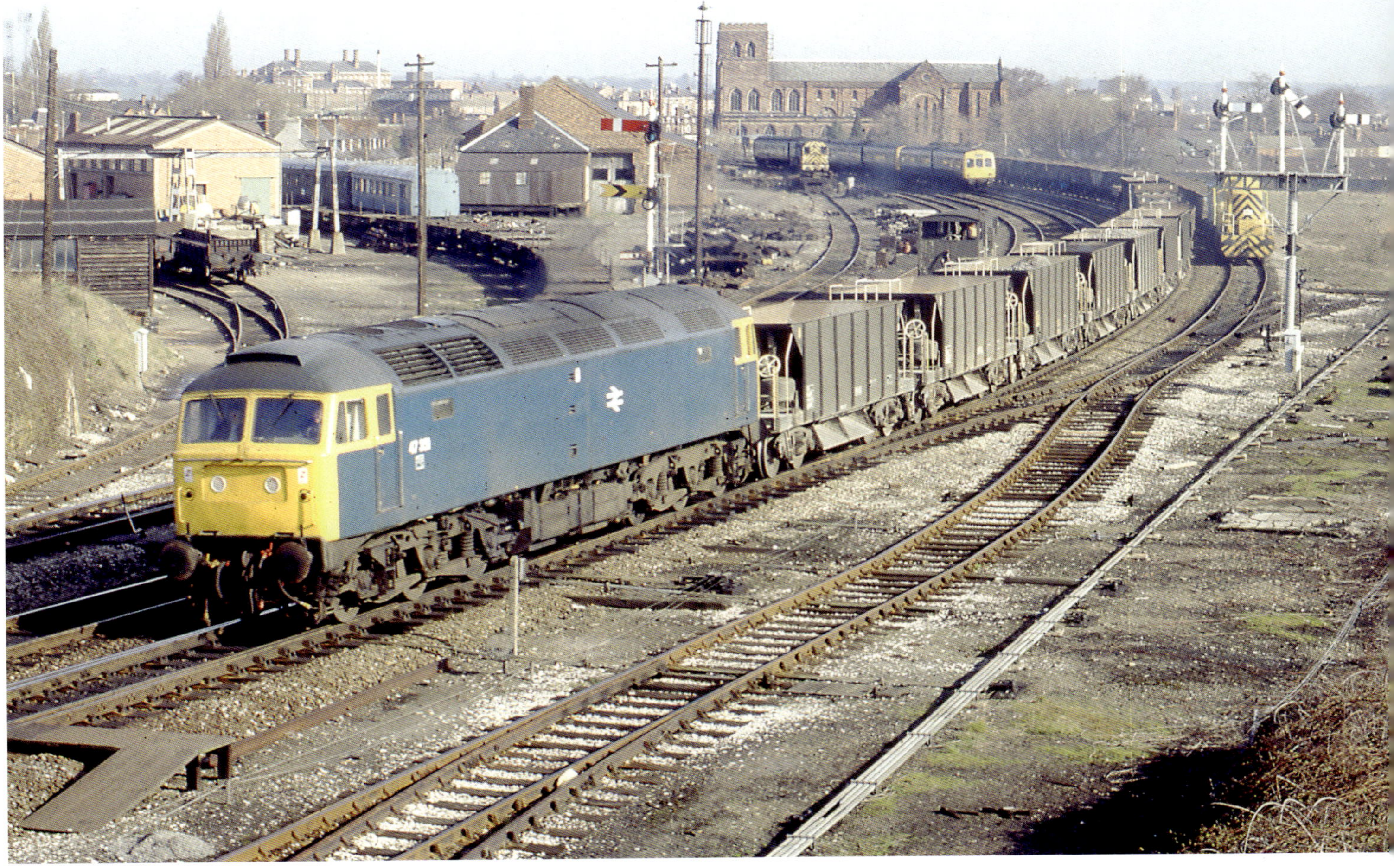

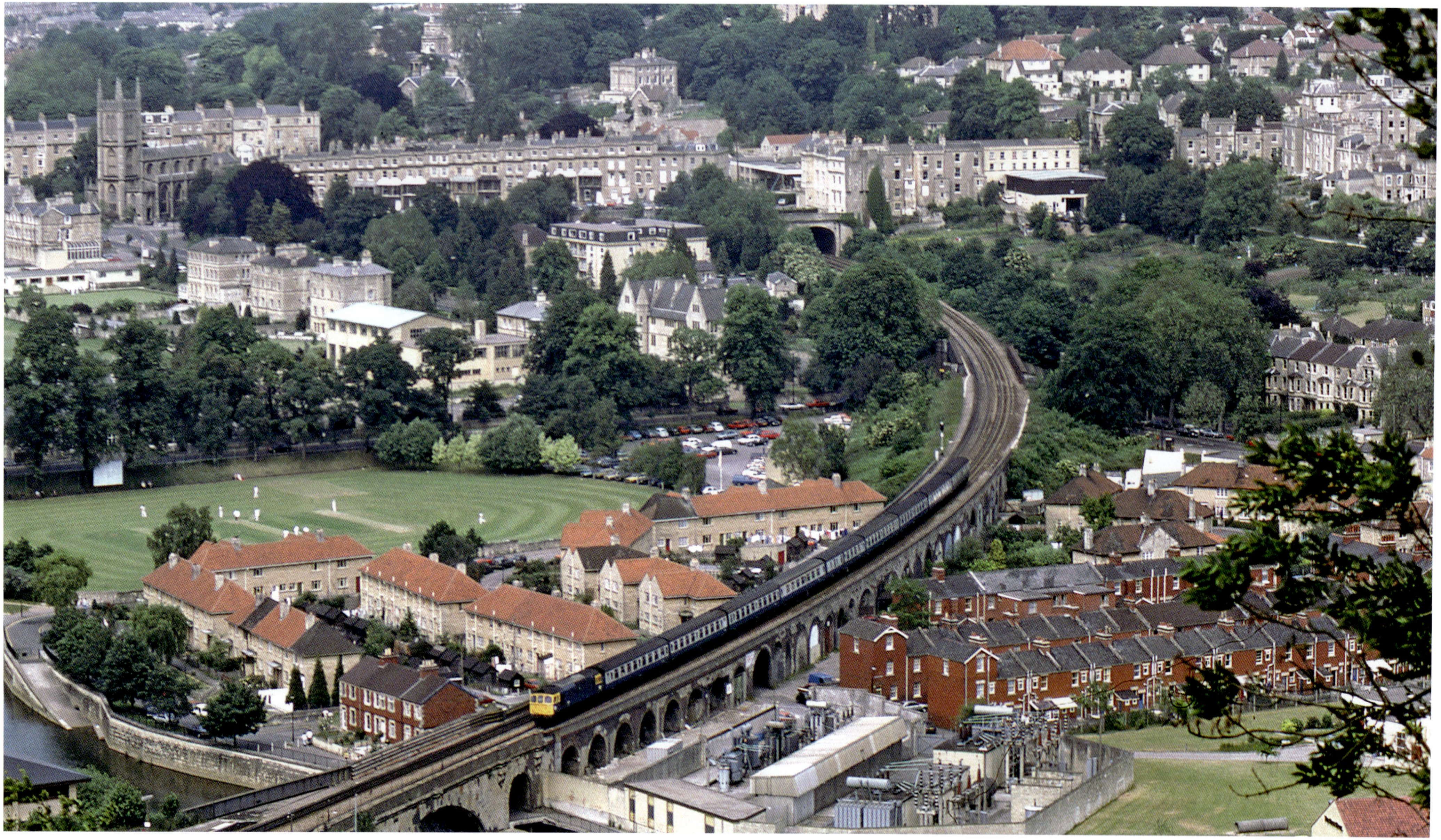

A Class 33 approaches Bath Spa station with a Brighton to Cardiff train on 21 June 1986. In the background we can see the city of Bath with the Church of St. John the Baptist standing proudly amongst the city's famed architecture. Bath was to suffer during World War Two with the Baedeker air-raids conducted by the Luftwaffe on 25 and 26 April 1942. They targeted strategically relatively unimportant but picturesque cities in England. These cities were reputedly selected from the German Baedeker Tourist Guide to Britain, meeting the criterion of having been awarded three stars (for their historical significance), hence the English name for the raids. Baron Gustav Braun von Stumm, a German propagandist is reported to have said on 24 April 1942 following the first attack, "We shall go out and bomb every building in Britain marked with three stars in the Baedeker Guide." ***Rail Photoprints/John Chalcroft***

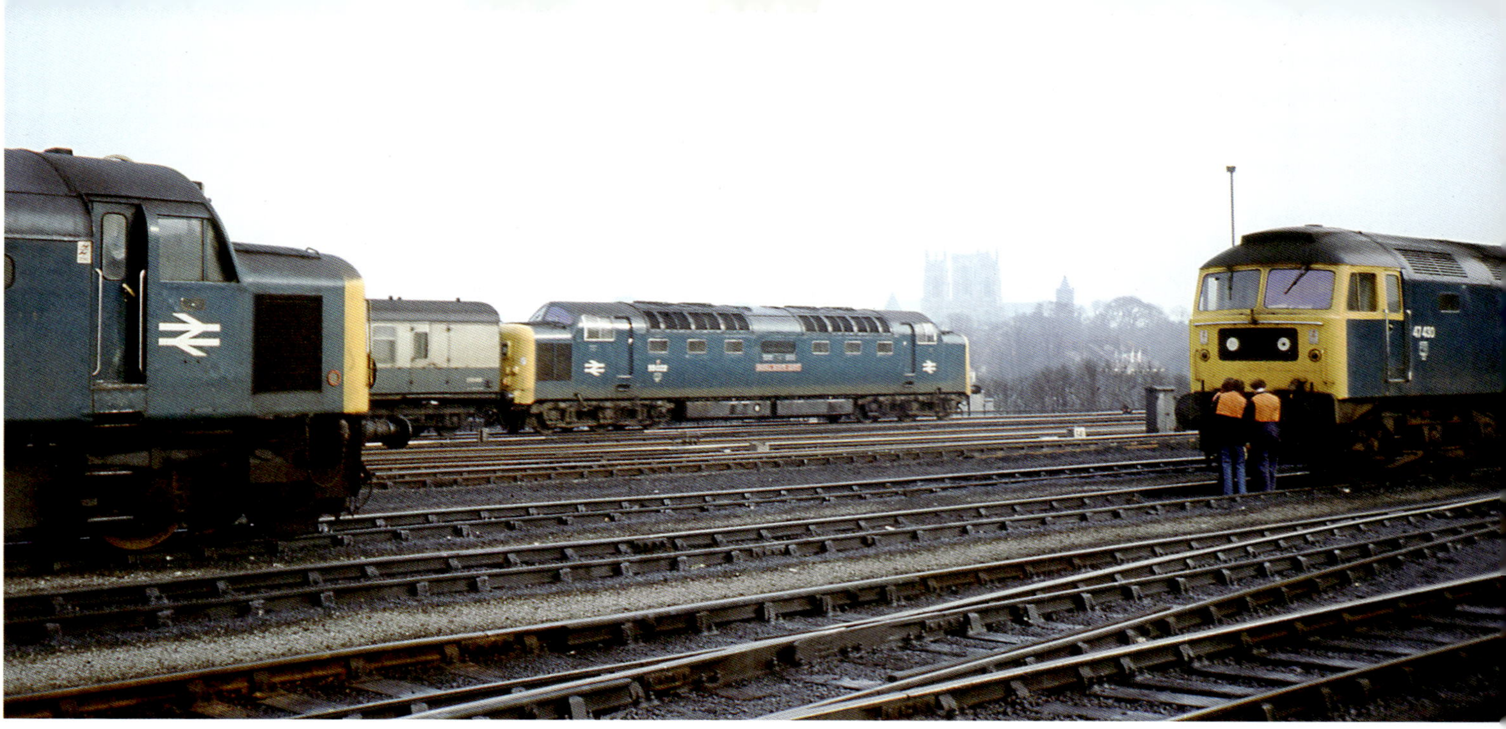

Other cities to suffer these Baedecker Raids were Exeter, Norwich and here in York where the ancient city's famous Minster graces the skyline from all angles. In the depot yard a Class 40 and Class 47 were on hand to watch a Deltic arrival from the north on 19 February 1980. ***Ken Gambles***

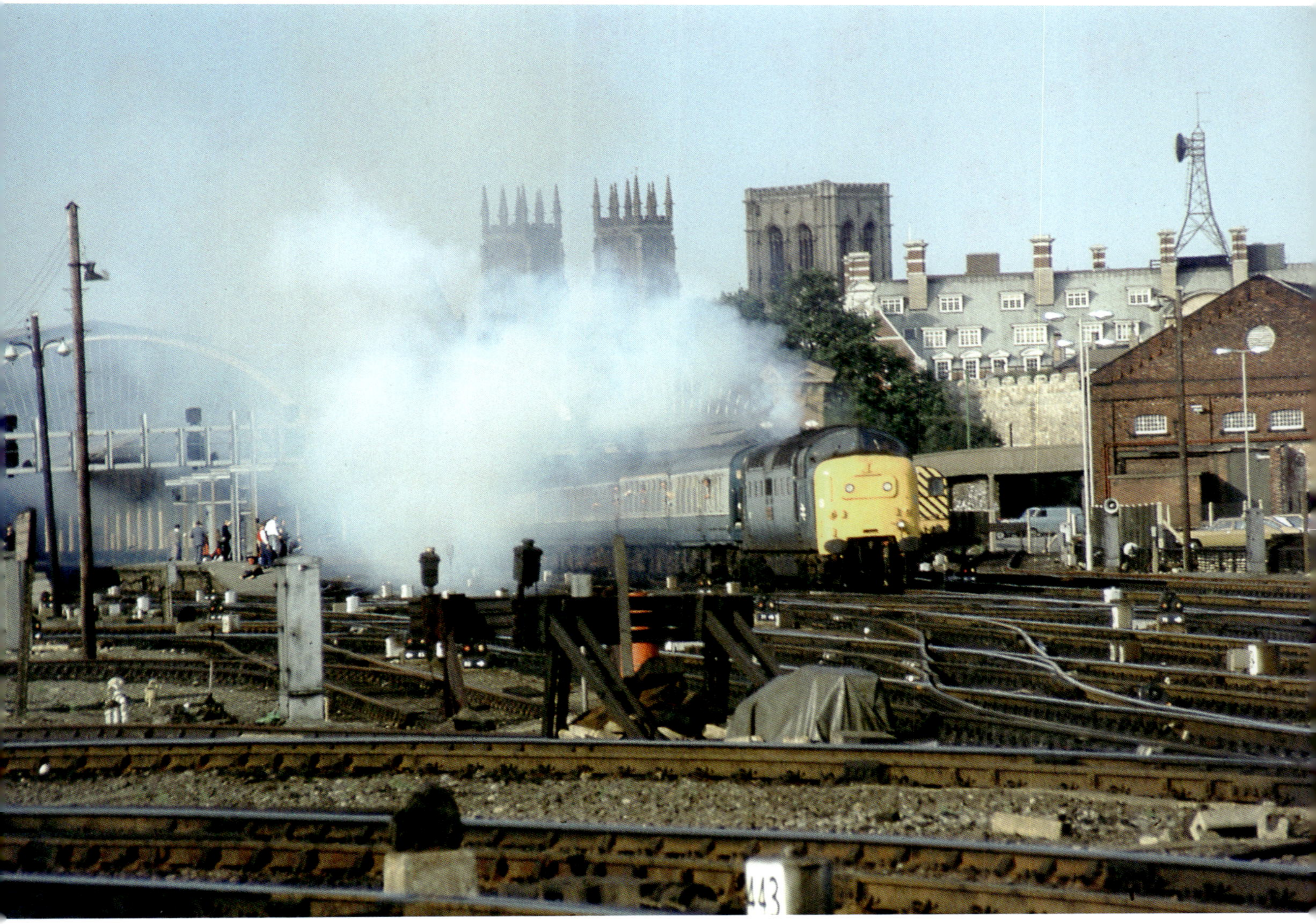

The platform enders and best part of the south end of York's station are obscured in a typical Deltic haze as 55017 The Durham Light Infantry marches off southwards towards Holgate Bridge at speed in July 1981. ***Mike Howarth/Strathwood Library Collection***

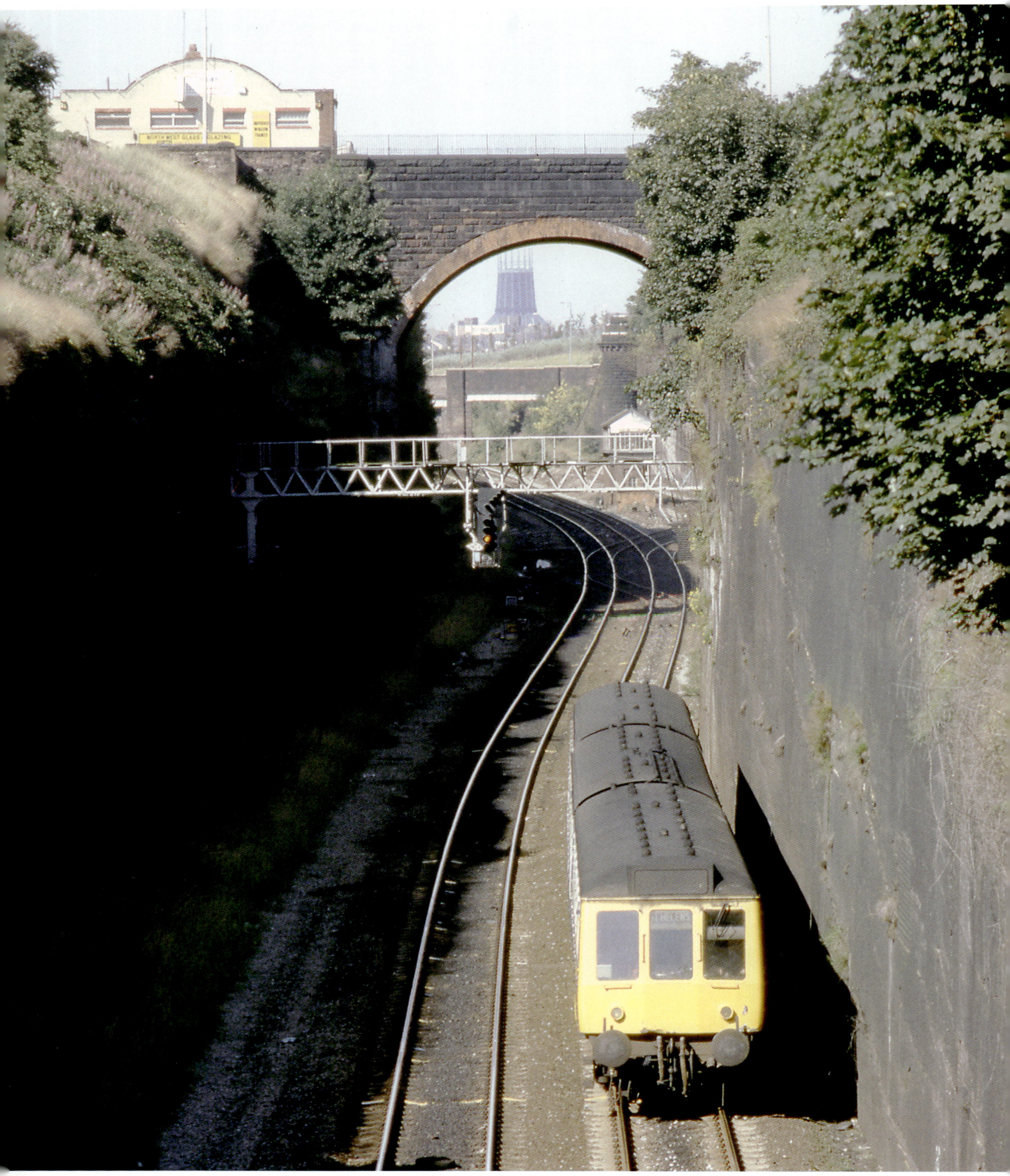

Liverpool has two cathedrals, with the Roman Catholic one being the most famous and distinctive. Often referred to irrevantly as Paddy's Wigwam or The Mersey Funnel its offical title is the Liverpool Metropolitan Cathedral Church of Christ the King and is seen through the arch in the distance in September 1986. In July 1981 the suburb of Toxteth erupted into riots, one of the main causes of poverty in the area was containerisation at the nearby Liverpool Docks, destroying thousands of waterfront-type jobs which had been associated with the city of Liverpool for generations. With the economy in recession, unemployment in Britcin was at a 50-year high in 1981, and Toxteth had one of the highest unemployment rates in the country. ***Mike Auerswald***

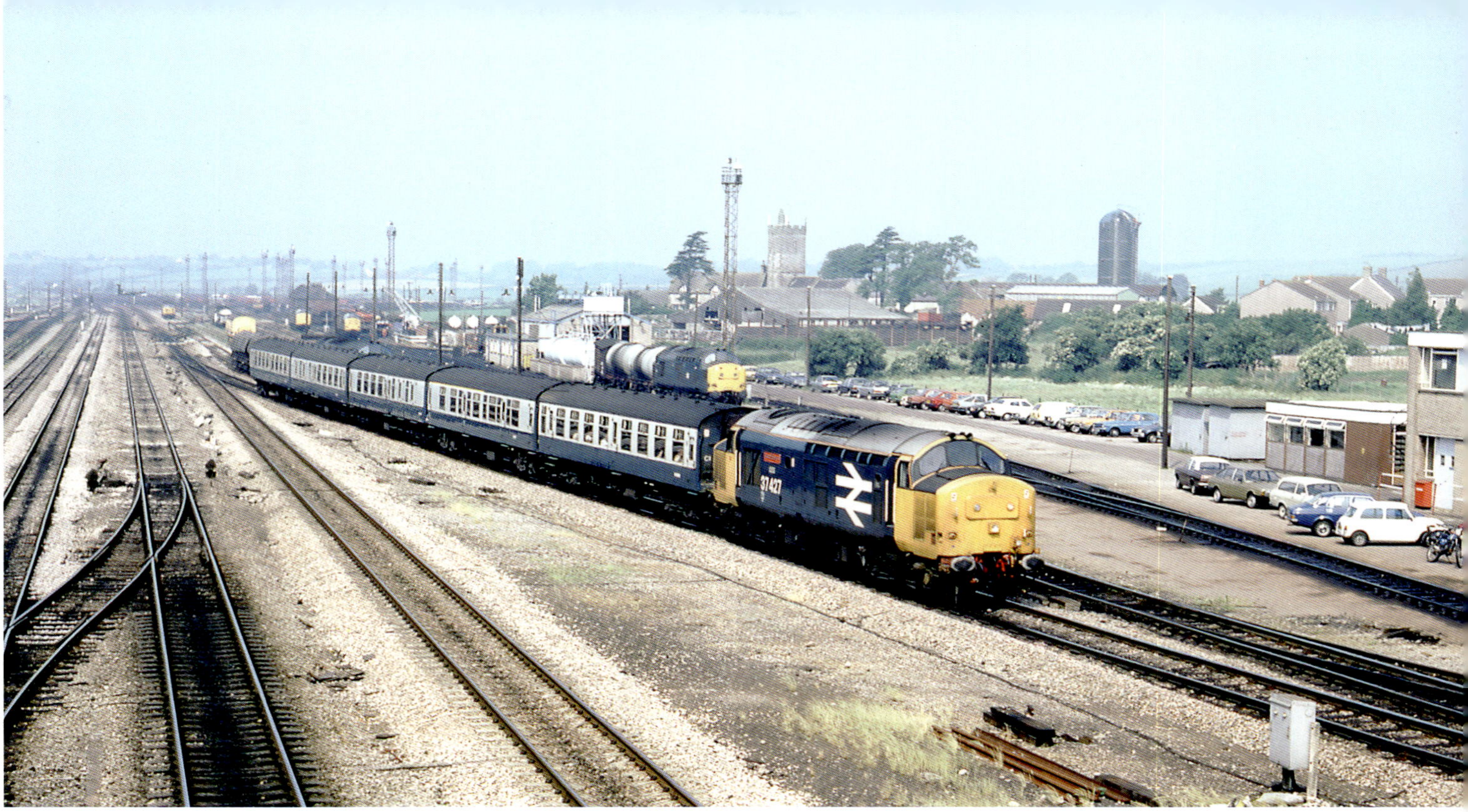

Another location to feel the winds of change during the decade was Severn Tunnel Junction, seen here in July 1986 with 37427 drawing in off the mainline. As a result of reduced coal and industrial production from the mid-1980s from South Wales, Severn Tunnel Junction goods yard and locomotive depot would close on 12 October 1987. St. Mary's church at Rogiet in the background looks out now on the toll booths to the second Severn Bridge Crossing instead. ***David T. Williams***

Much has been said on the plight of the Settle & Carlisle through the seventies and eighties. In the face of adversity the line remains open today for passengers to enjoy and for railway management to be quietly thankful for when the WCML is closed. This was the everyday scene at Skipton on a sunny January day 1988. ***Rick Harvey***

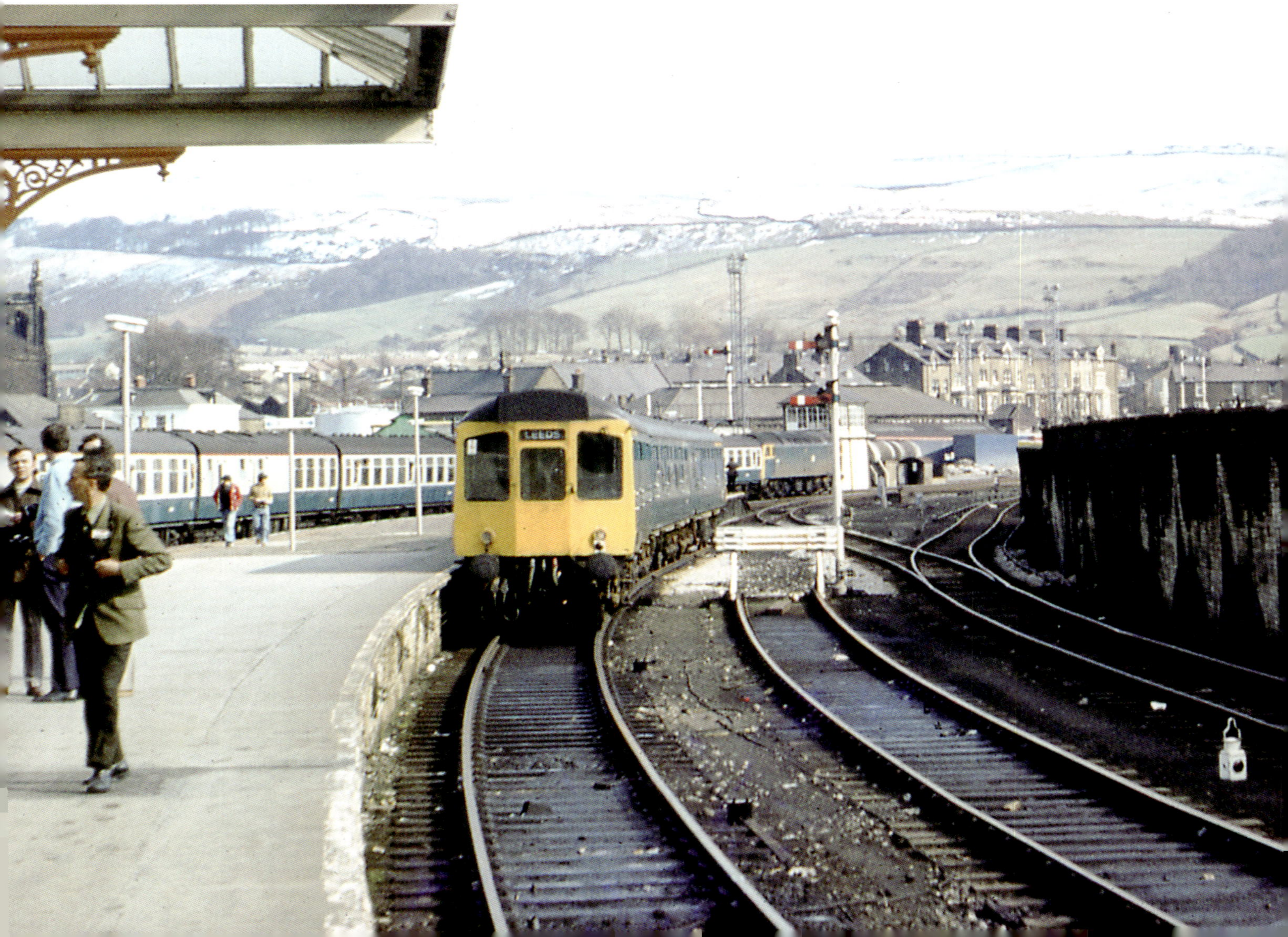

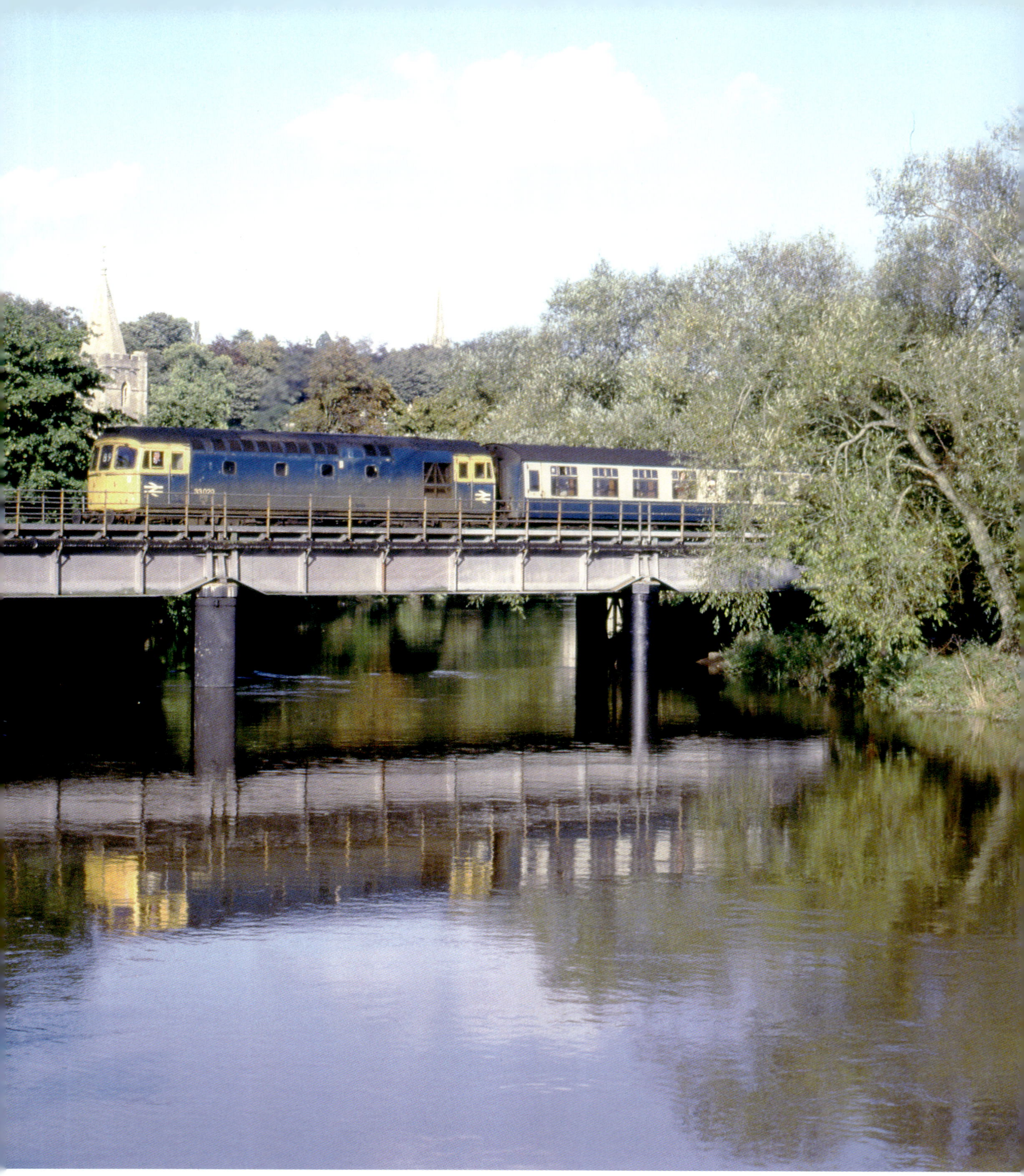

The traditional church tower or steeple continues to be very much a part of the British landscape whilst the sights and sounds of locomotive hauled passenger trains has since been becoming a rarity. On 17 October 1987, 33020 rumbled across the river at Bradford-on-Avon with a Portsmouth Harbour to Cardiff service. This shot was taken the day after the great storm that Michael Fish found fame for predicting wrongly! ***Gilroy A. Kerr***

Depot Panoramas

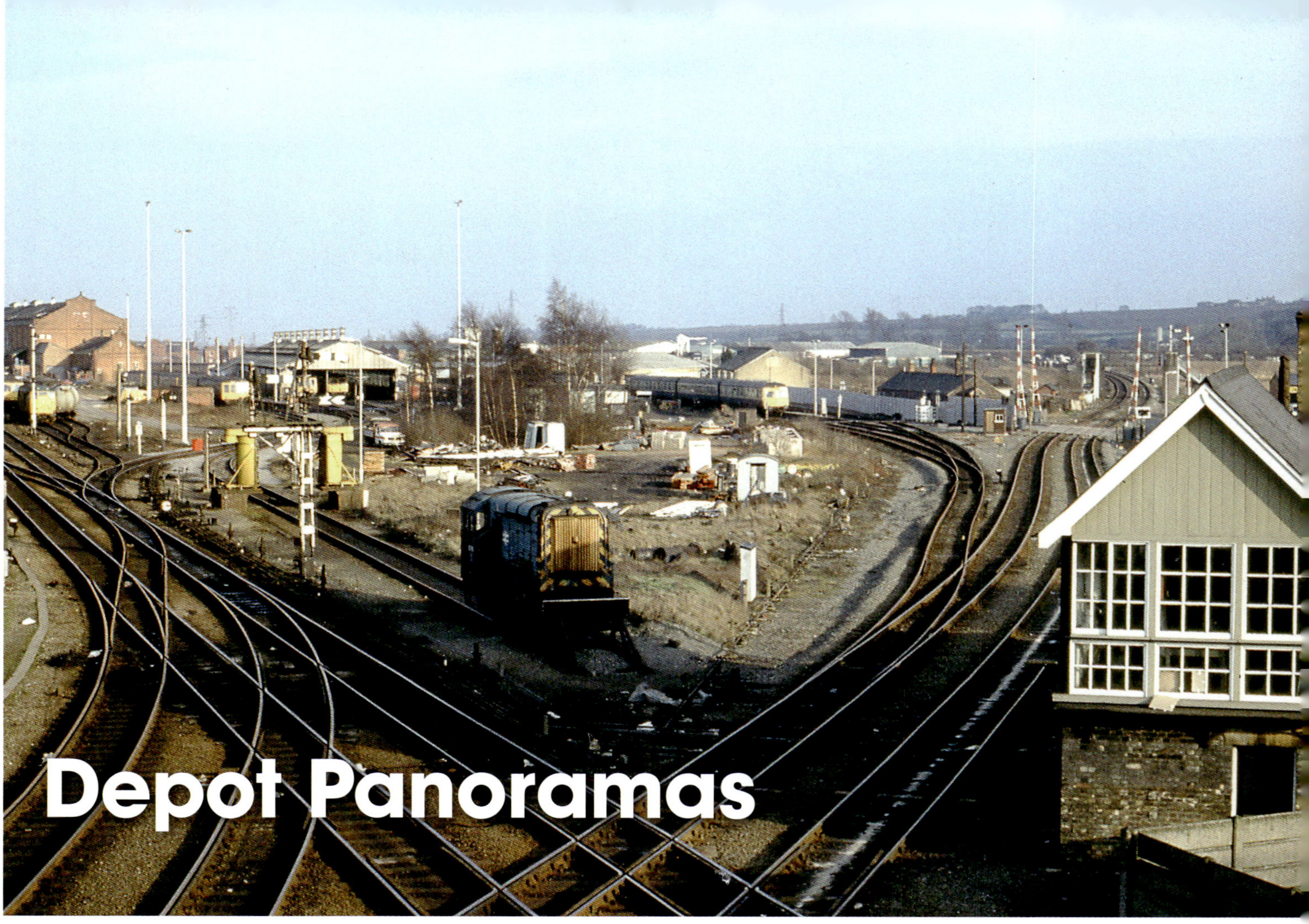

One location that sees very little coverage is Lincoln's motive power depot this was the view towards it on 23 February 1985, I would say it was worth a look around wouldn't you? ***Arthur Wilson***

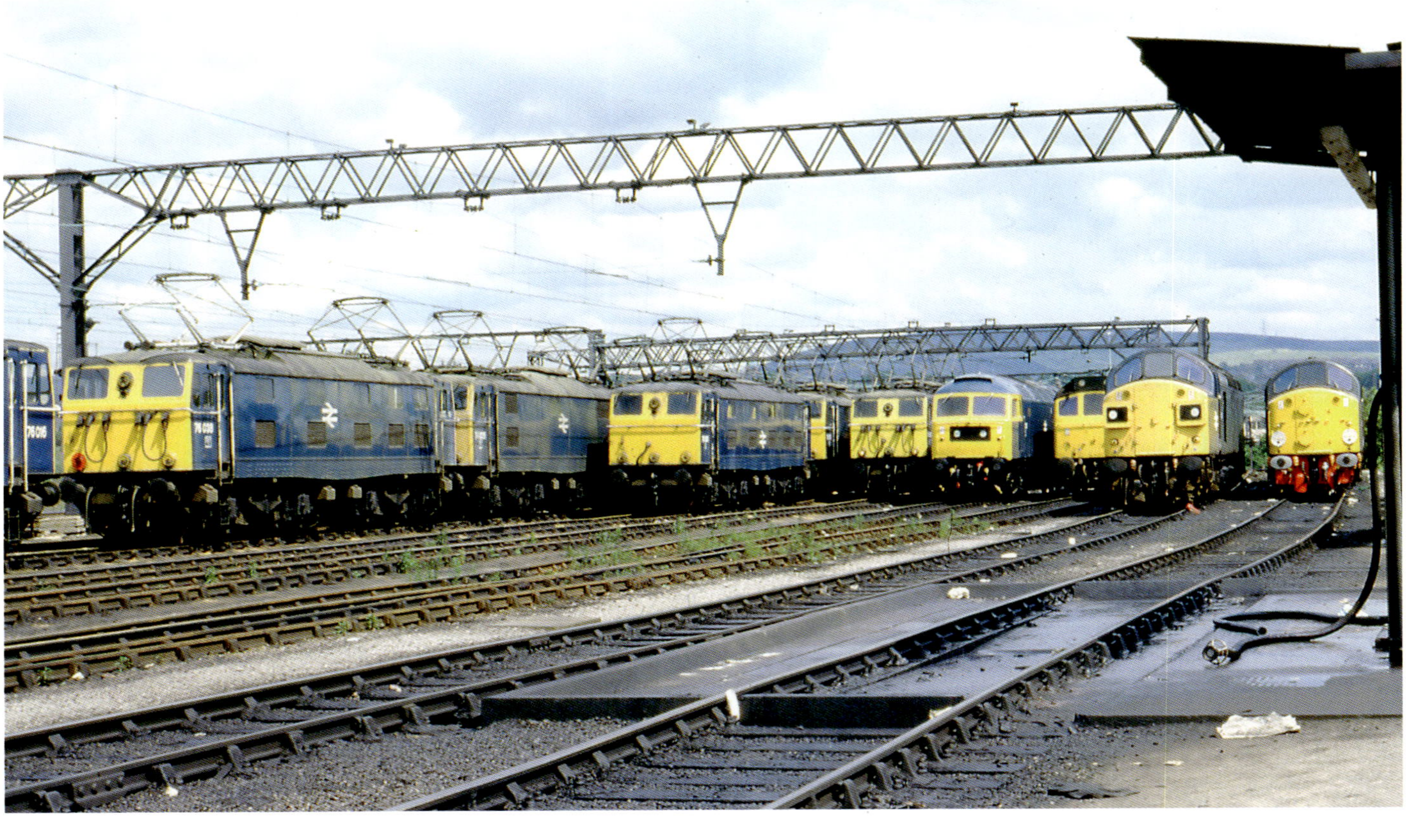

Many enthusiasts will have made the trip to enjoy and record moments like this at Guide Bridge with 76016, 76038, 76035, 76001, 76003, 76026, 47225, 25216, 40140 and 40106 all visible on 30 May 1980. ***Colin Whitbread***

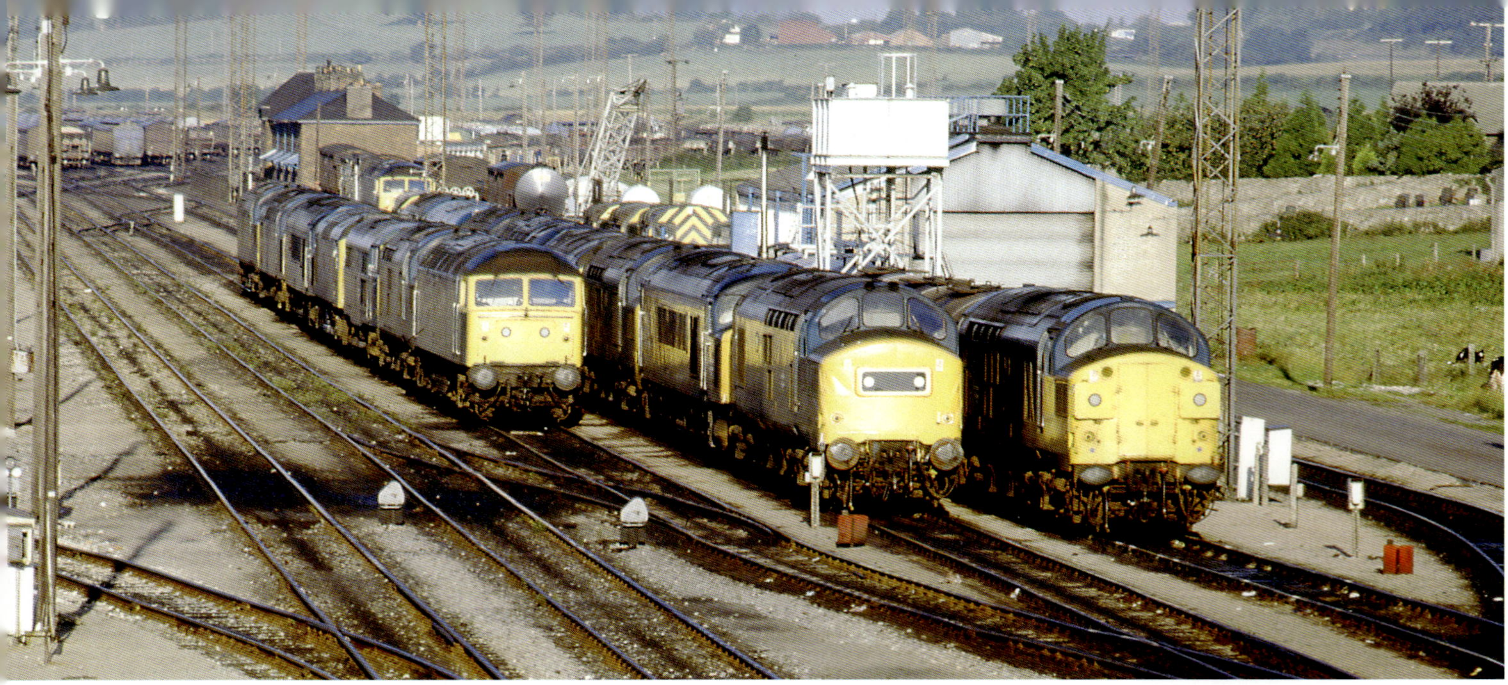

On 29 August 1982 a visitor to Severn Tunnel Junction would have had this tempting line up to record. ***Sid Steadman***

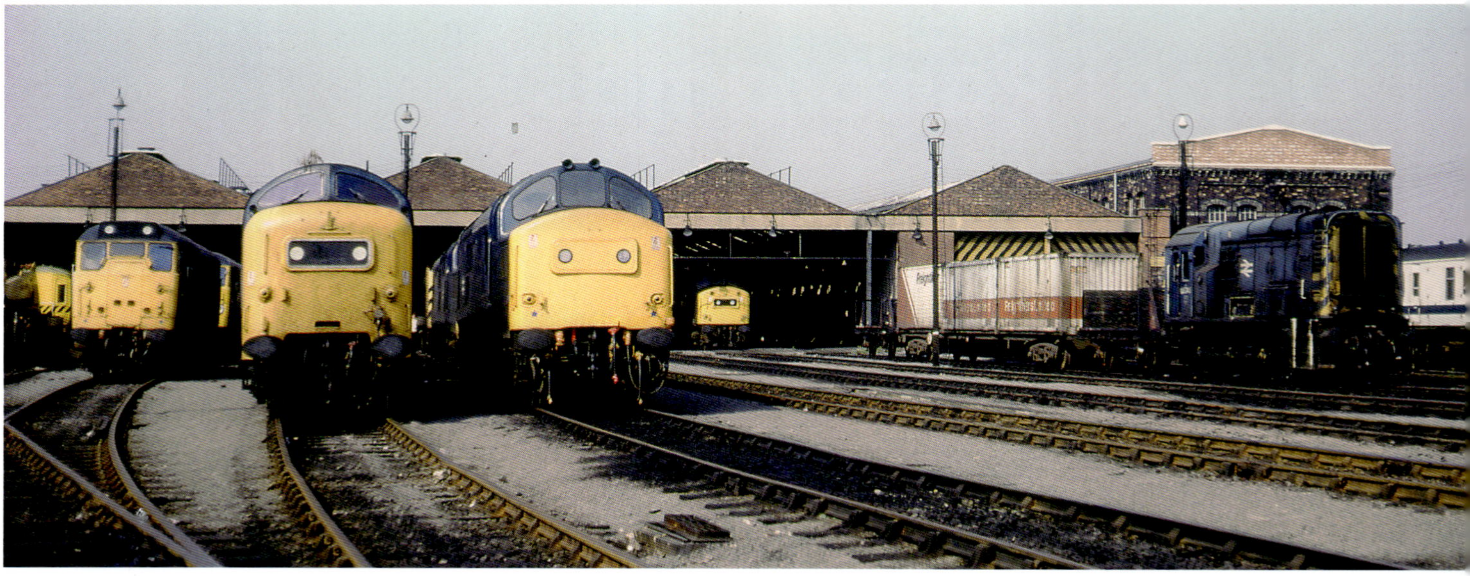

Whereas Doncaster's shed offers a good variety of types to the cameraman on 6 September 1981. ***Strathwood Library Collection***

Below: Most views of Colchester's depot are inevitabley taken from the station platforms as here on 6 December 1986. ***Late Derek Whitnell/Strathwood Library Collection***

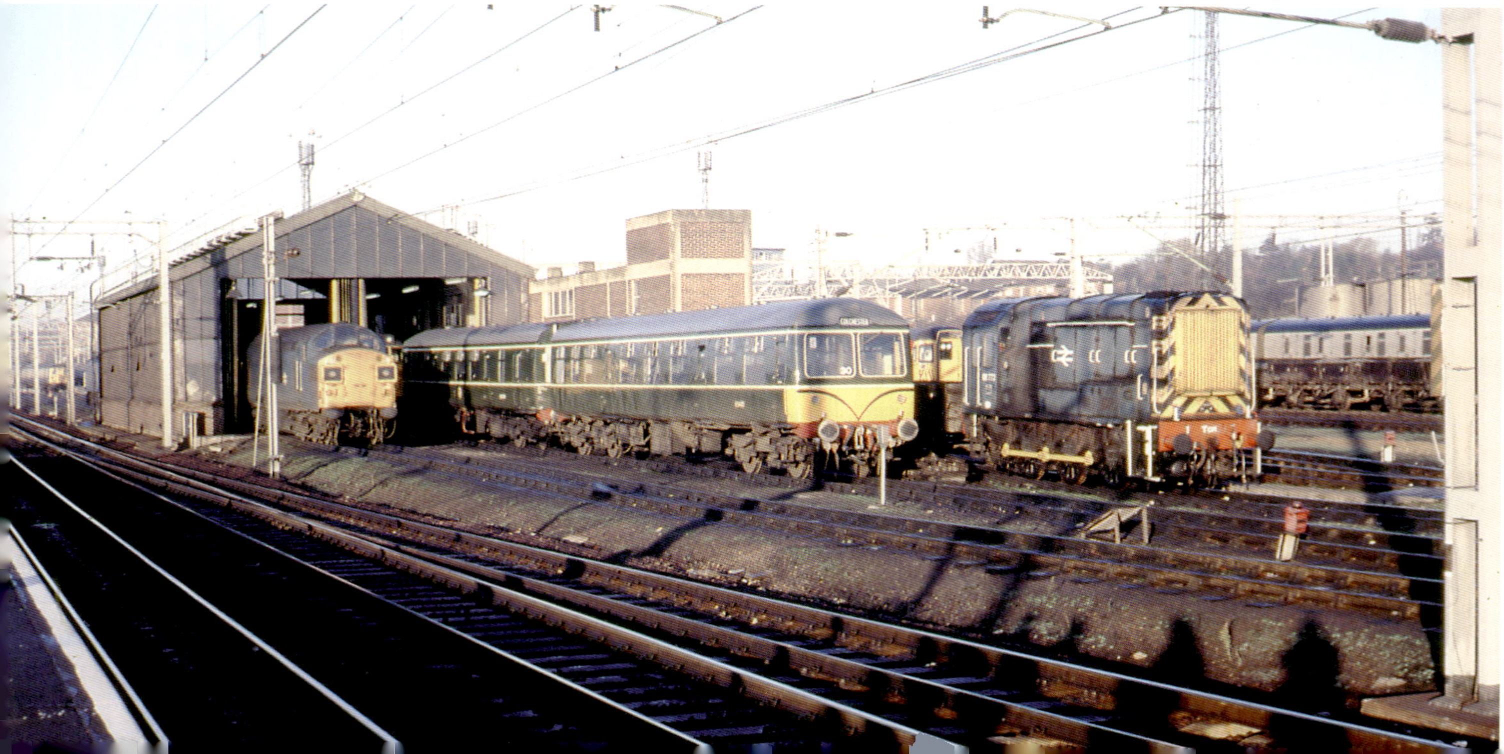

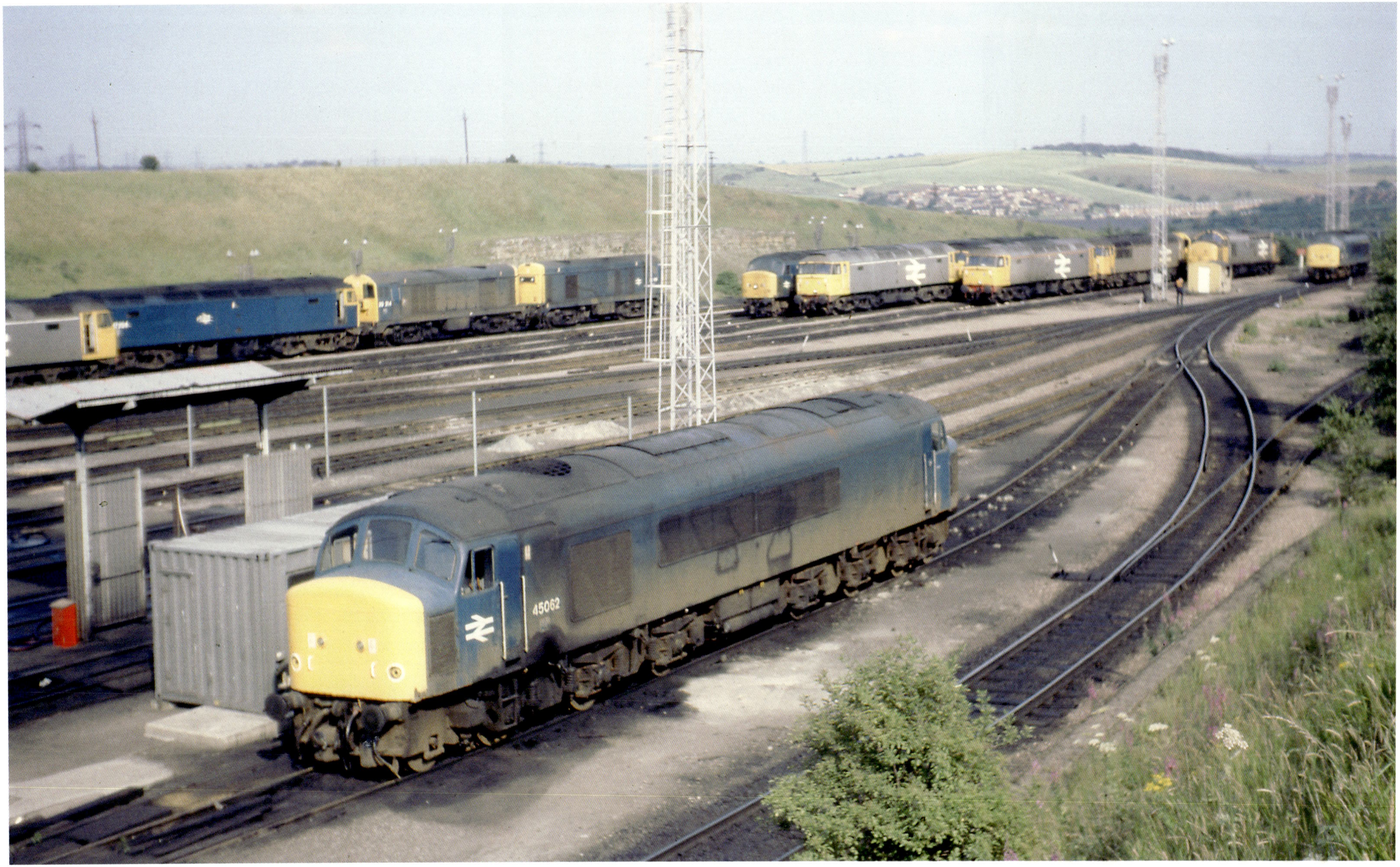

A real favourite depot for many since it opened in 1965 was Tinsley for its wide variety of locomotives, and the huge numbers of engines always to be found on shed, as here in August 1987. As the eighties progressed more and more withdrawn locomotives could be seen dumped here among the deliveries of Class 56s that had began in 1976 and ended with 56135 arriving new on 4 November 1984. Finally Tinsley would close completely in 1998 and the site would be levelled a few years later. ***Mike Auerswald***

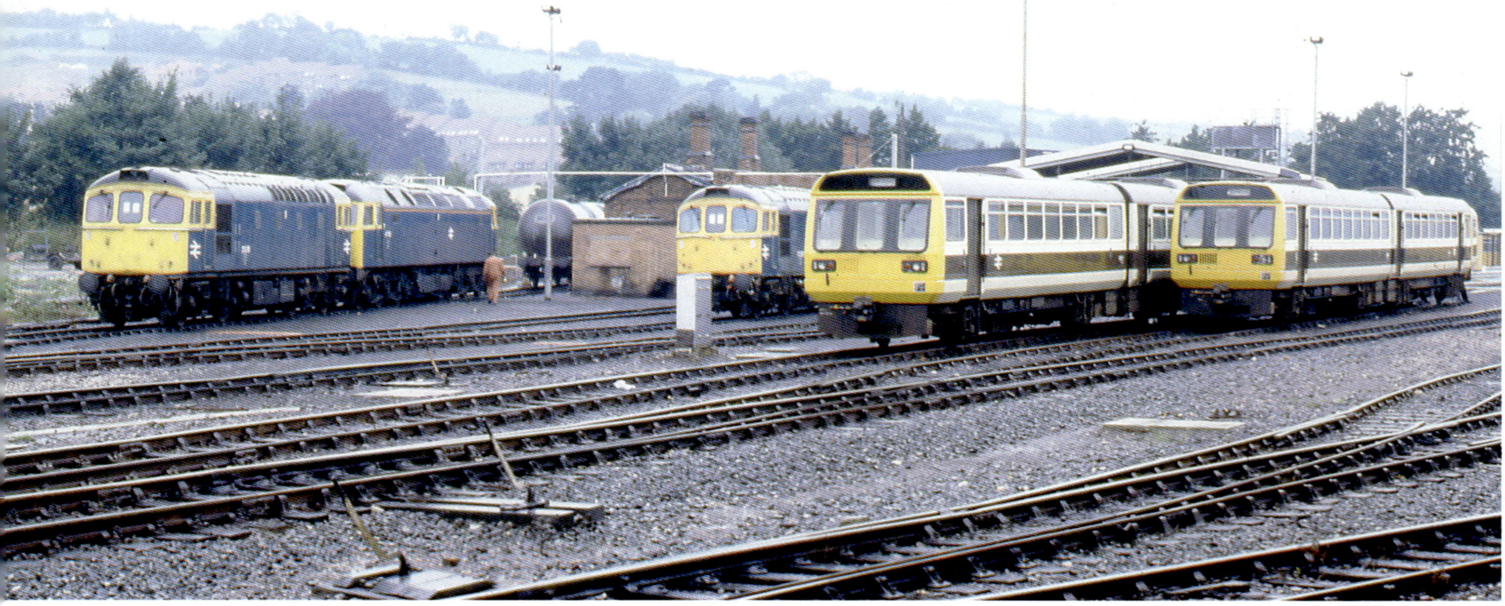

The stabling point at Exeter during September 1986 is another location best viewed from under the platform canopy when its raining. ***Dave Southern***

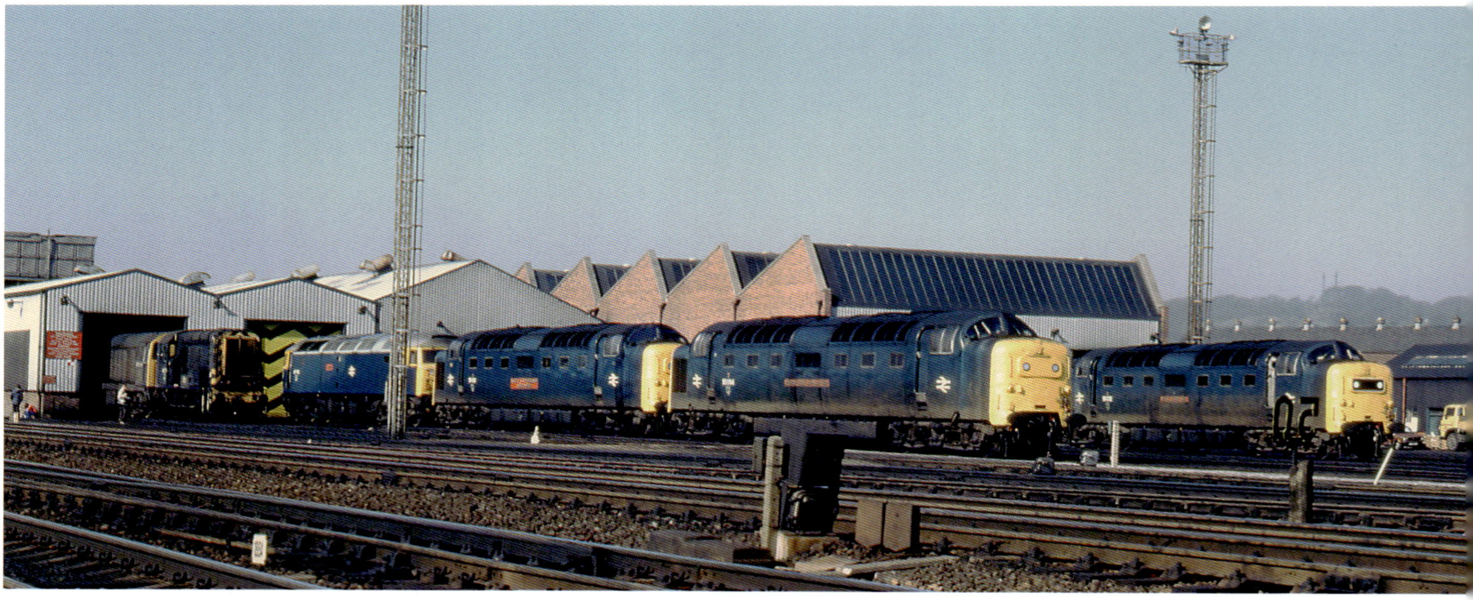

Haymarket famous for its prestige locomotive fleet over the years does not dissappoint with 55004, 55021, 55022 and 47705 displayed on 5 April 1980. ***Sid Steadman***

Below: Whereas Healey Mills with its plethora of freight turns offers 31321 in October 1982. ***David T.Williams***

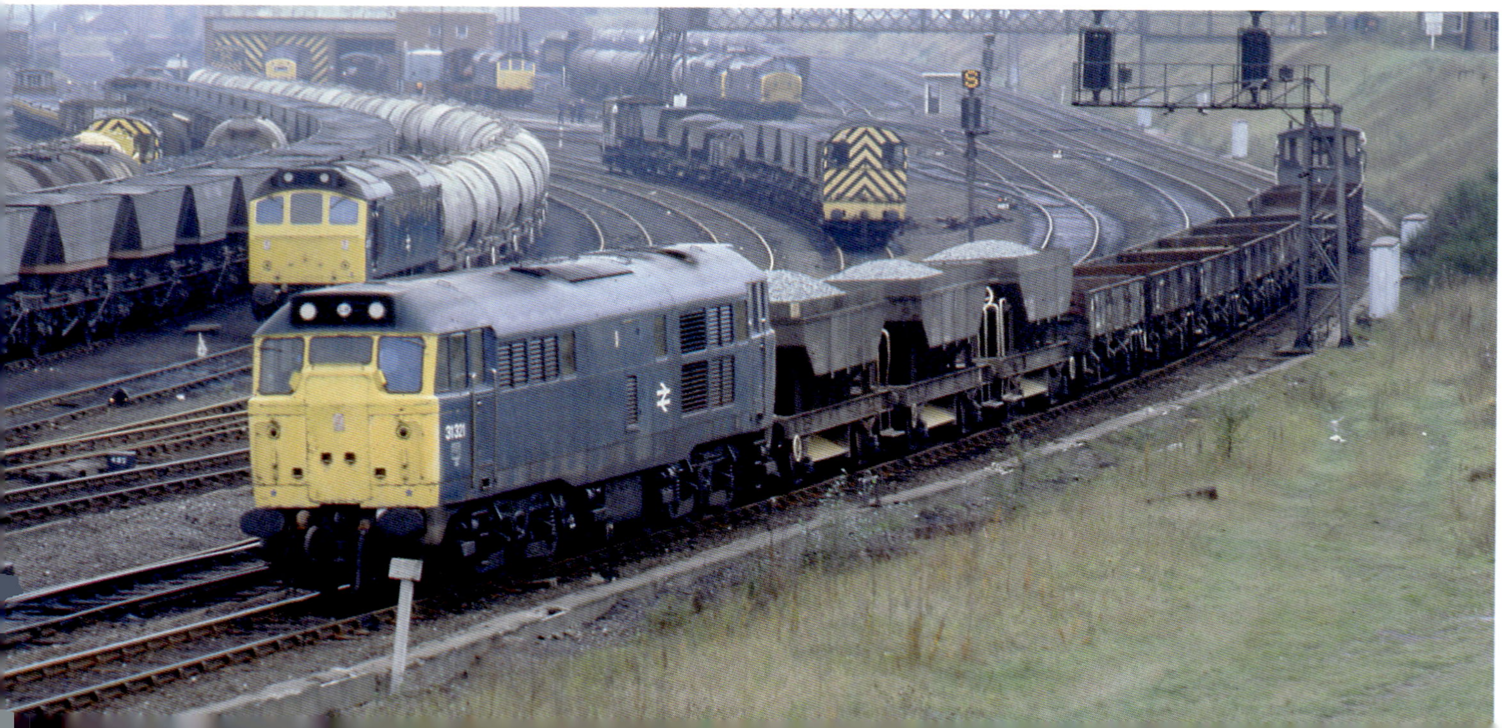

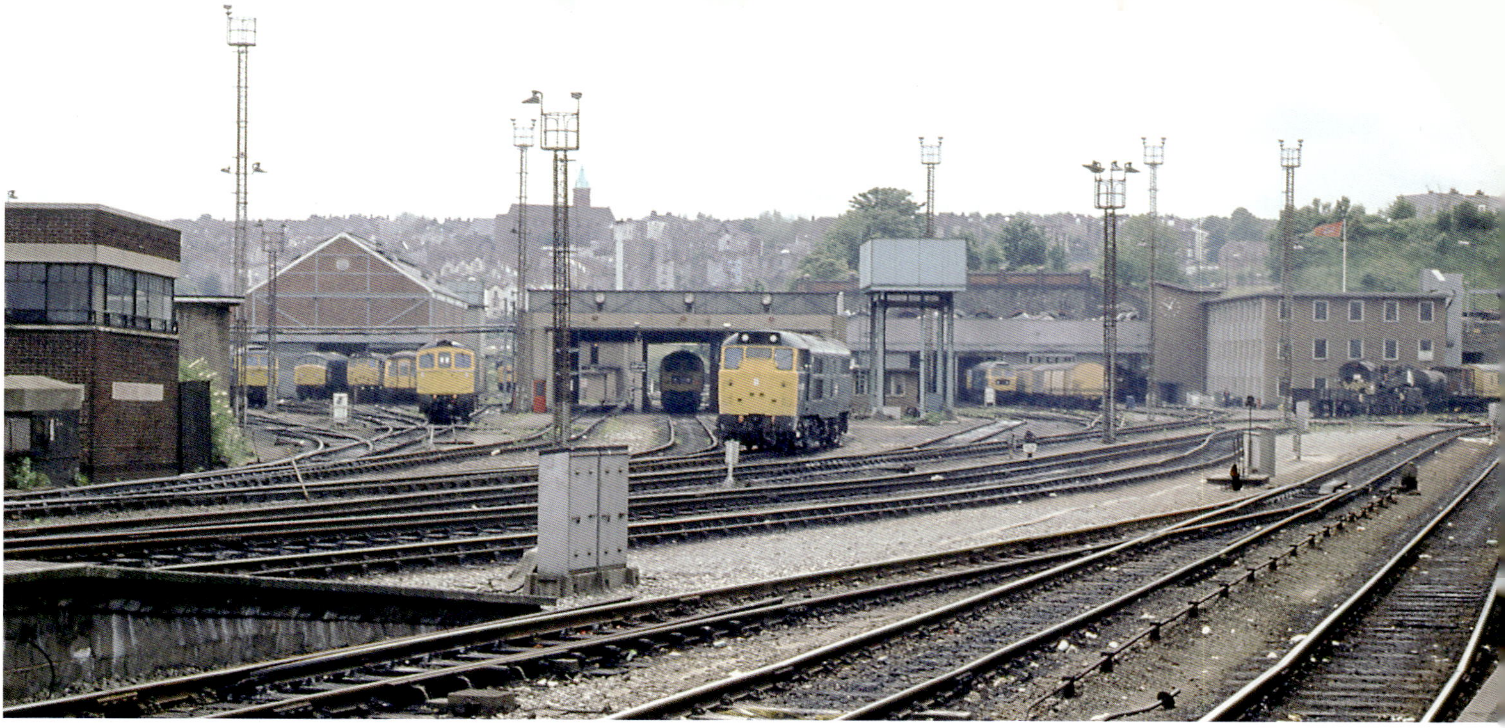

Three more depots viewed from station platforms now, firstly Bristol's Bath Road on 15 June 1981. Then to Suffolk for Ipswich on 31 July 1982. ***Photos: Arthur Wilson and John Arthur Bennett/Strathwood Library Collection***

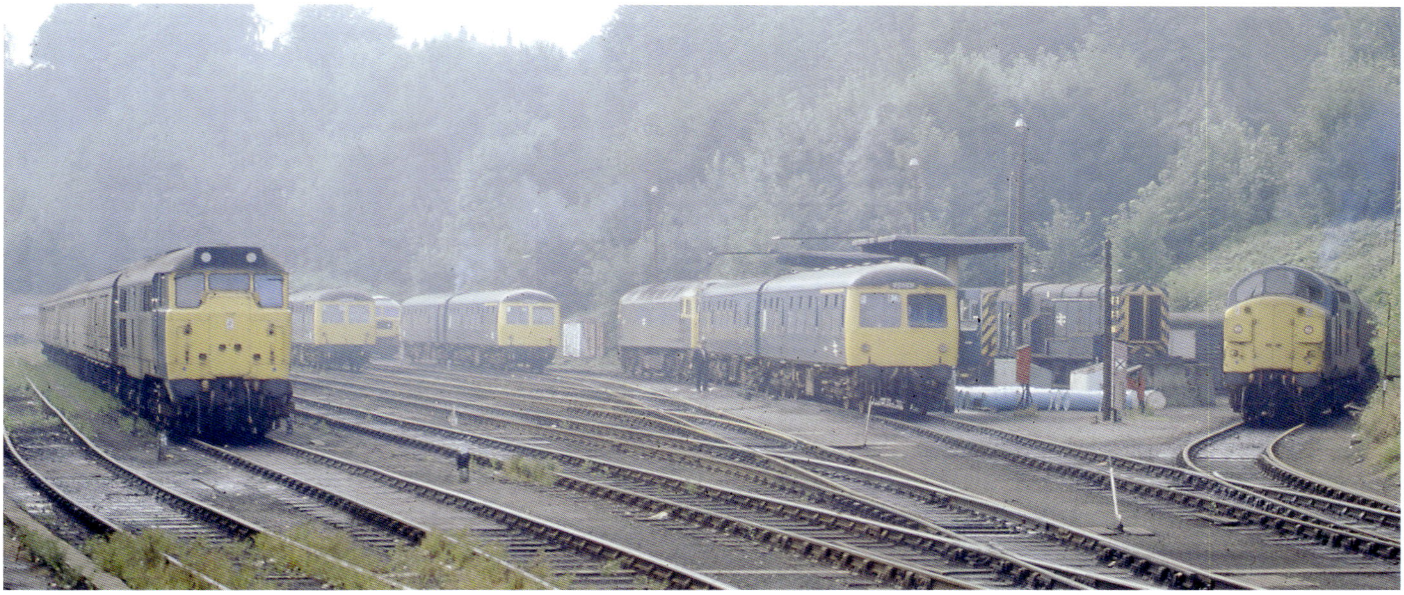

An unusual view of Willesden in November 1980 from the High Level station platforms. ***Alan Rintoul***

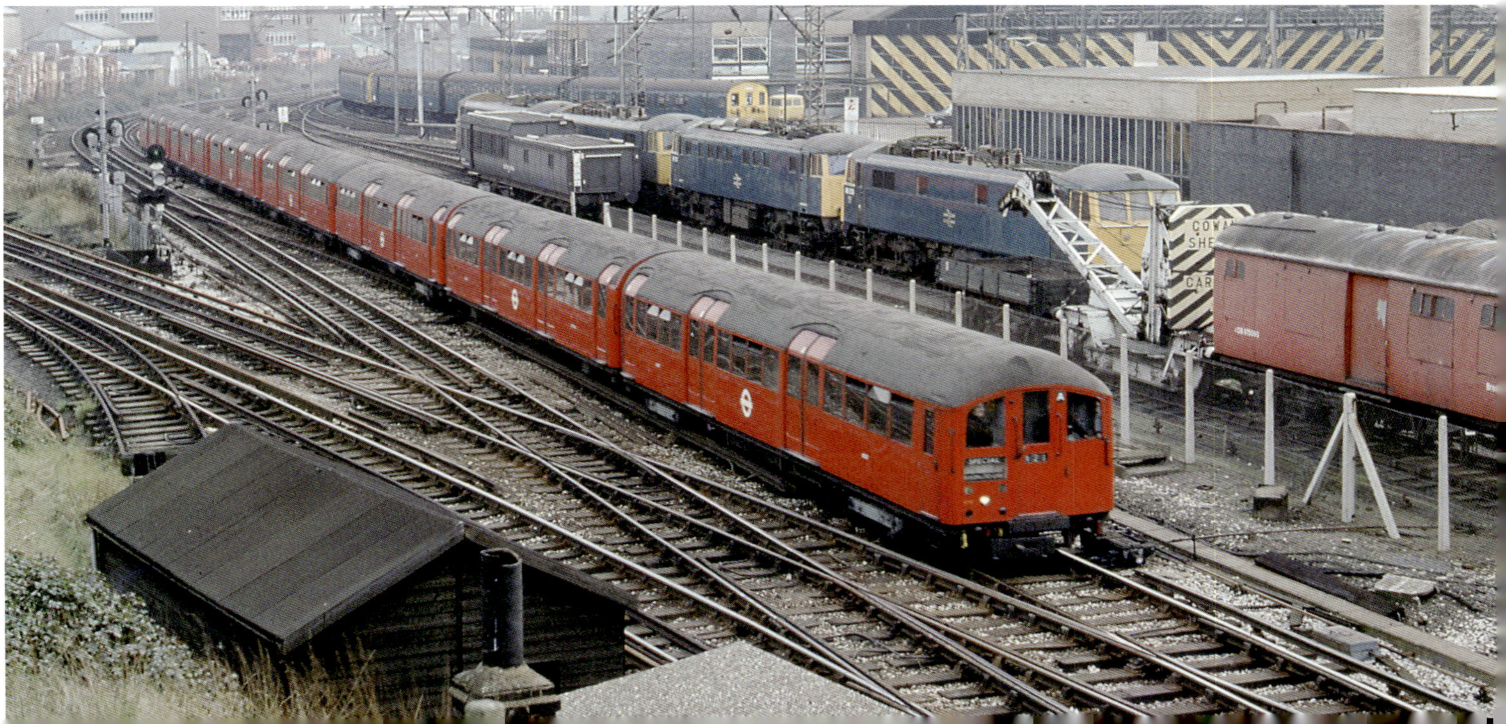

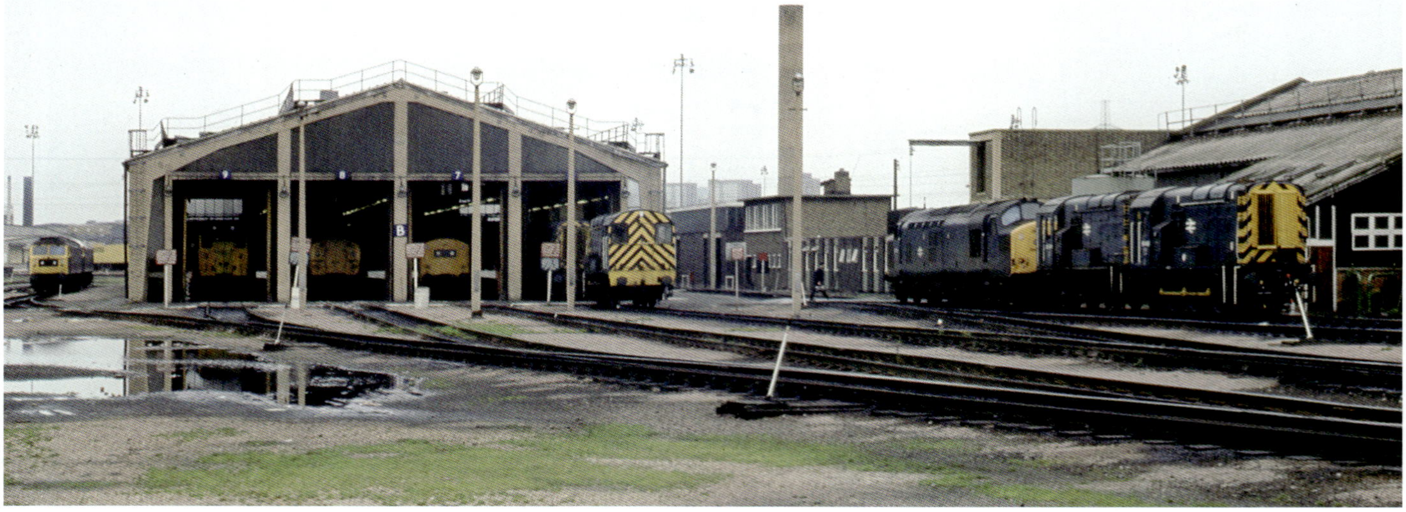

Another mecca for spotters was Stratford which once boasted the largest allocation in London and could also be relied upon to fill our notebooks with any visit even on quiet days as here on 10 October 1981. Although it hosted an Open Day in the eighties the depot would not survive the following decade. ***Arthur Wilson***

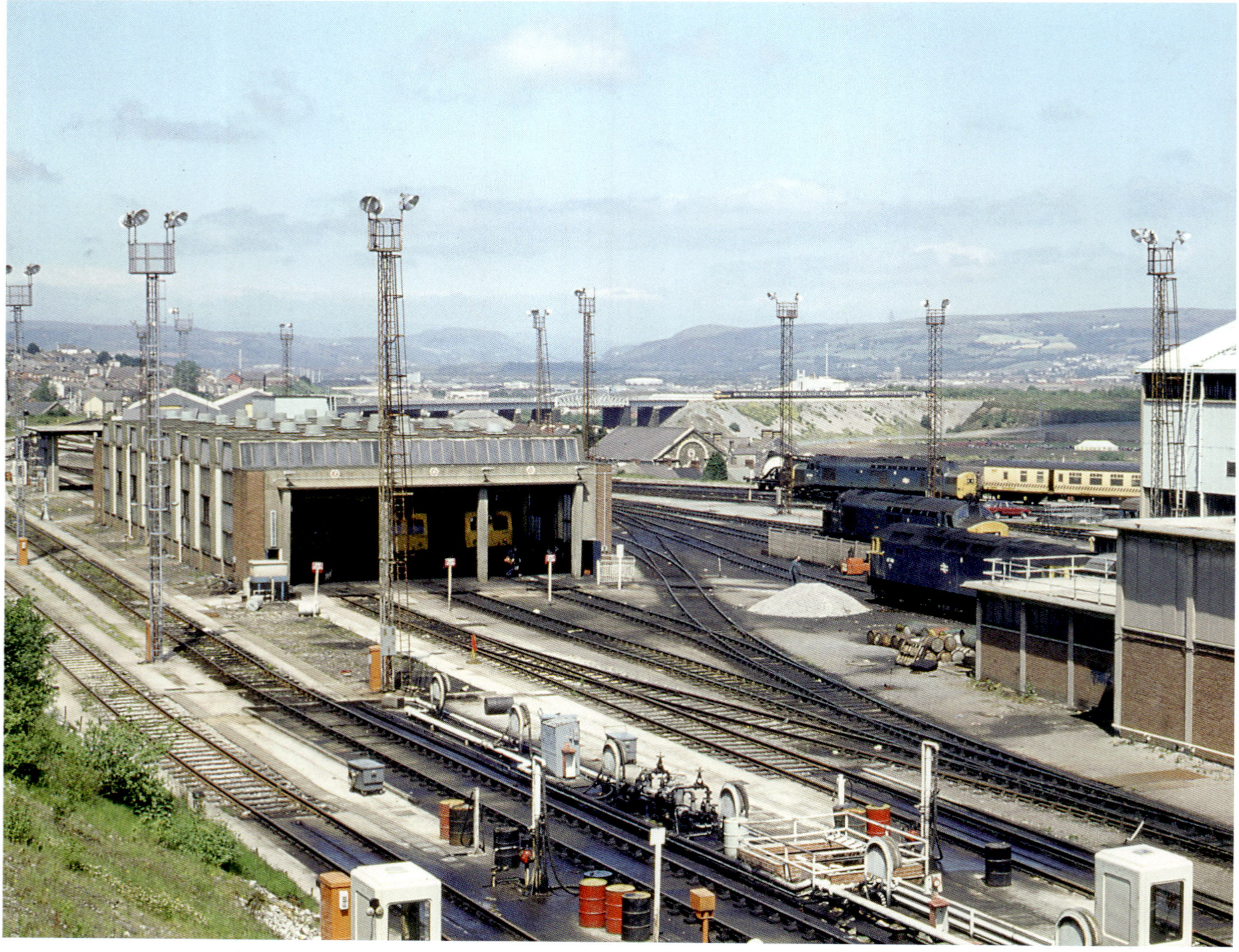

One depot that would fare better was Landore seen on 20 June 1981. The purpose built diesel servicing depot was built on the site of the old steam sheds coded 87E. The conversion work took almost two years and the depot fully re-opened to the new traction in May 1963. It remains open whilst so many other once busy locations in South Wales have vanished completely. ***Arthur Wilson***

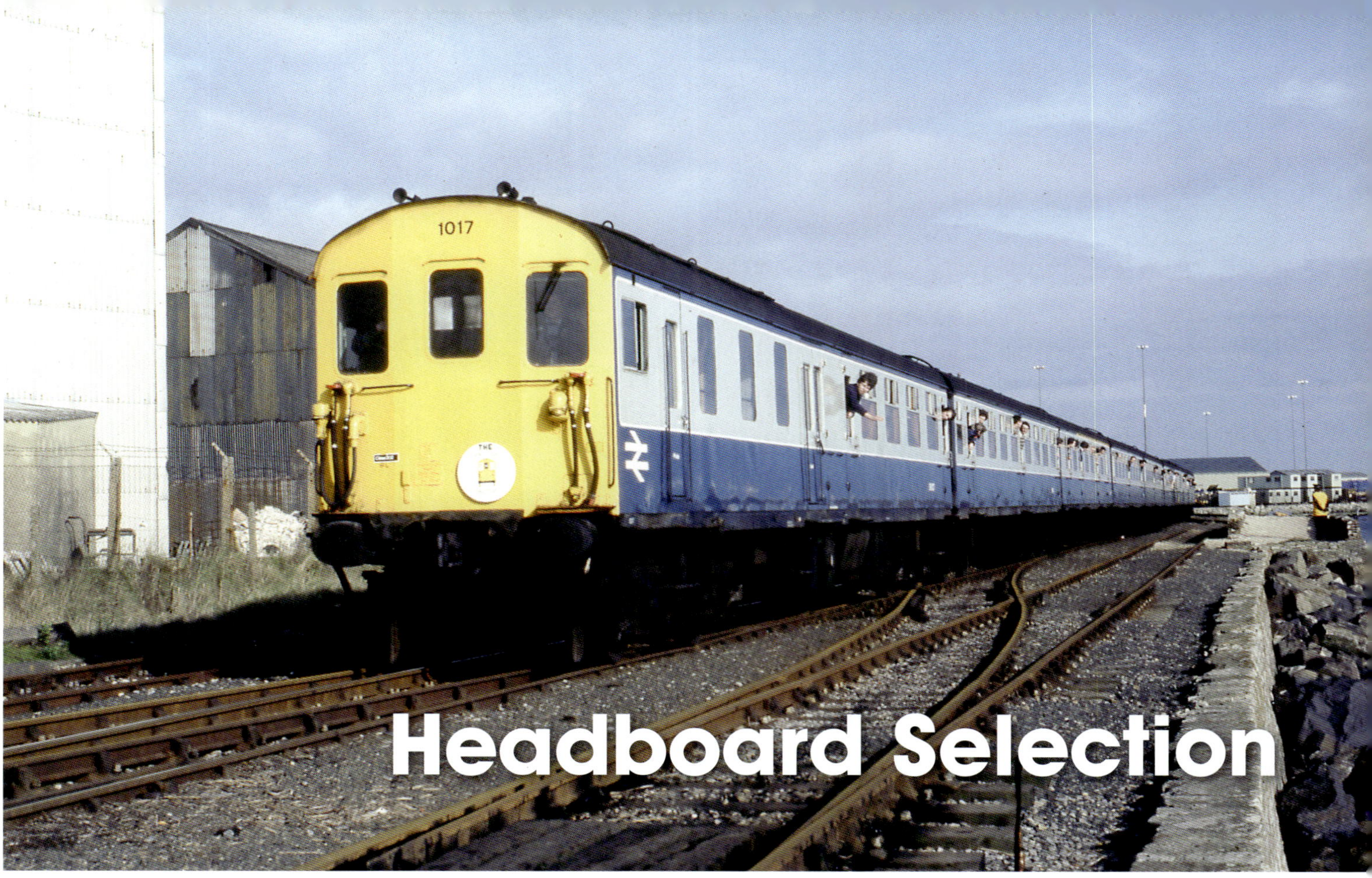

Headboard Selection

On 19 March 1983 Hertfordshire Railtours ran The Thames - Piddle Executive from Watford Junction taking in as many branches as possible in Hampshire and Dorset including Hamworthy. ***John Sansom Strathwood Library Collection***

The freshly painted D200 shows off at Bethnal Green in March 1988 recalling the headboard from 1958 when it was new on this route. ***Strathwood Library Collection***

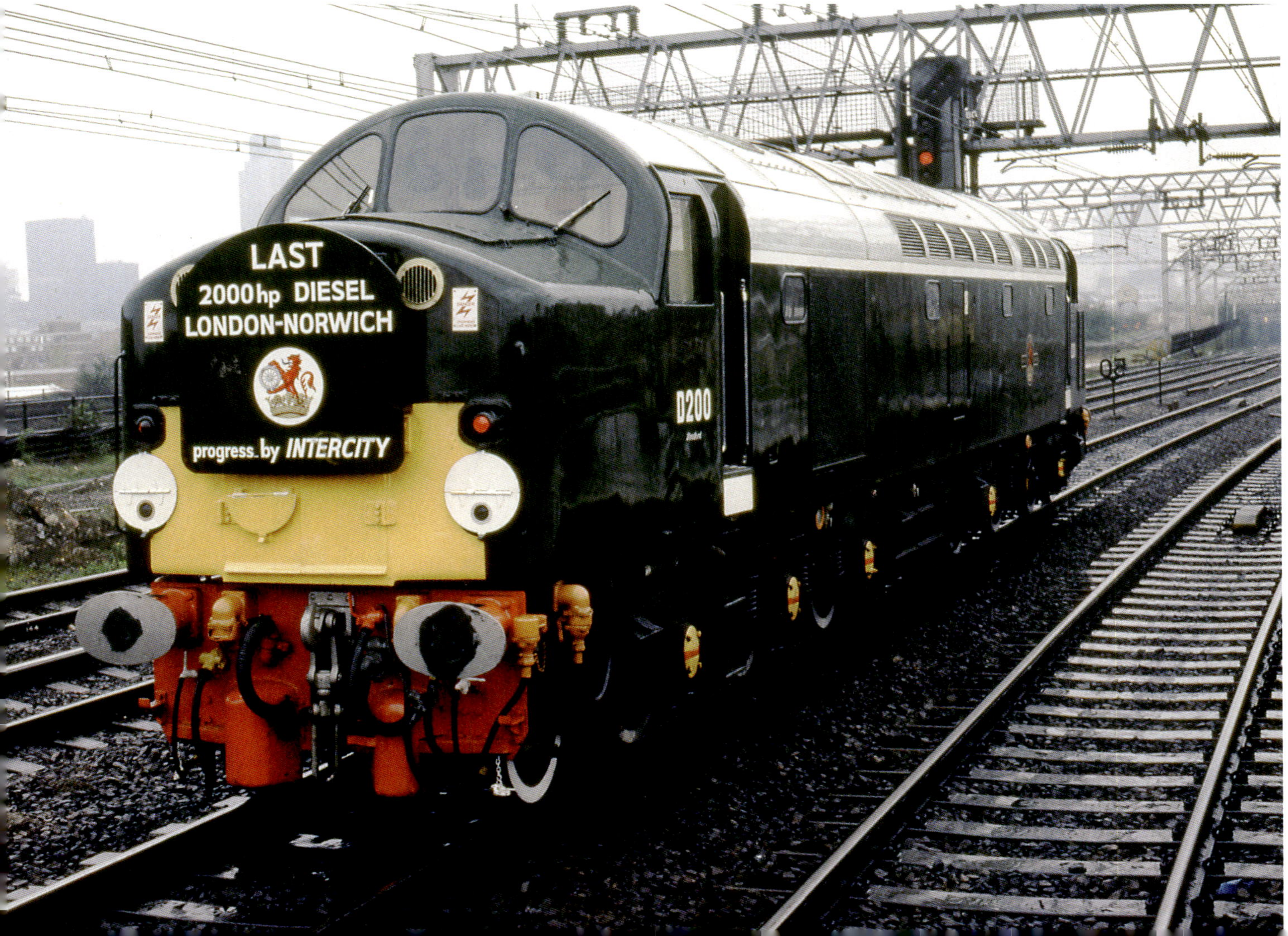

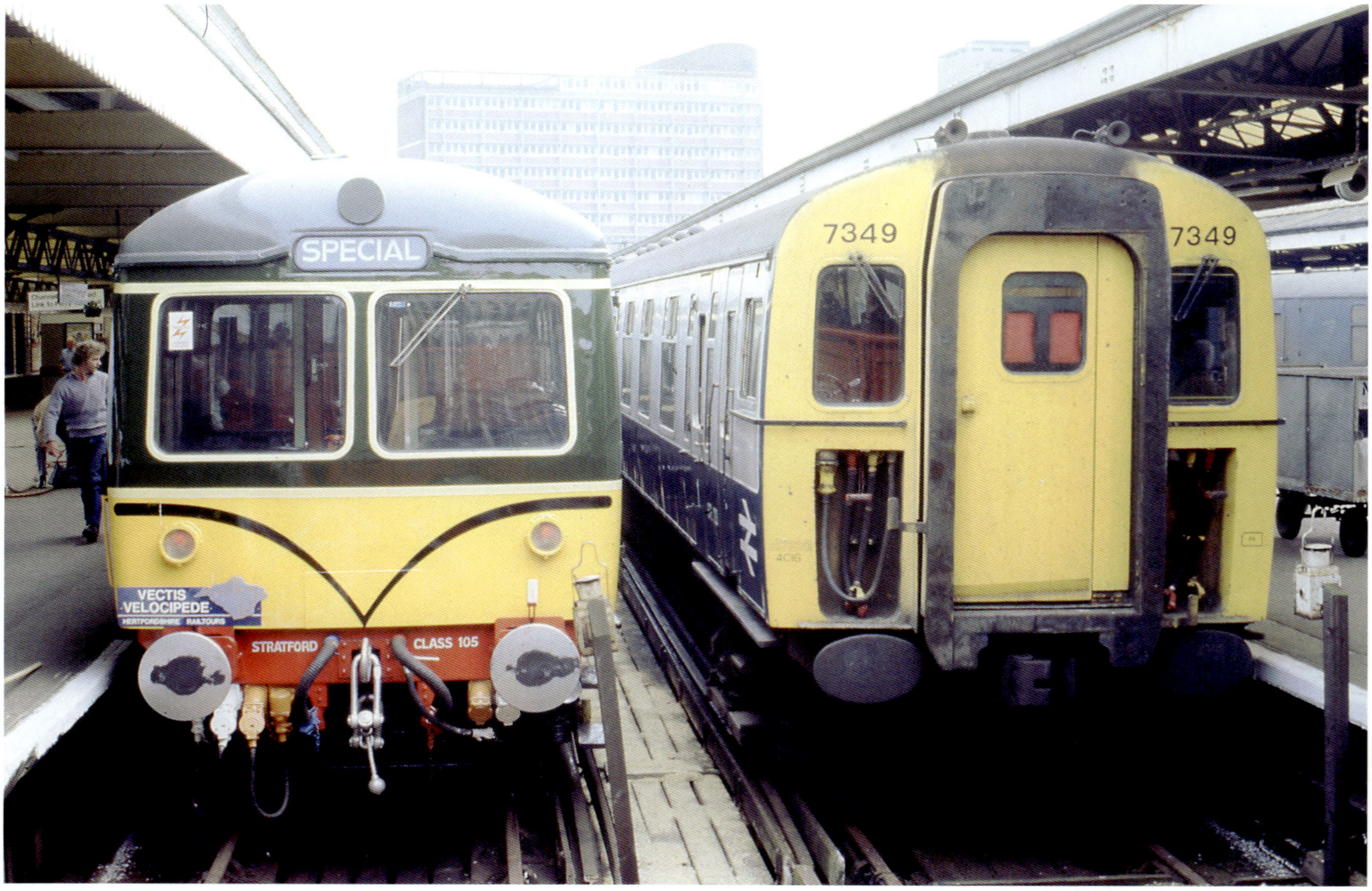

Who fancies being vibrated around in a venerable Cravens unit from Stevenage in 1986 to here at Portsmouth Harbour and back for 260 miles of travel on what was the very first Network Day when you could travel anywhere for just £5 this was later reduced to just a pound! ***Strathwood Library Collection***

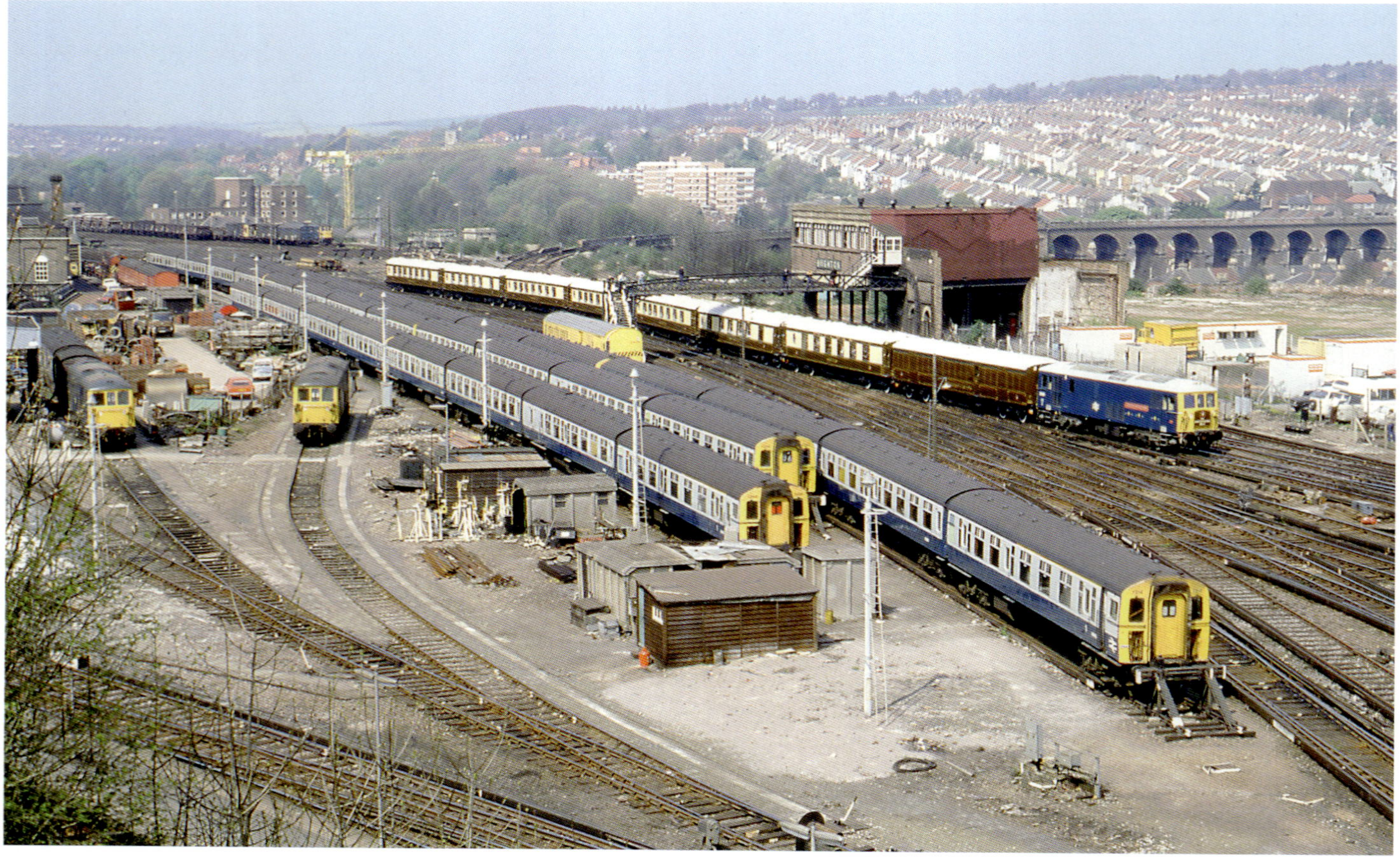

One fears the fare for travelling in luxury behind 73101 Brighton Evening Argus the 51 miles from London's Victoria station to Brighton onboard a Pullman special as the Brighton Festival Belle on 28 April 1982 was considerably more. Although you would have seen a good number of Class 73s on arrival at the Sussex terminus. ***Colin Whitbread***

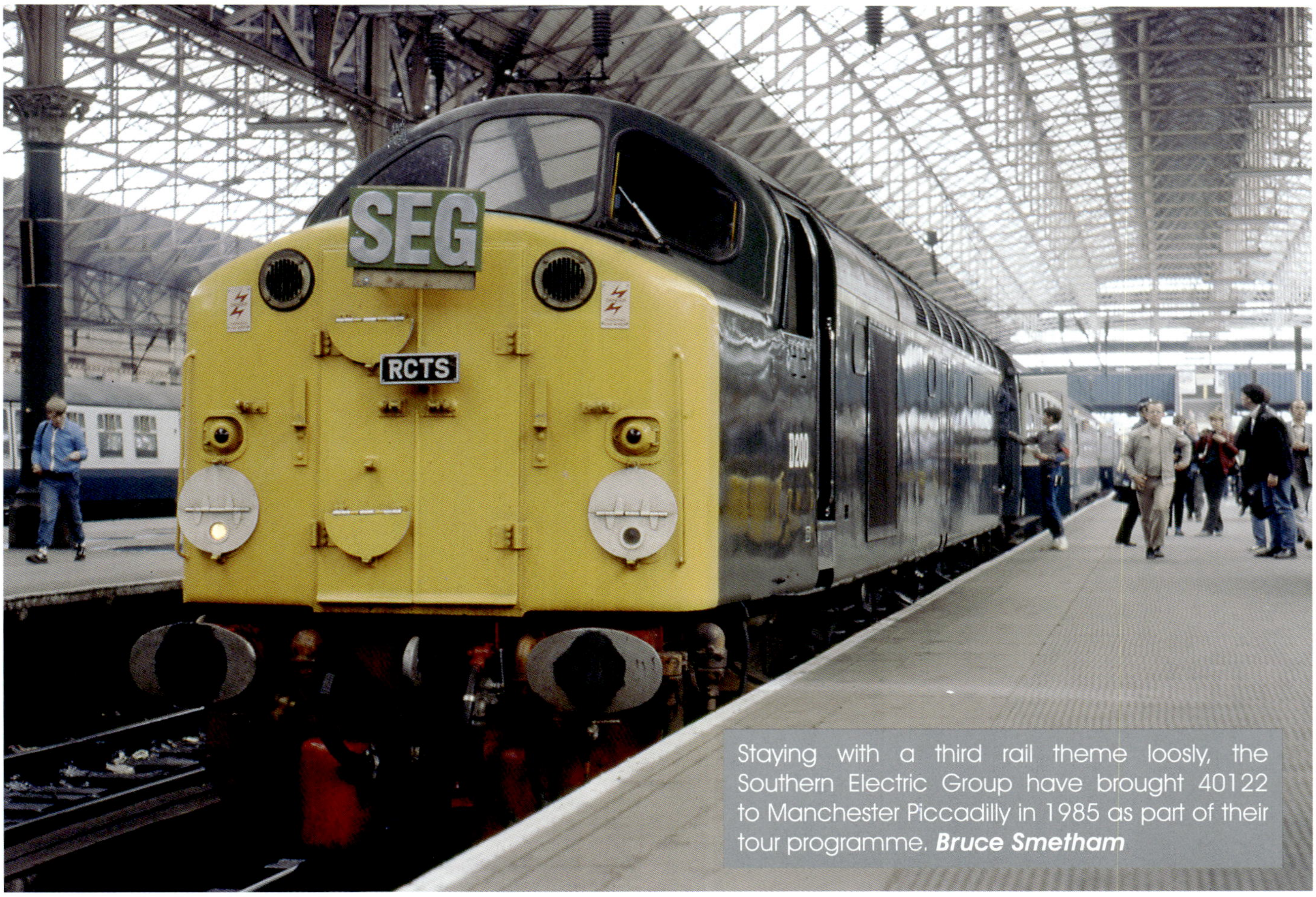

Staying with a third rail theme loosely, the Southern Electric Group have brought 40122 to Manchester Piccadilly in 1985 as part of their tour programme. ***Bruce Smetham***

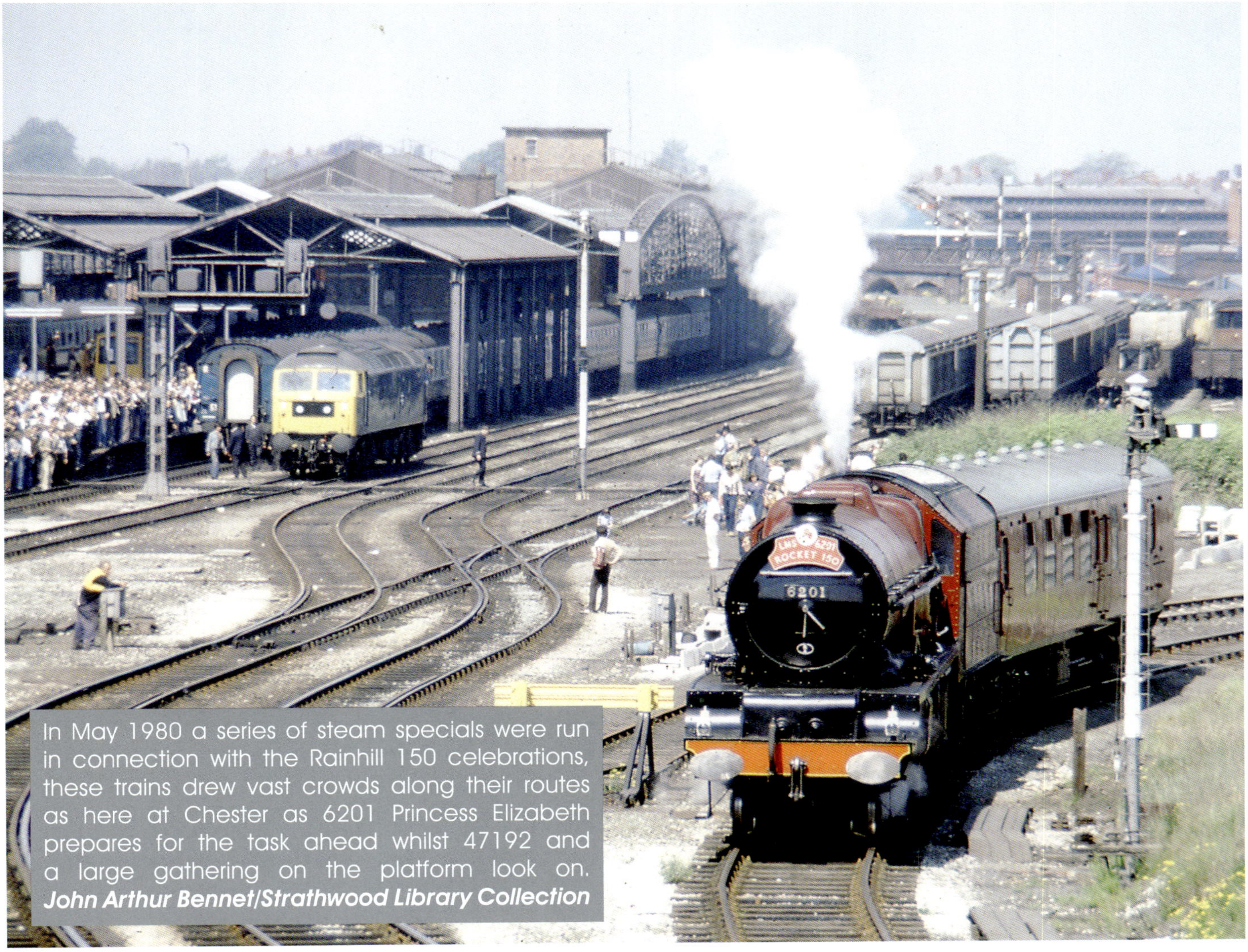

In May 1980 a series of steam specials were run in connection with the Rainhill 150 celebrations, these trains drew vast crowds along their routes as here at Chester as 6201 Princess Elizabeth prepares for the task ahead whilst 47192 and a large gathering on the platform look on. ***John Arthur Bennet/Strathwood Library Collection***

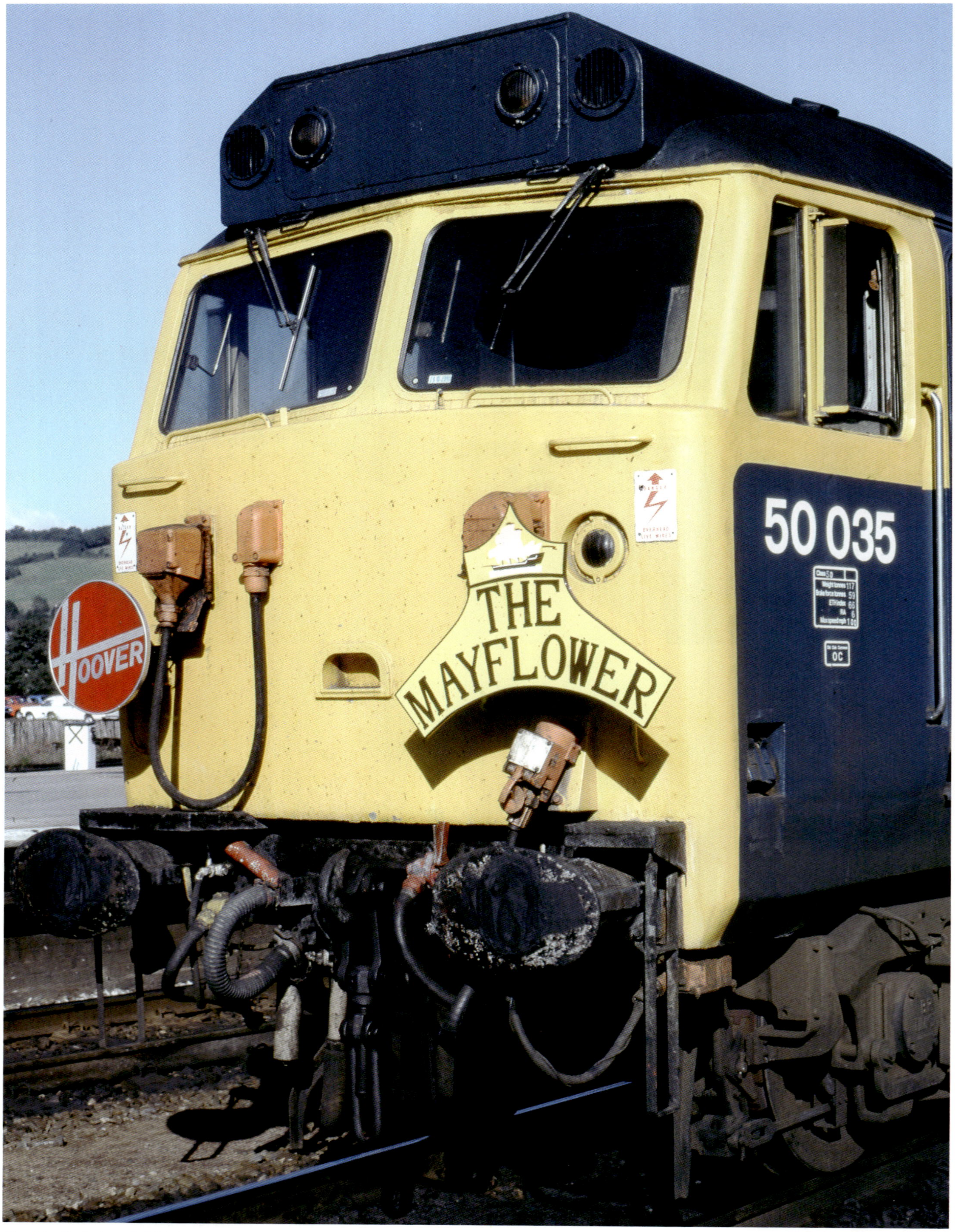

On 12 October 1980 the R.P.P.R. organised Mayflower tour headed west from Paddington behind 50035 Ark Royal which made a brief stop here at Honiton on its way to Newton Abbot to meet up with a DMU which would take passengers on a tour of Devon and Cornwall's branchlines. The day did not go to plan, as the severe curve out of Tavistock Yard, Plymouth was too great for the DMU and as the buffers were fully compressed and the wheel flanges were riding up onto the rail, the train inspector stopped the special. After the delays the tour returned with 47050 up front in lieu of 50035 Ark Royal which had been re-diagrammed elsewhere, although 50023 Howe was found at Bristol Temple Meads to continue journey to London. ***Strathwood Library Collection***

Open Days

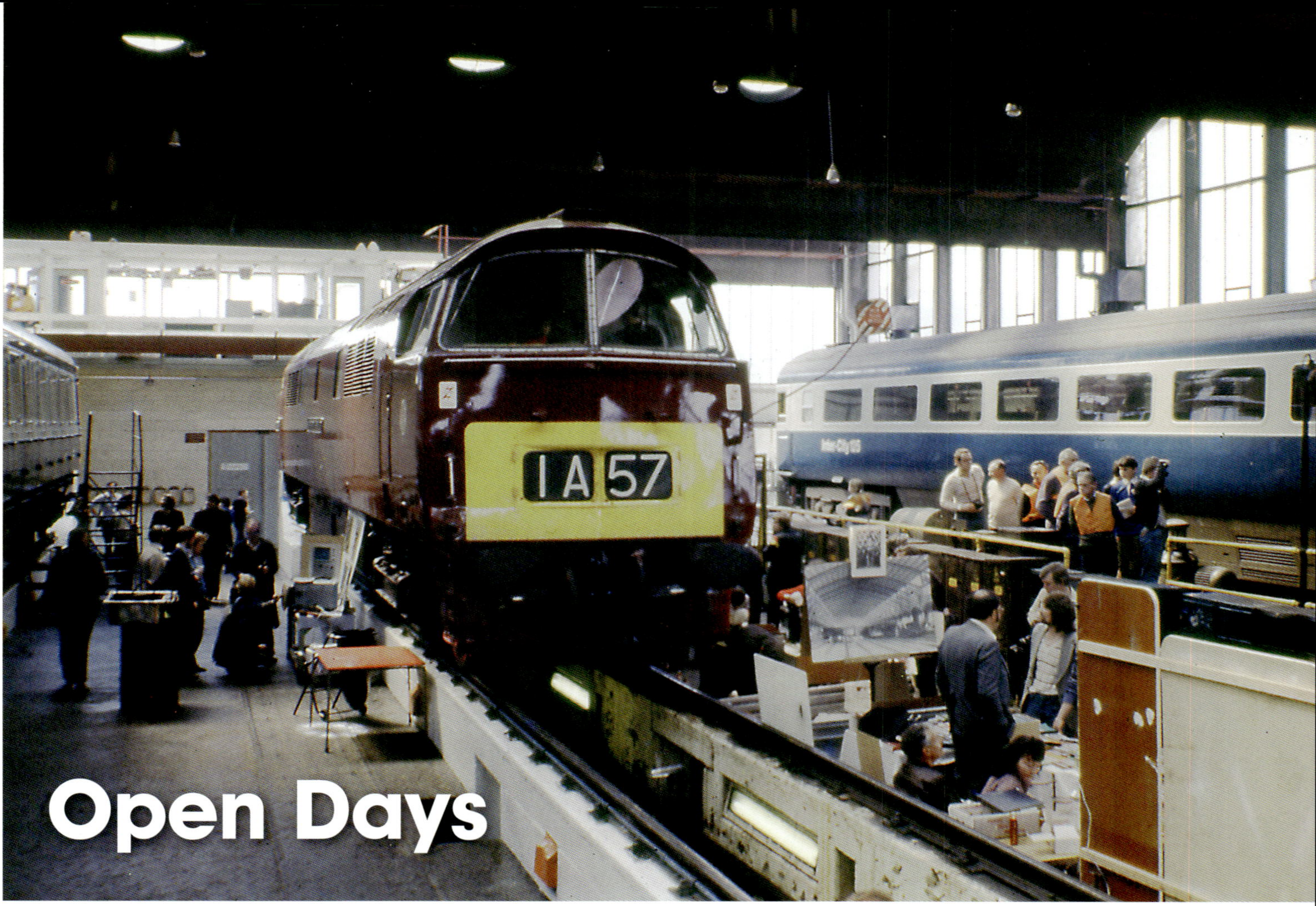

All is quiet before the crowds arrive on 25 April 1982 inside Laira for the Open Day as D1023 Western Fusilier is parked up inside the inspection sheds as some of the sales stands set up for the day. ***Phil Bidwell***

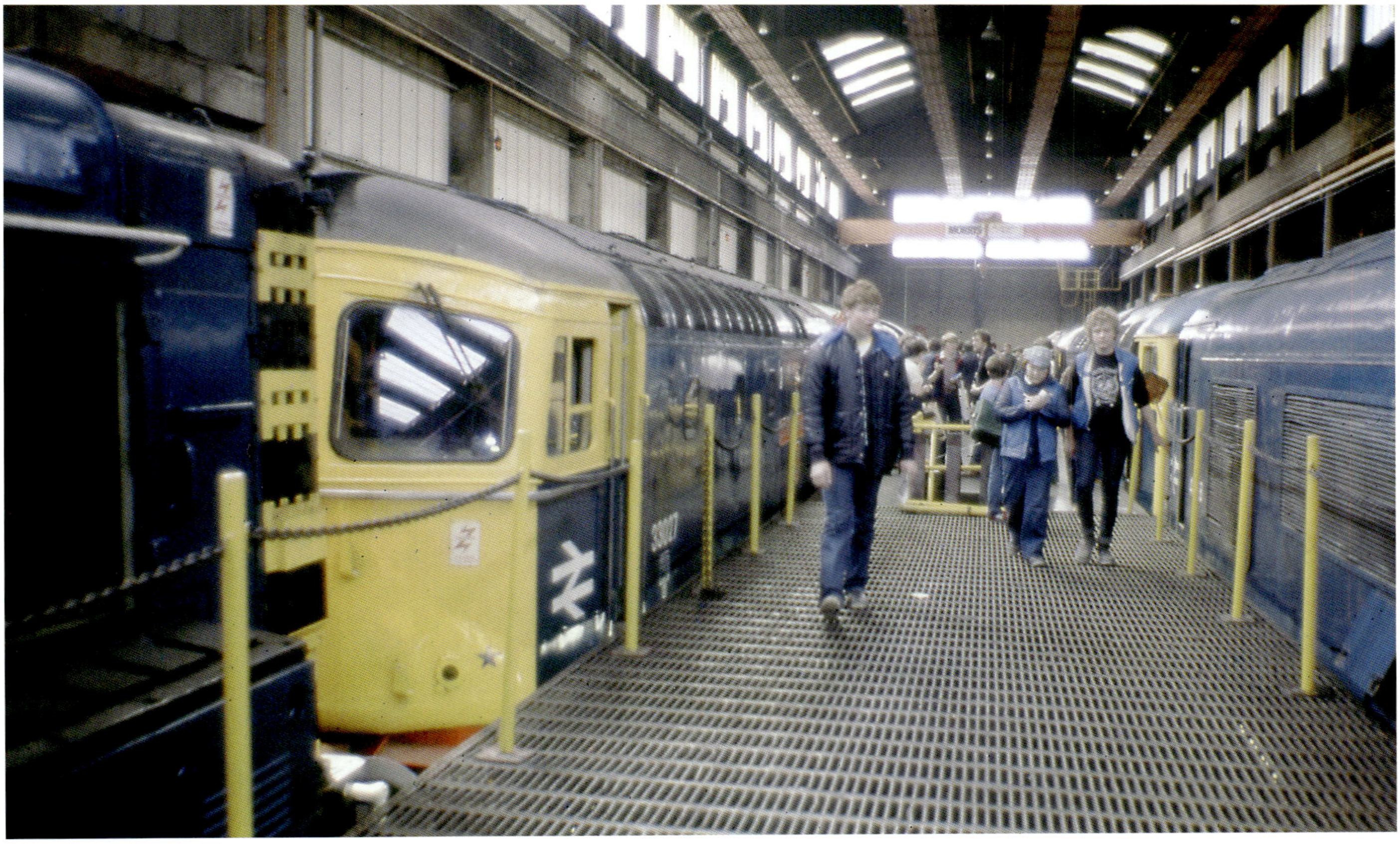

Elsewhere inside the maintenance sheds a selection of cleaner locomotives than normal has been assembled for the day including 33027 Earl Mountbatten of Burma brought in for display. ***Phil Bidwell***

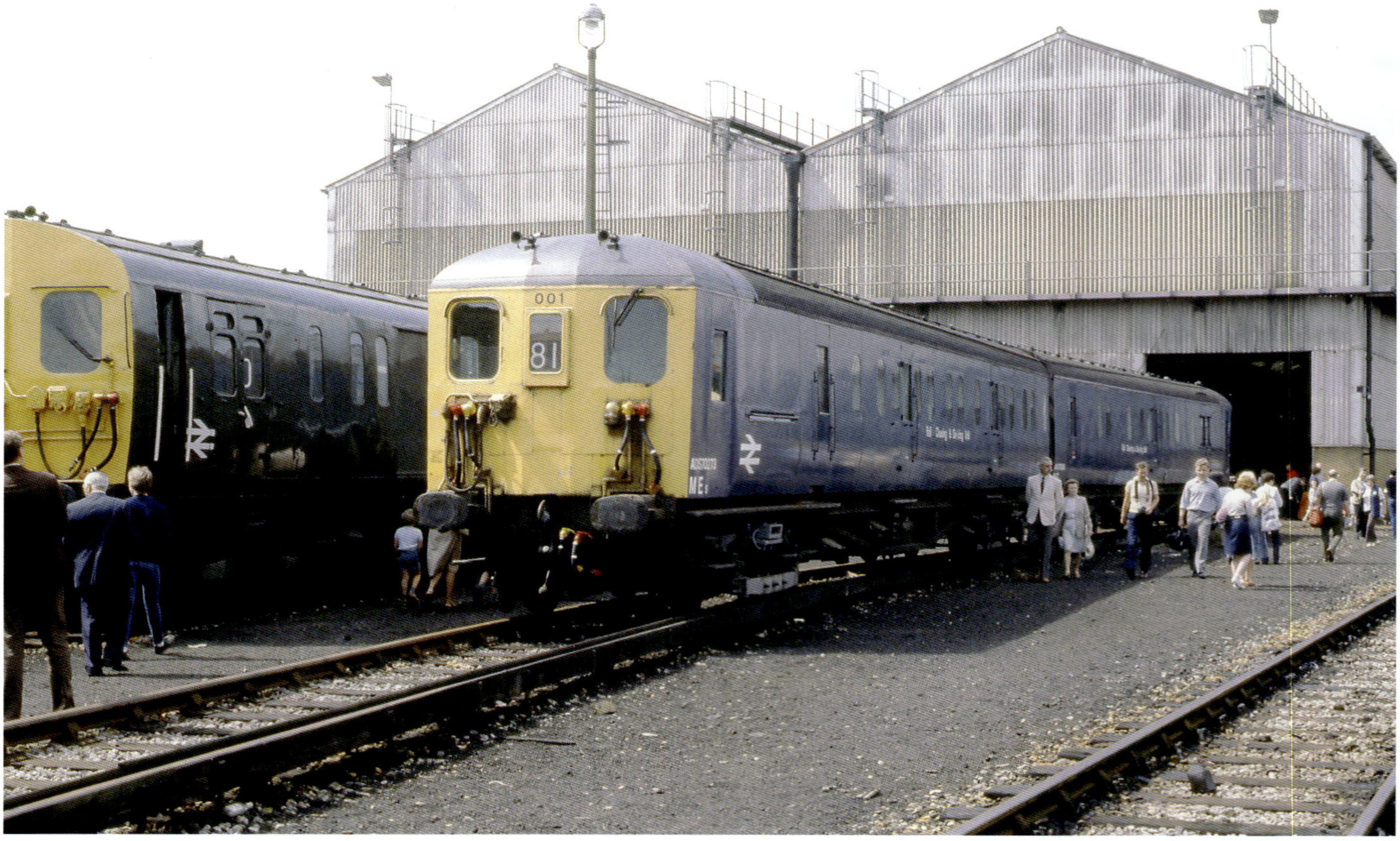

A traditional home of Class 33s on the Southern Region next, with a visit to Ashford Works Open Day on a sunny 14 August 1982. With the third rail thankfully isolated for the day two of the region's departmental units have been smartened up for display to the public. ***Ian James***

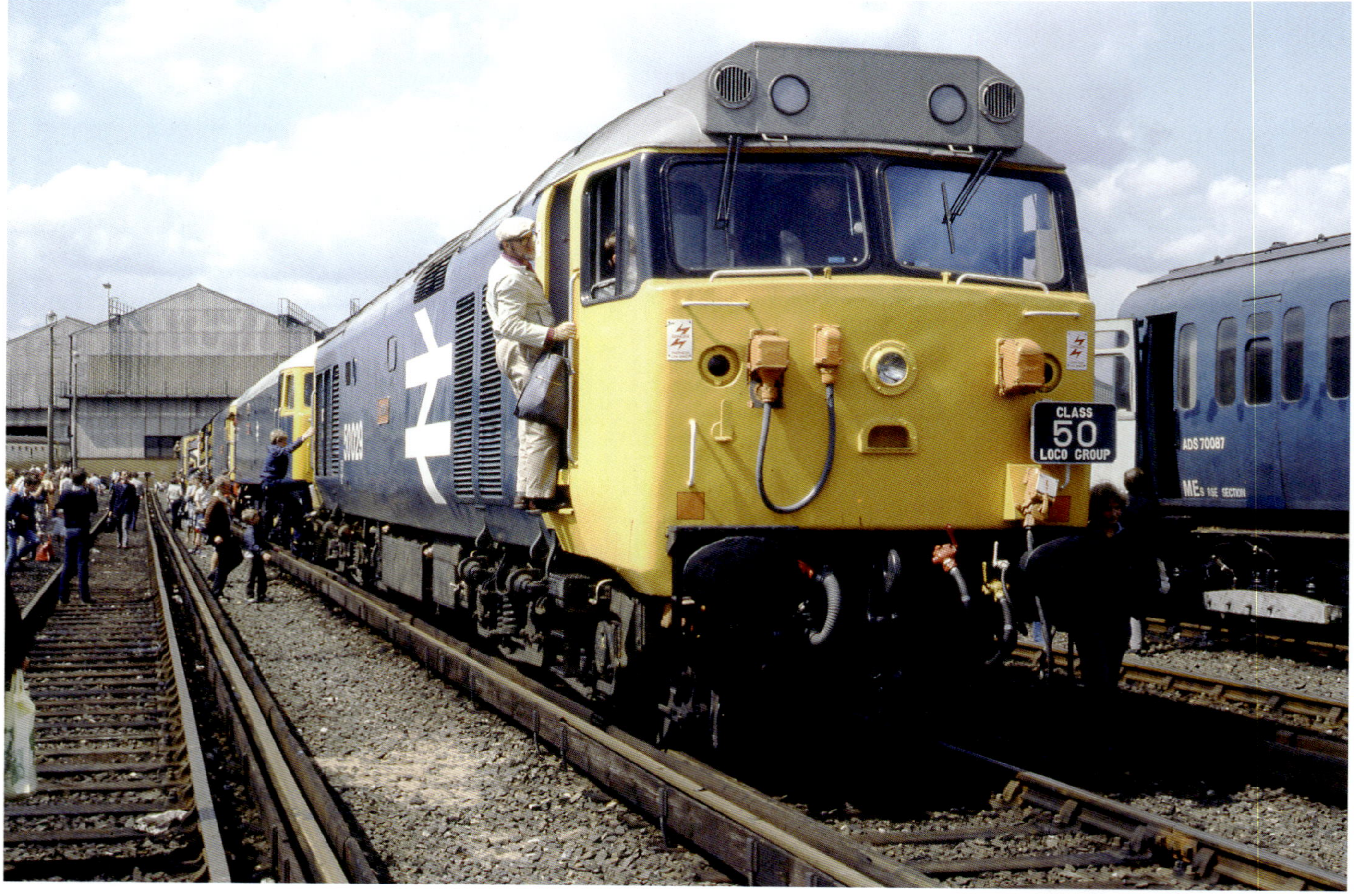

As is often the case for such events unusual motive power for the area is drafted in to put on a show, and here it is the return favour of the Western Region who provided 50029 Renown, which was among the locomotives parked up in the works yard for inspection. ***Ian James***

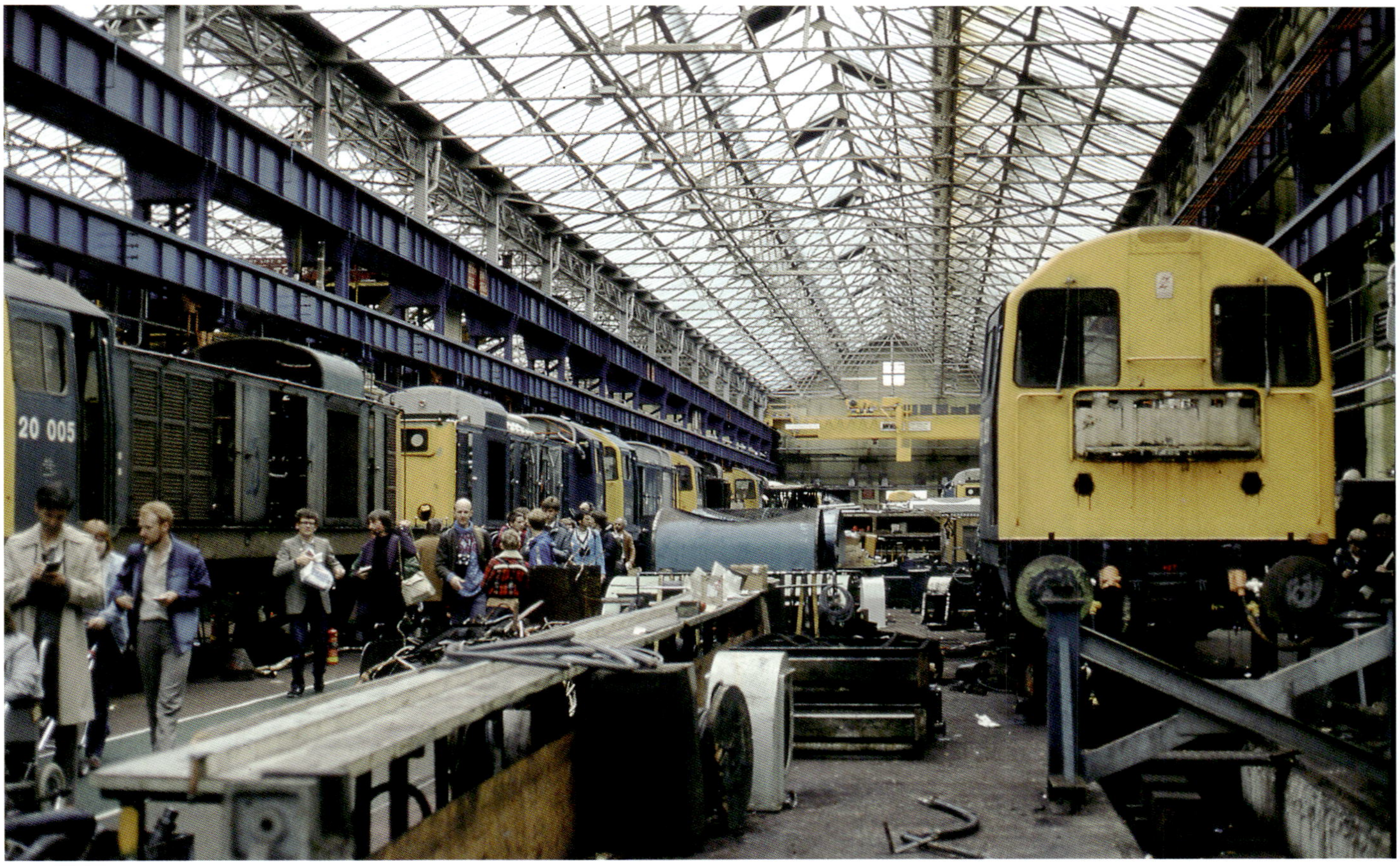

The great erecting shops at Crewe have been tidied up for the day with all tools and small componants safely tucked away in order to host visitors on 2 June 1984. Where a good selection of Class 20s were to be in the works for repairs at the time. ***Arthur Wilson***

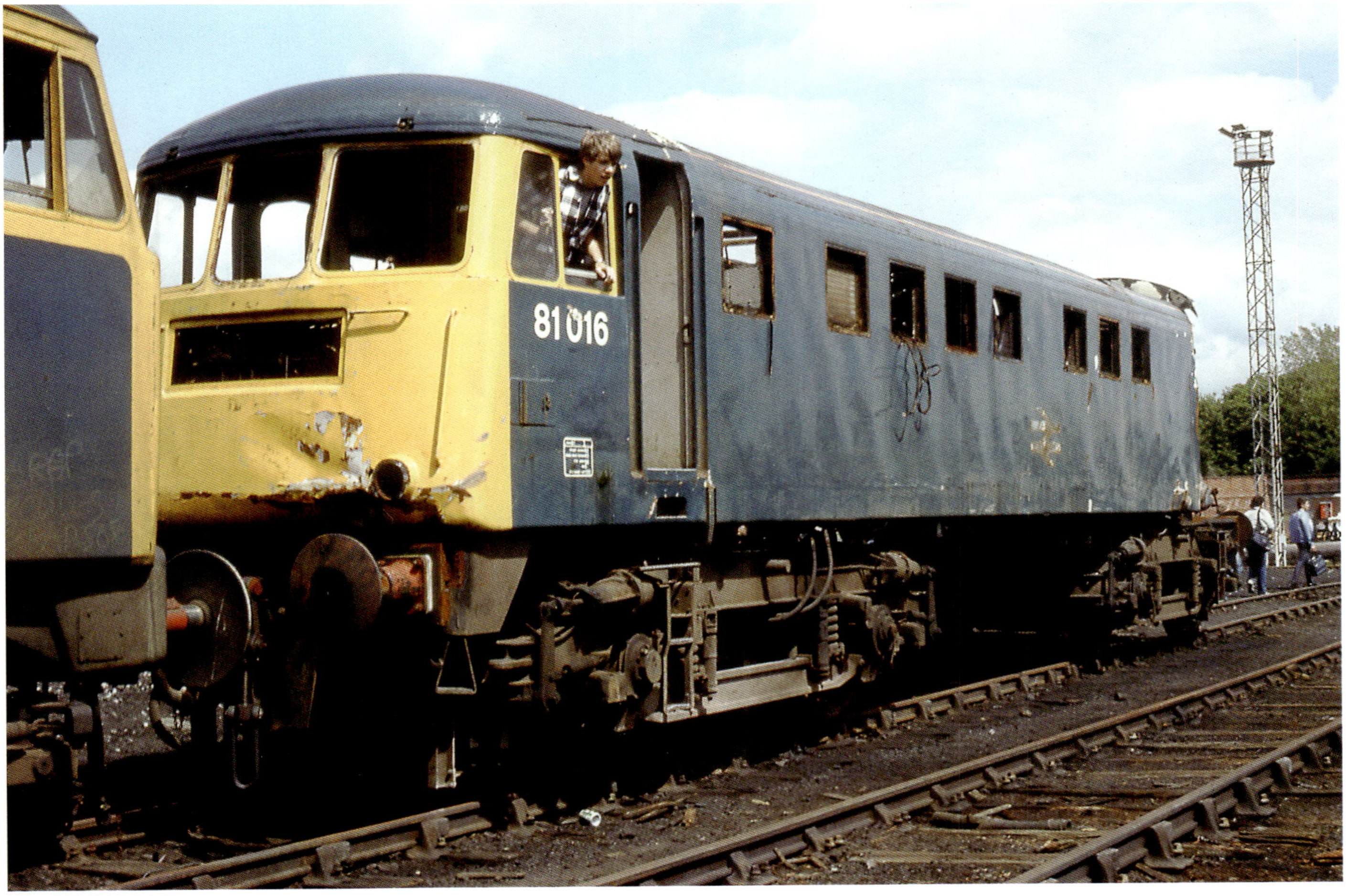

Also in the works yard that day was the remains of 81016 which had come to grief at Linslade in late 1982. No repairs were to be sanctioned and the unfortunate locomotive was cut in the works during January the following year. ***Edward Dorricott***

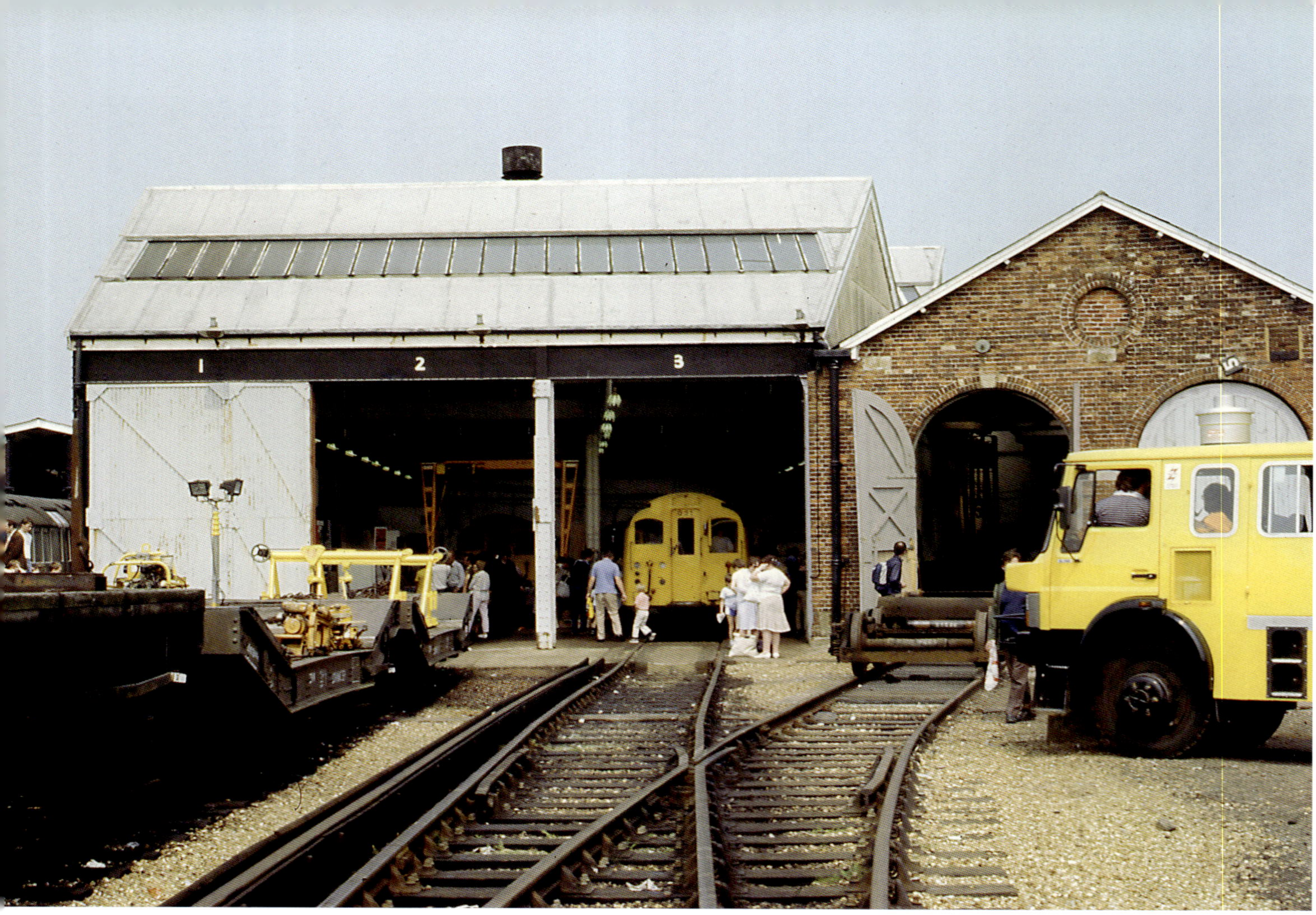

Little publicity exists for the Open Day held at the workshops in Ryde during the decade, perhaps it was thought not too not many enthusiasts would journey across the Solent from the mainland for it. ***Strathwood Library Collection***

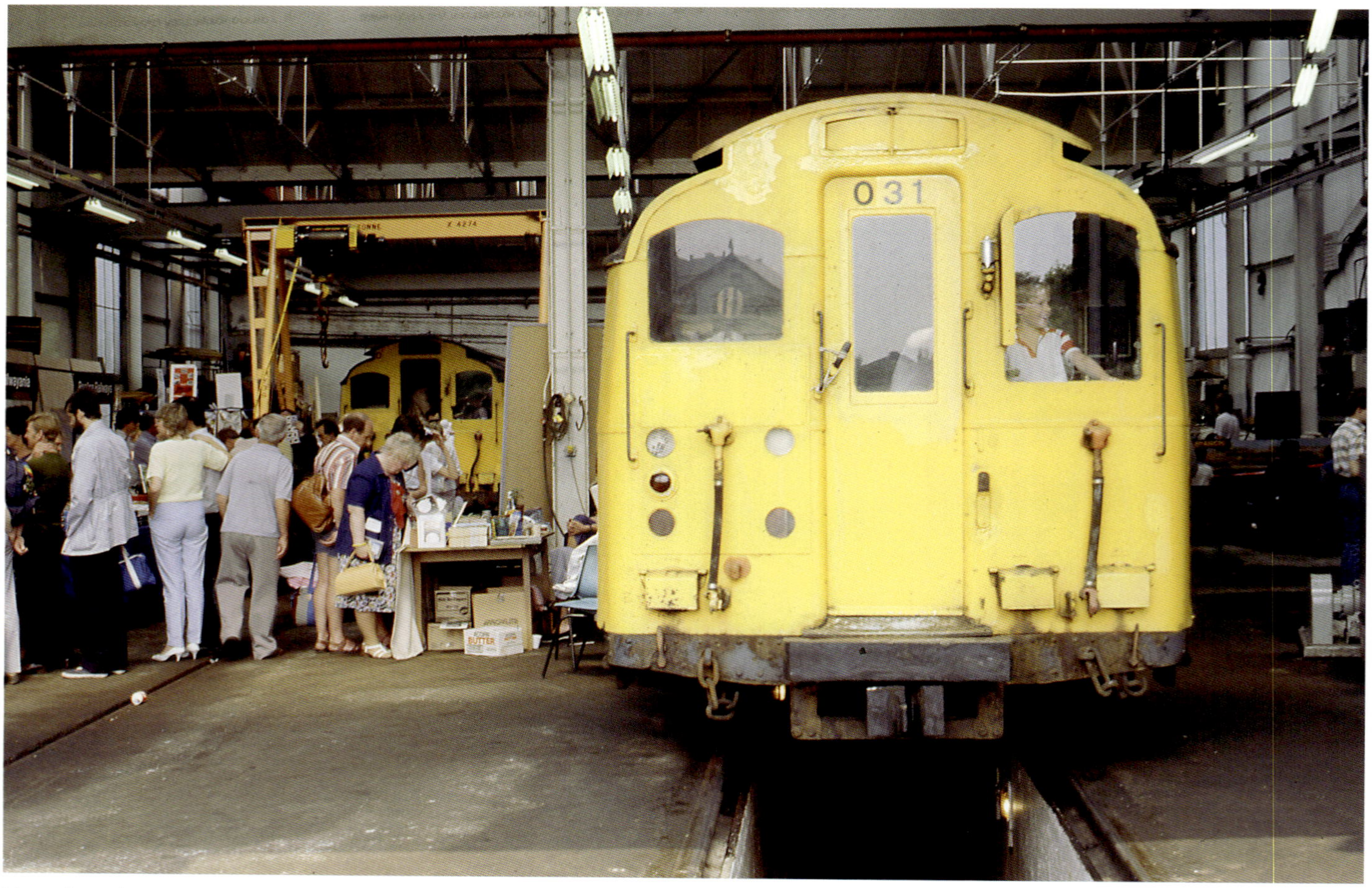

Needless to say there would be no chance of drafting in any visiting star attractions from other regions. However it gave visitors on the day a chance to explore the former Ryde Works which had maintained the fleet of the island's O2s before the ex London Transport stock ousted steam in 1966/7. ***Strathwood Library Collection***

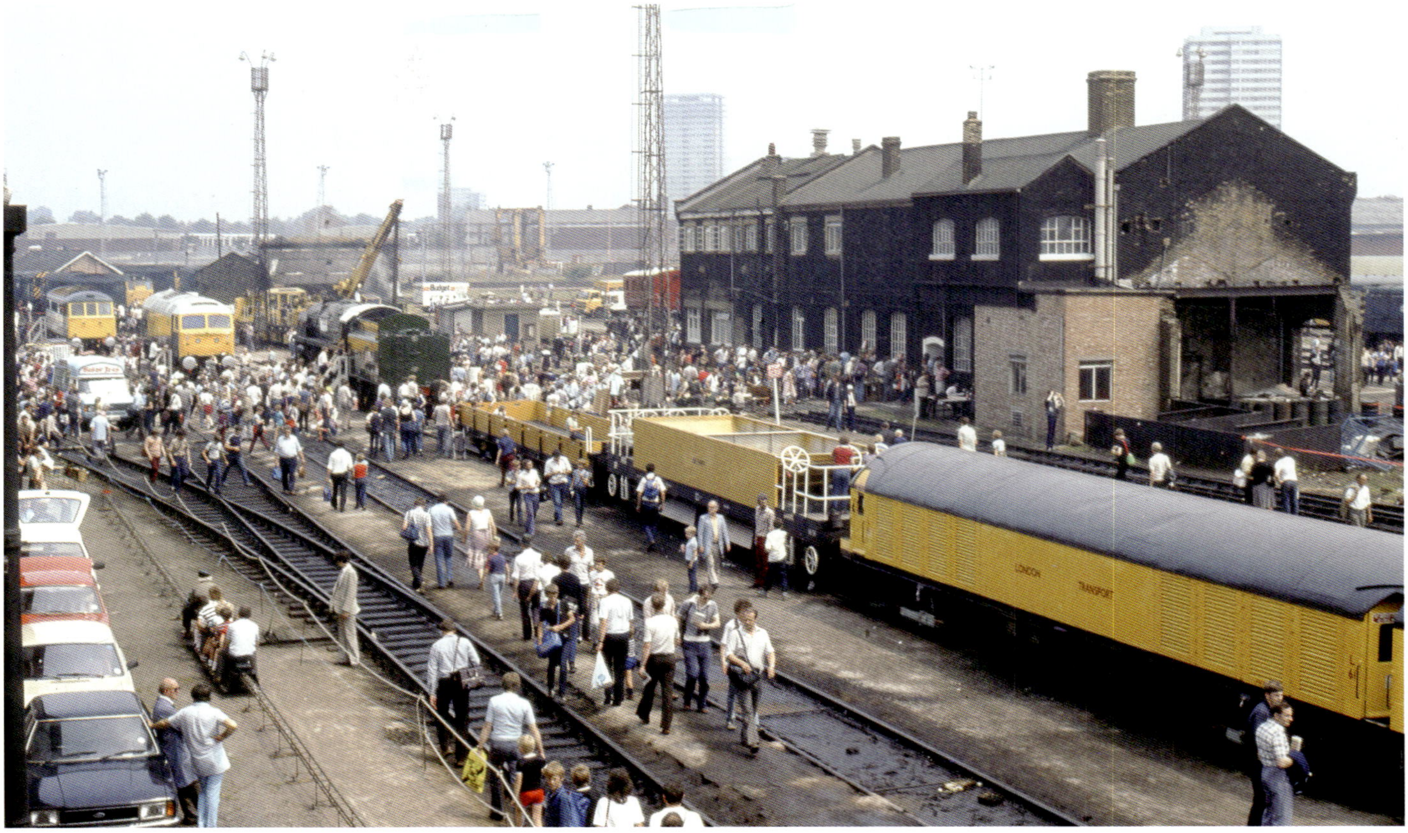

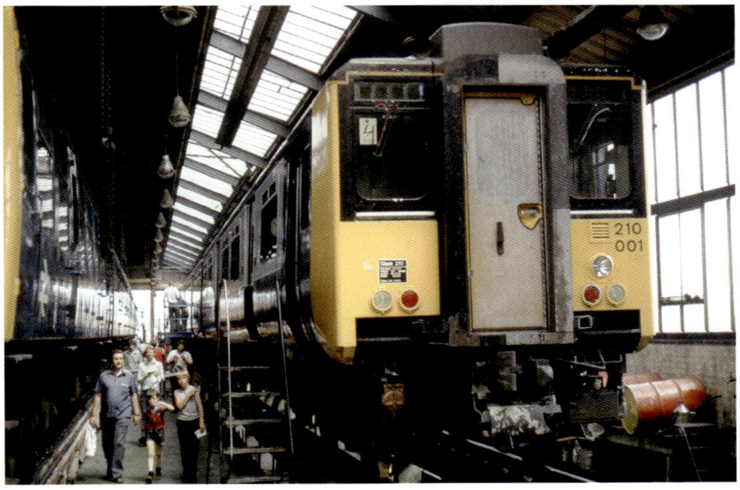

Crowds have decended upon Stratford for their Open day held on 9 July 1983. A lot of work goes into preparing and getting things back to normal when the day is over for such events which is often overlooked. The tidying up, making safe, special stock movements, staff rosters, etc. Making a welcome return to the depot was 70000 Britannia, whilst 47377 and 86224 Caledonian can be glimpsed afar beyond the London Transport battery locomotive.

As ever at such a large event a wide range of exhibits have been assembled for all the visitors to enjoy all suitably prepared for showing off such as 58002 and 56023 also the experimental DMU 210001. ***All: Arthur Wilson***

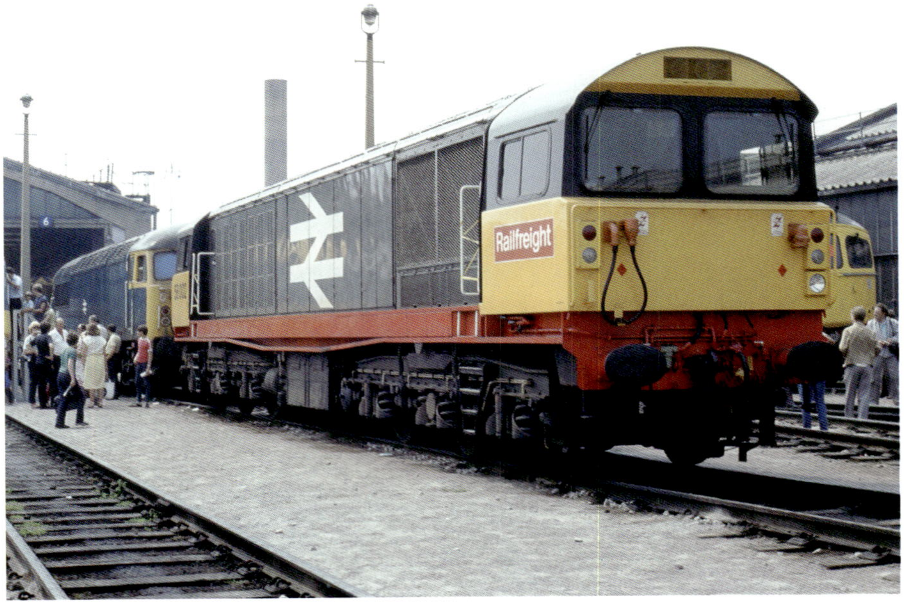

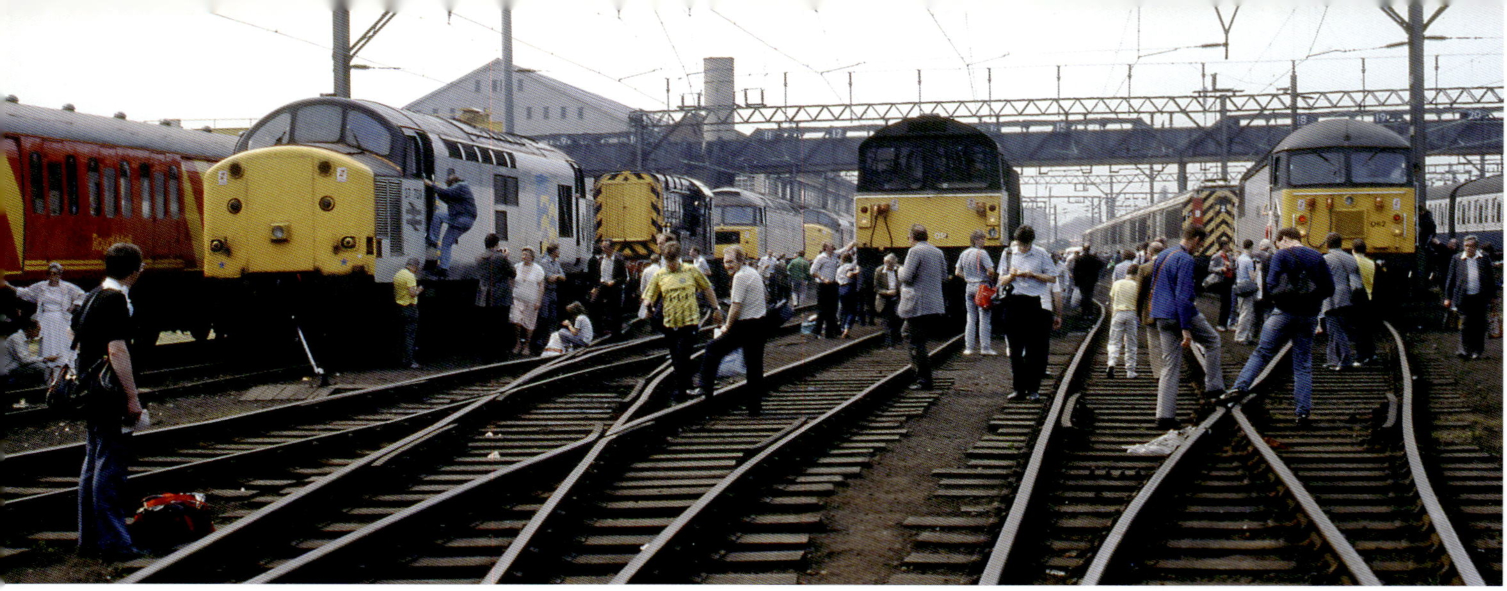

Staying in East London we visit Ilford on 20 May 1989 for their Open Day which brought together a selection of exhibits in the then new liveries of the time, including the unique 89001.

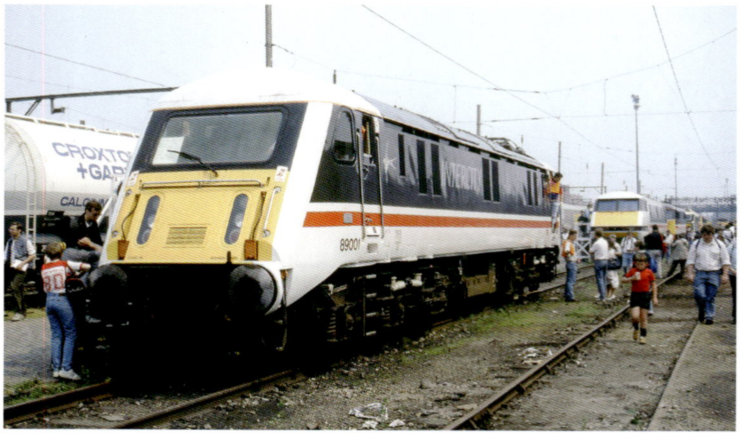

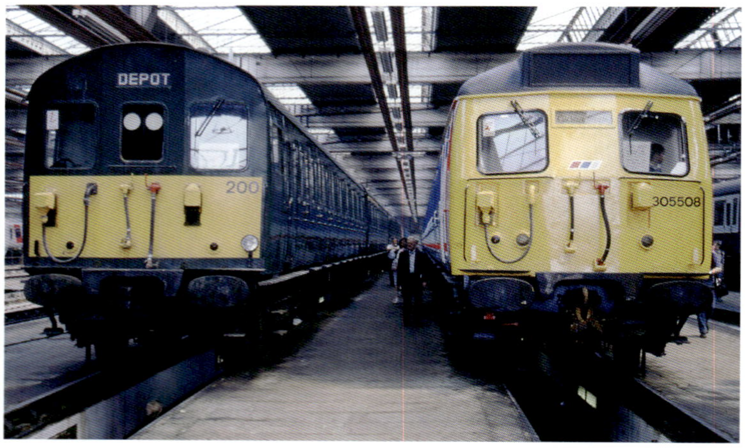

Also on show were the depot's two heritage livery repaints, although I must suggest that the green on 017 looks lighter than how they were twenty years beforehand. ***All: Arthur Wilson***

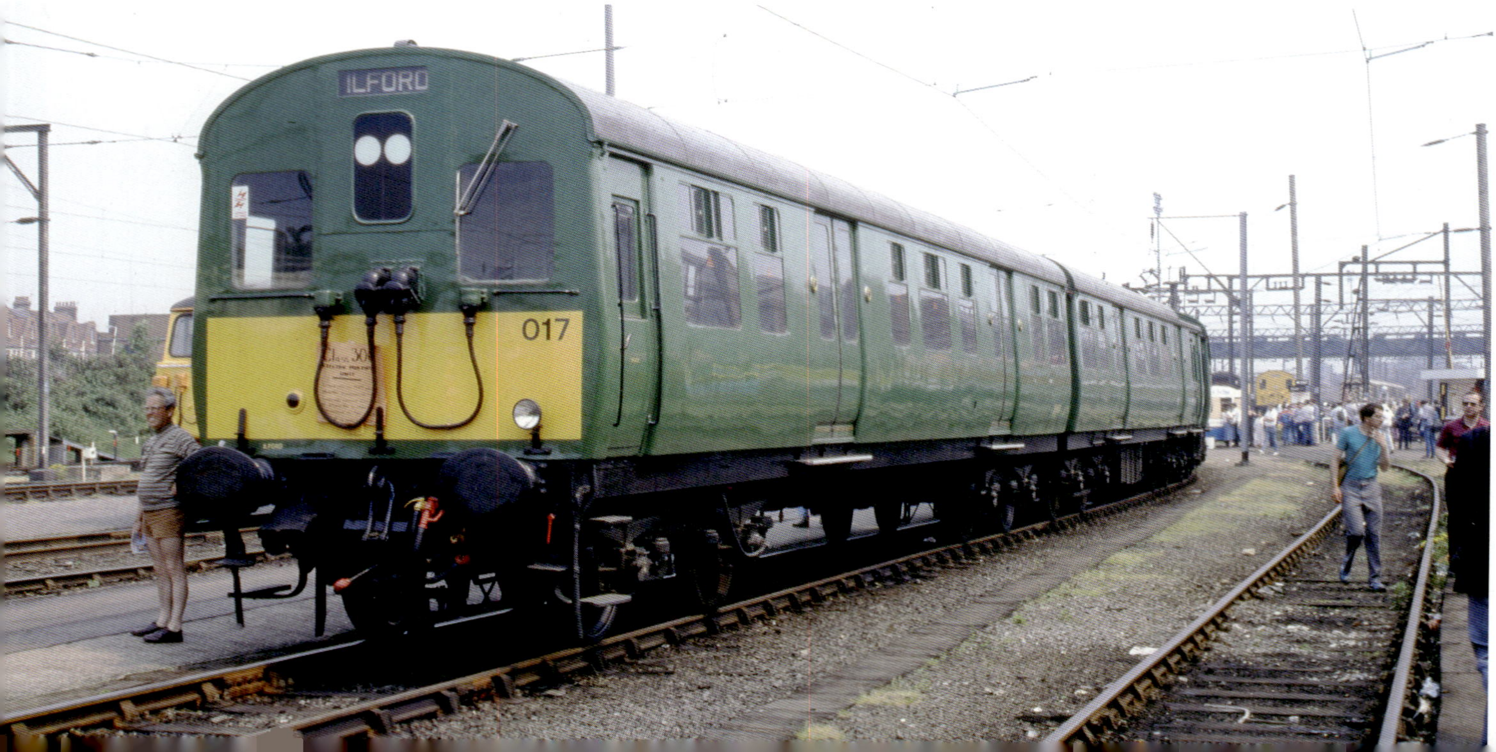

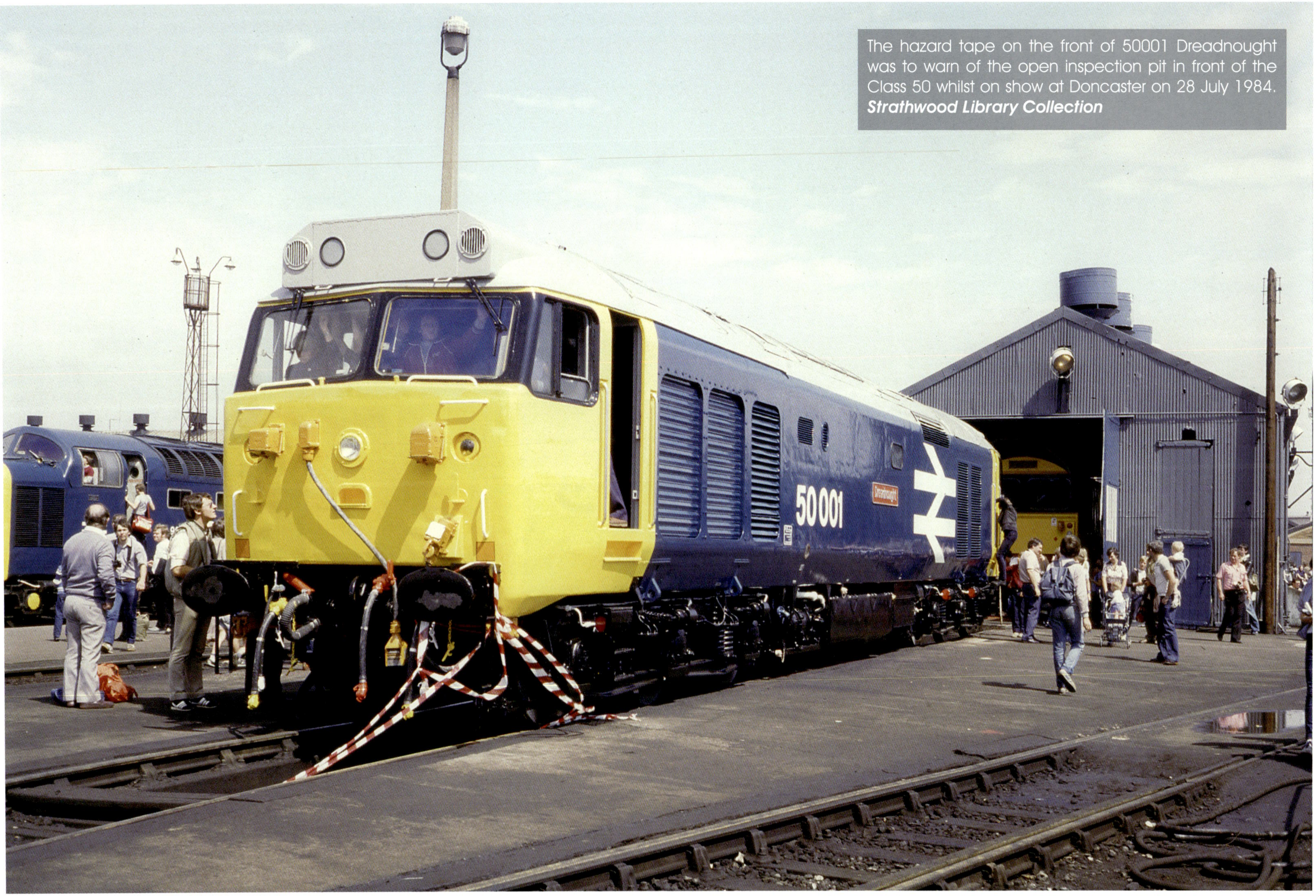

The hazard tape on the front of 50001 Dreadnought was to warn of the open inspection pit in front of the Class 50 whilst on show at Doncaster on 28 July 1984. ***Strathwood Library Collection***

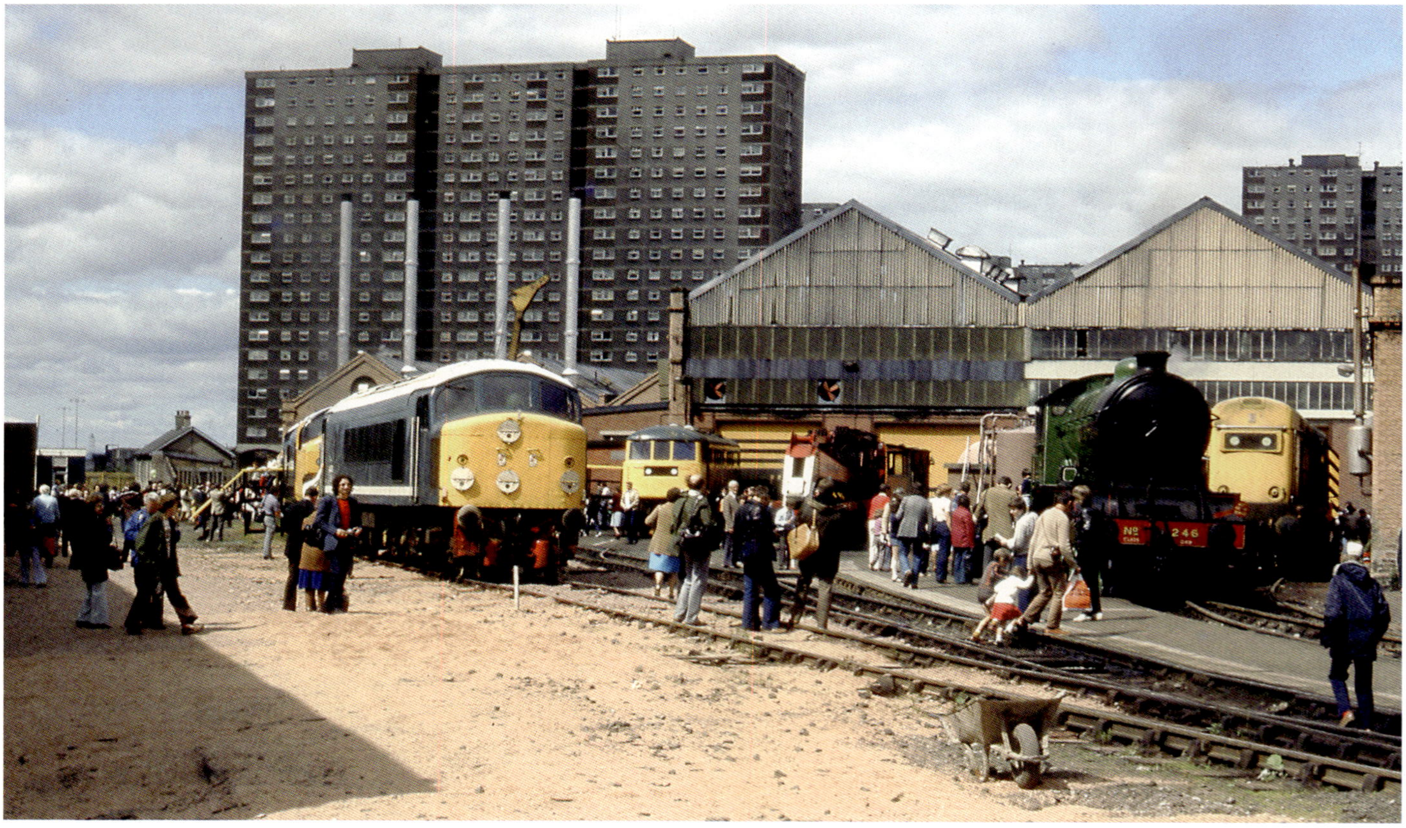

Staying with BREL Works for Open Days as by the start of the eighties the country's most northerly locomotive works was in Glasgow. Among the exhibits assembled for the day were the now preserved 44008 Penyghent and the sole surviving Class D49 Morayshire on 27 June 1981. ***Alan Rintoul***

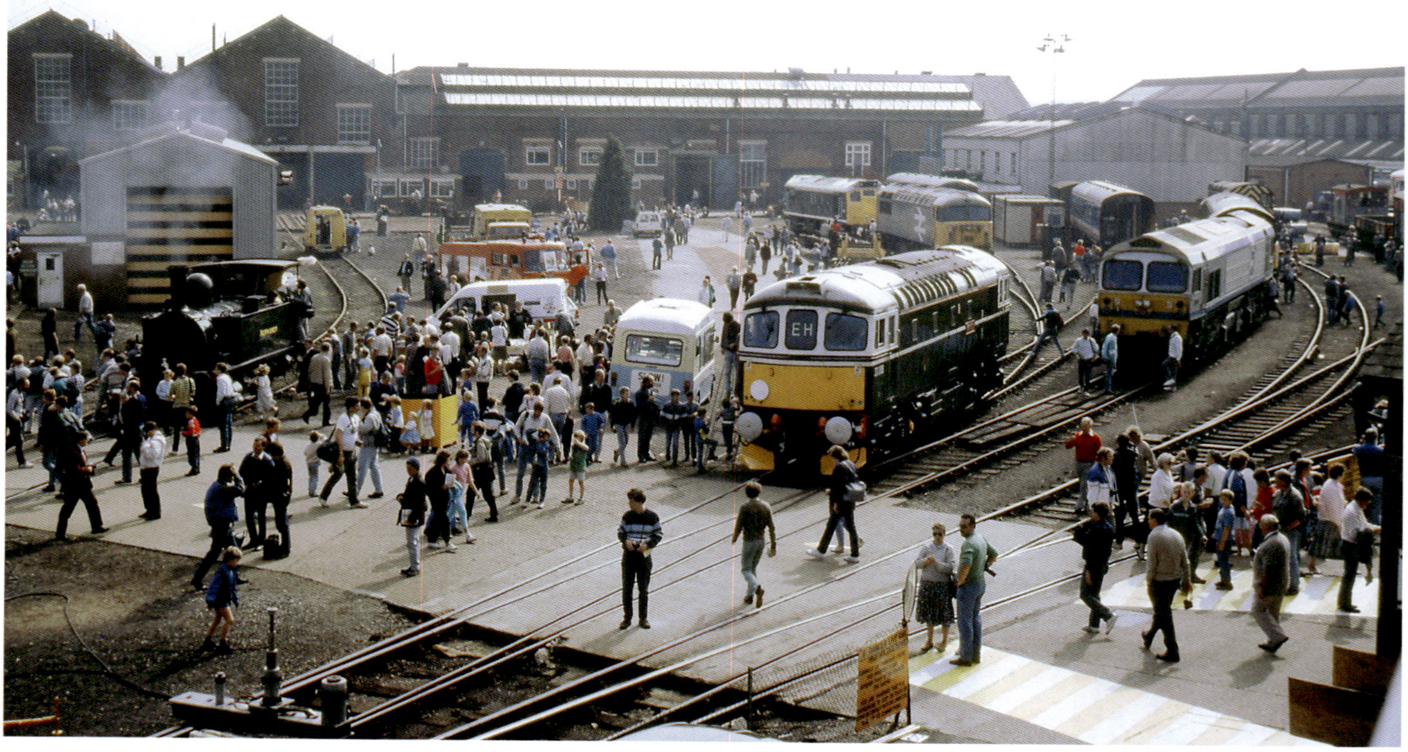

Seven years later and we are at the opposite end of the country for Eastleigh Works on 18 September 1988 to look down into the yard from the roadbridge that leads to both the workshops and the depot. ***Arthur Wilson***

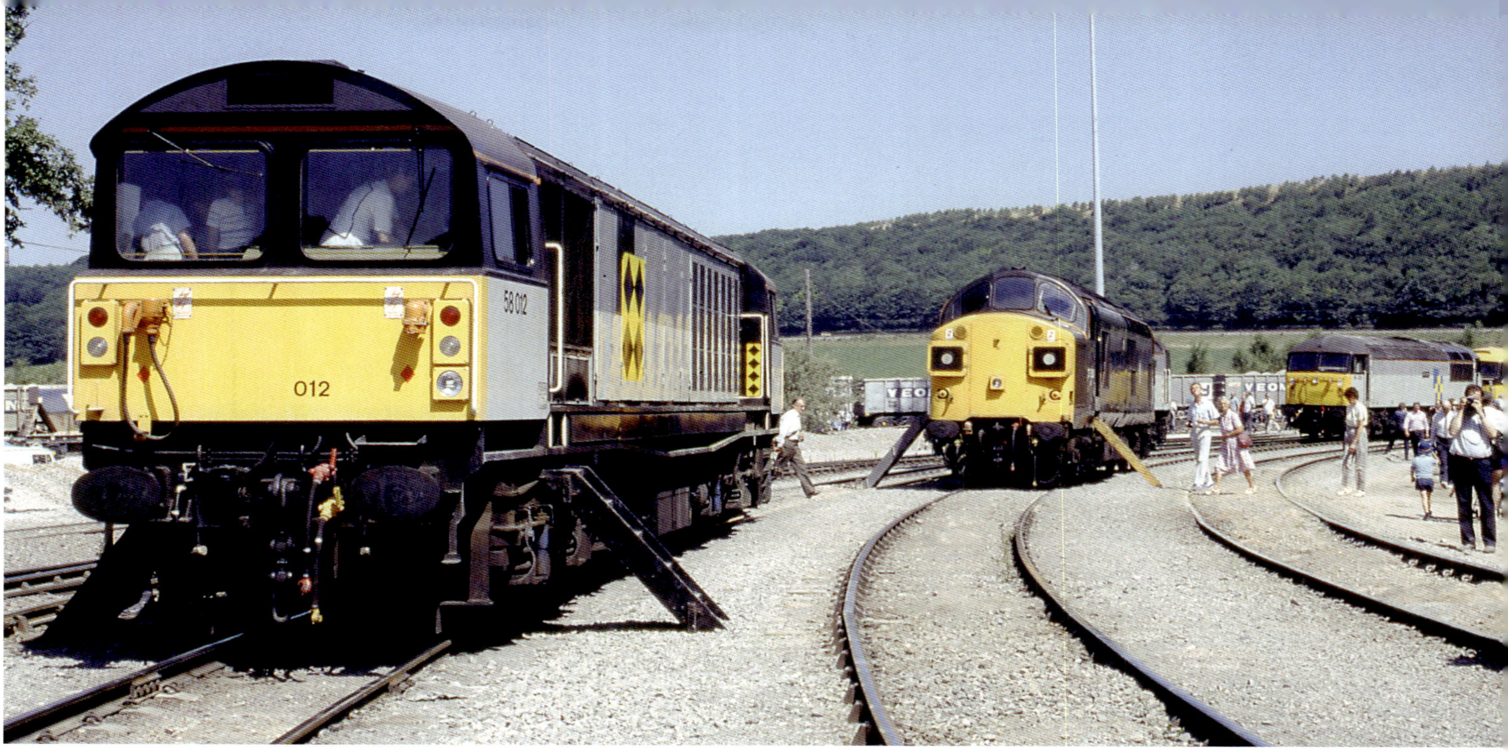

An encouraging venture for Foster Yeoman on 25 June 1989 as they threw open their doors to welcome the public as they laid on 58012, 37350, 47063, 33050 Isle of Grain, 33051 Shakespear Cliff and their own fleet of Class 59s at Merehead. ***All: Arthur Wilson***

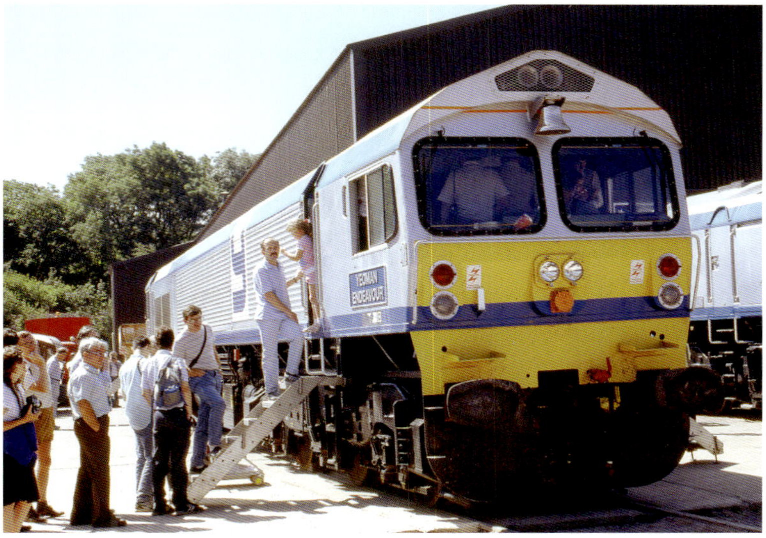

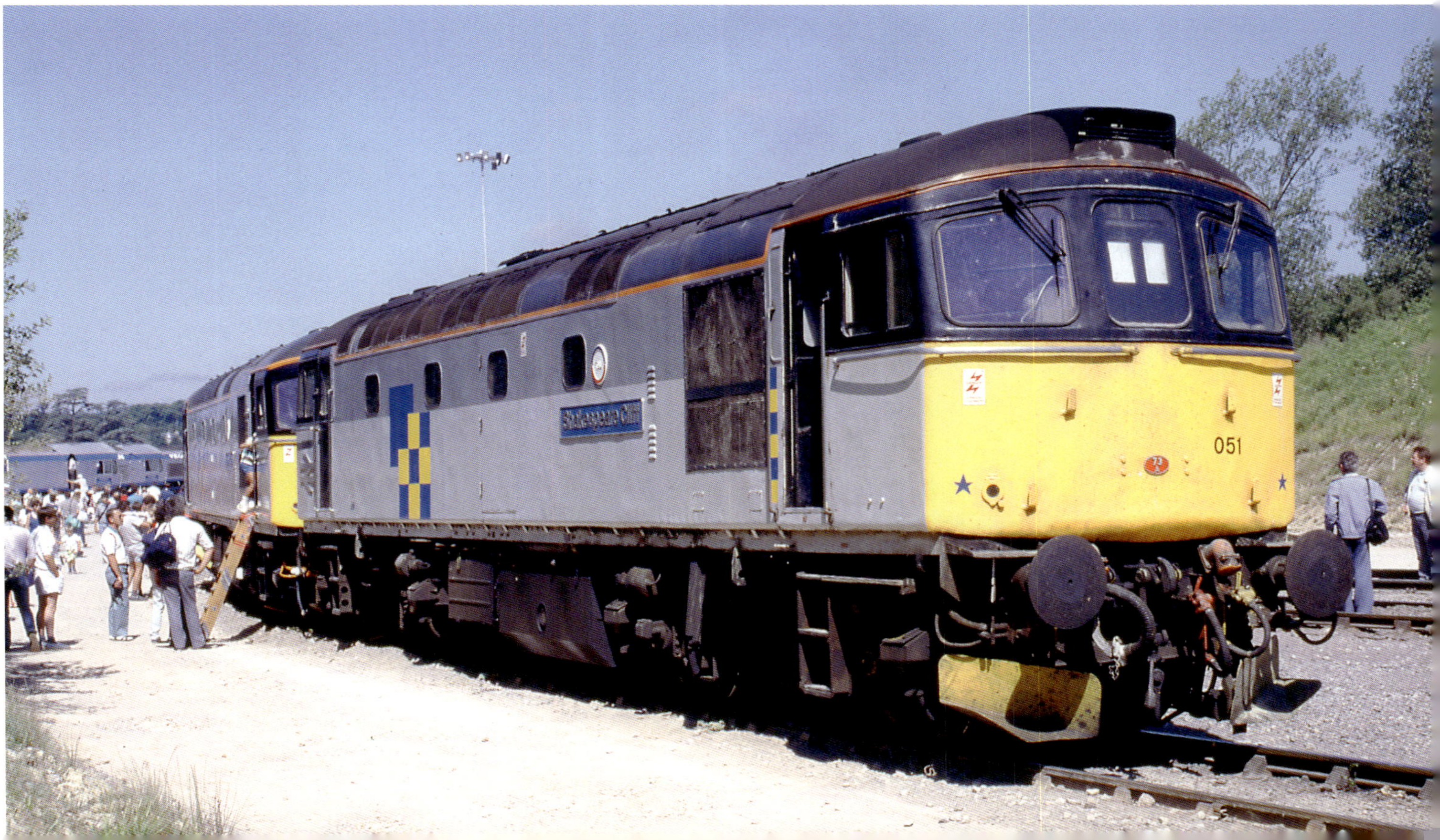

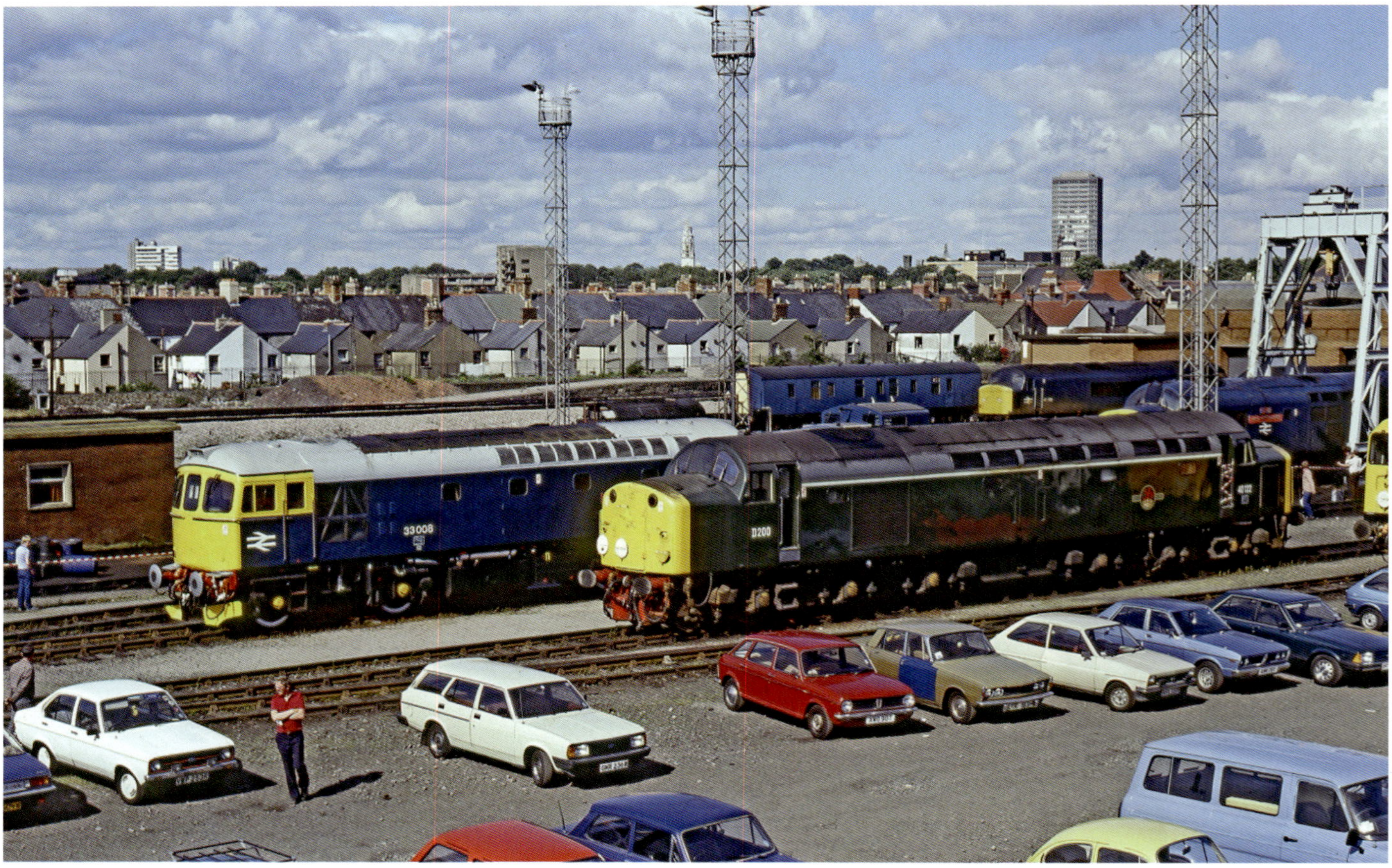

Venturing west to Cardiff Canton for their Open Day on 6 July 1985 rewards us with the then superstar attraction of the celebrated green liveried D200 alongside 33008 Eastleigh still in its embellished blue livery at this time. ***Rail Photoprints/John Chalcroft***

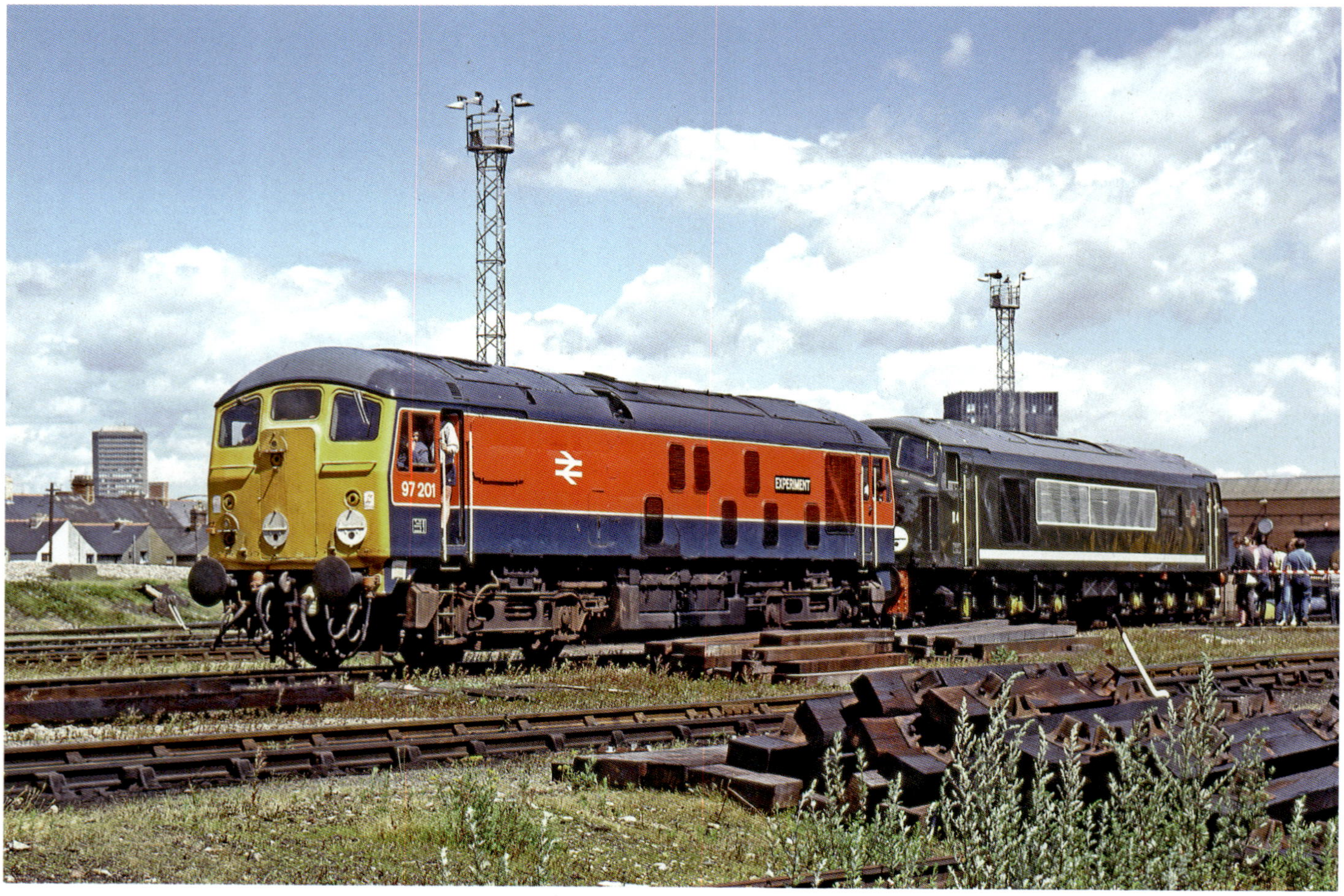

Also on show today were the one time D5061 disguised now as 97201 Experiment from the Derby Research Centre and the preserved D4 Great Gable, two relics from 1960 and 1959 respectively. ***Rail Photoprints/John Chalcroft***

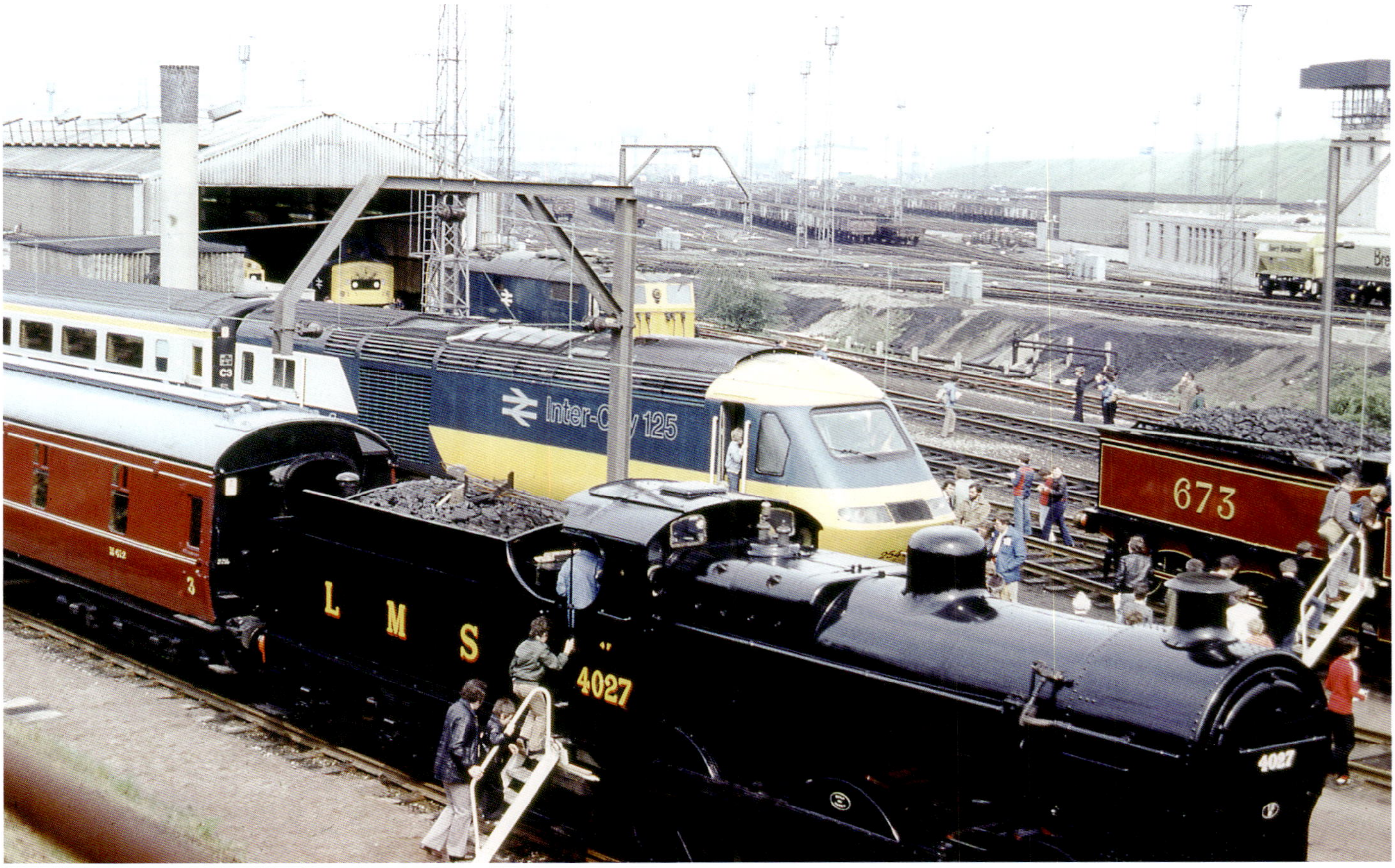

Off to Yorkshire next on 15 June 1980 and to Tinsley, not for the main depot but to the small running shed that was once down within the yard complex. which would be much easier to arrange and police! ***Phil Bidwell***

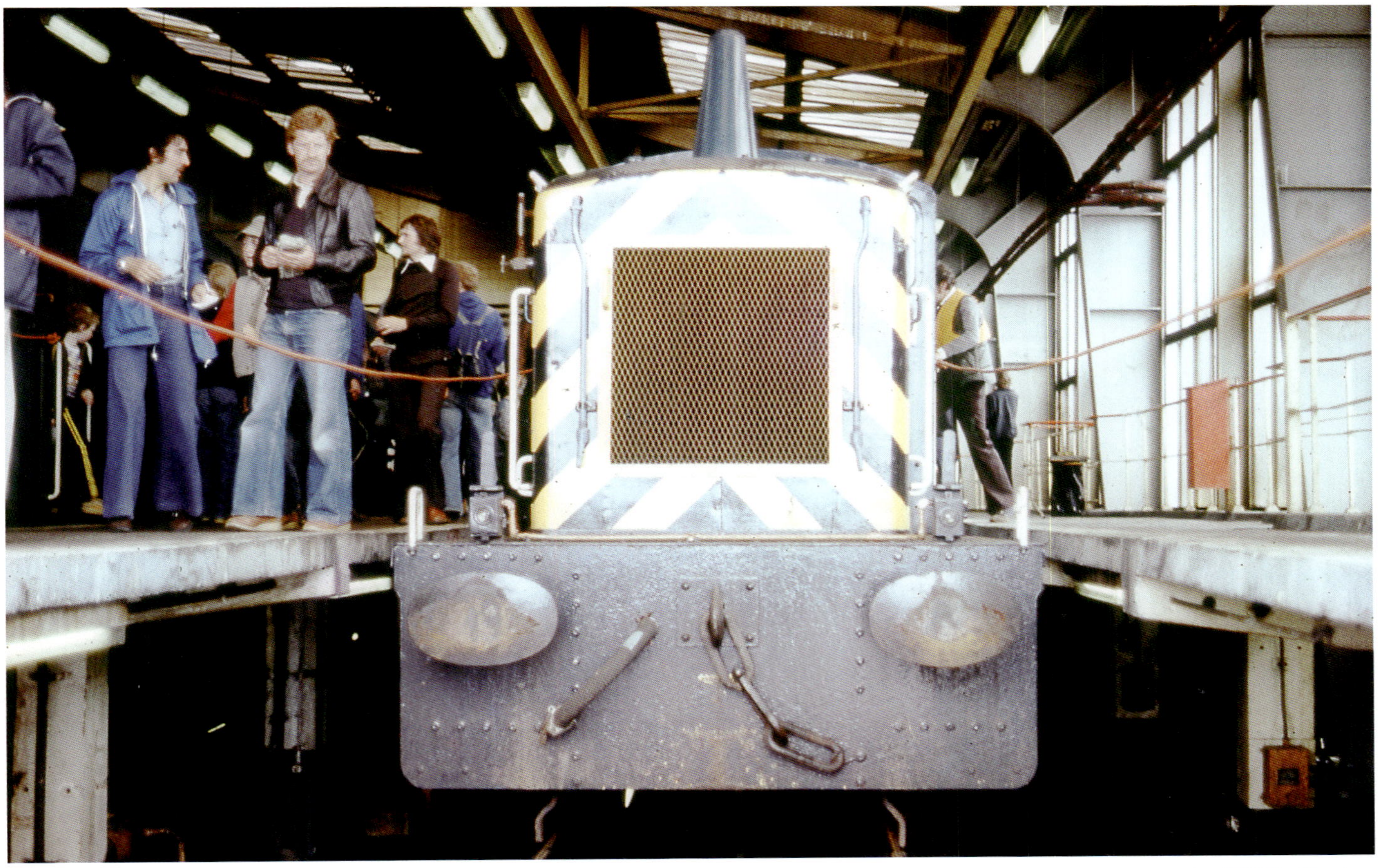

Inside the shed building was the unfortunate 03129, it had survived storage in 1969 to find work as the pilot within Barrow Hill's roundhouse, whilst this depot found salvation, the Class 03 did not as it went to Booth's scrapyard at Rotherham for cutting up in 1983. Tinsley as we have already mentioned succumbed to progress also, as it seems have Open Days generally. ***Phil Bidwell***

Bridging the Gaps

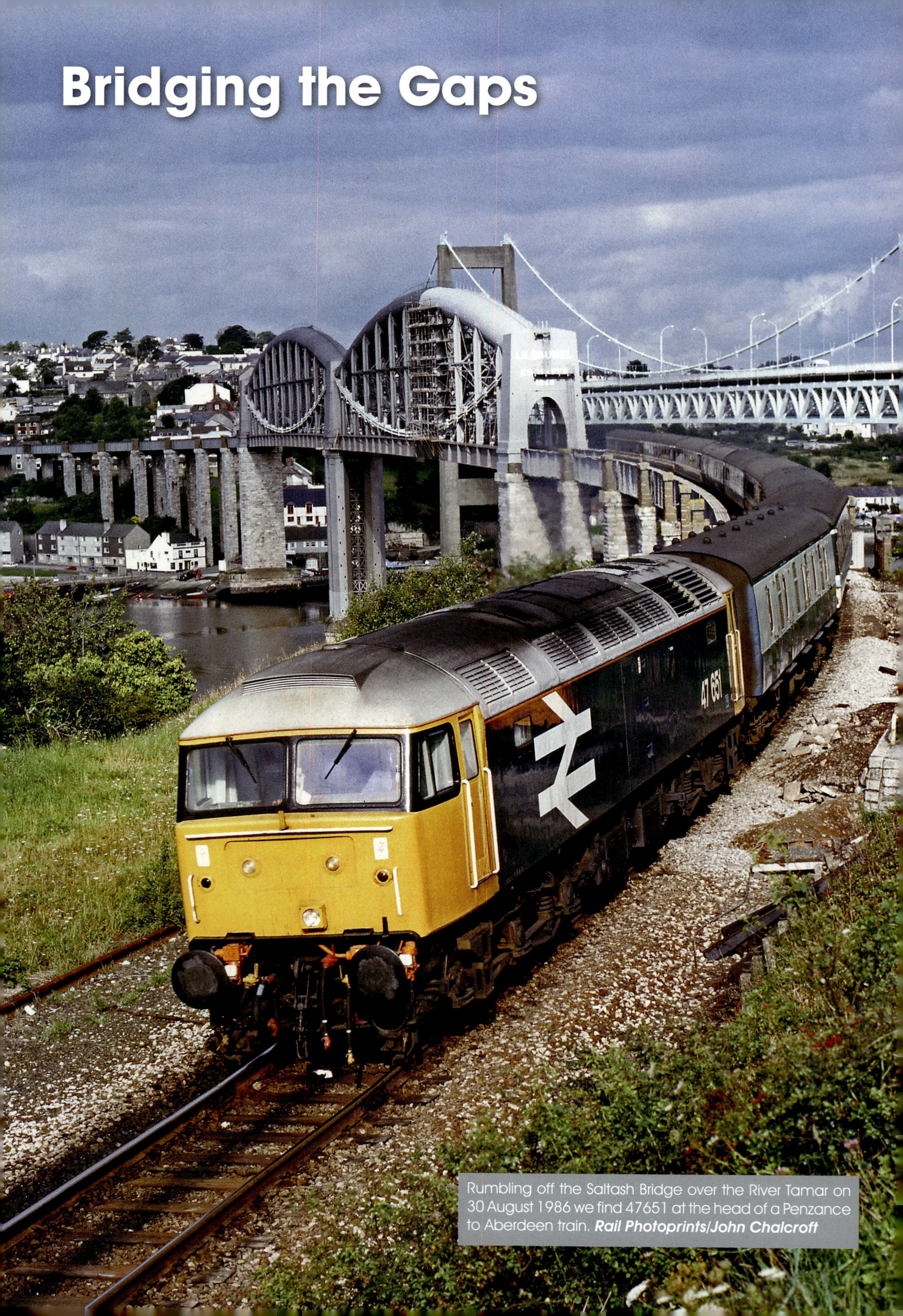

Rumbling off the Saltash Bridge over the River Tamar on 30 August 1986 we find 47651 at the head of a Penzance to Aberdeen train. ***Rail Photoprints/John Chalcroft***

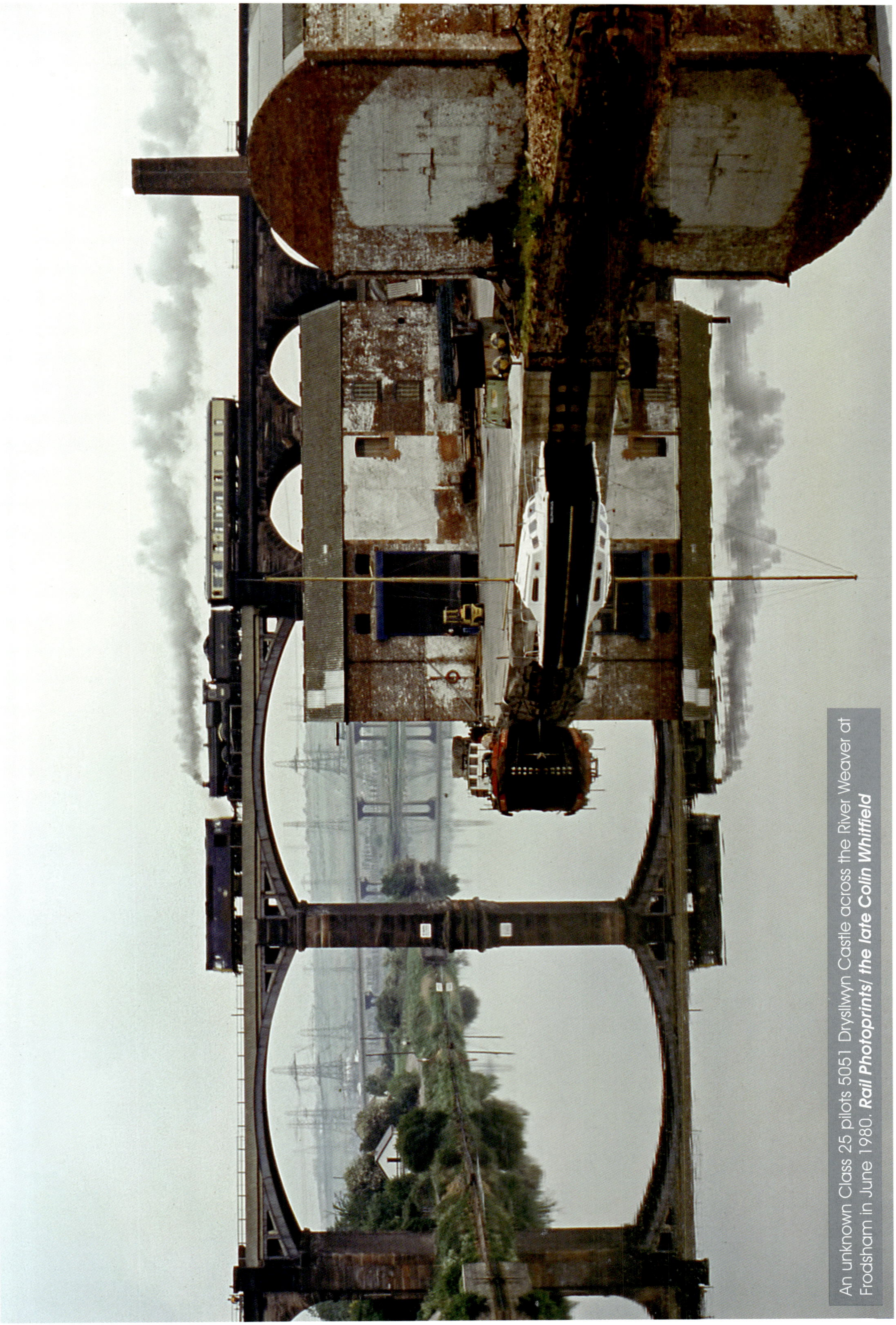

An unknown Class 25 pilots 5051 Drysllwyn Castle across the River Weaver at Frodsham in June 1980. ***Rail Photoprints/ the late Colin Whitfield***

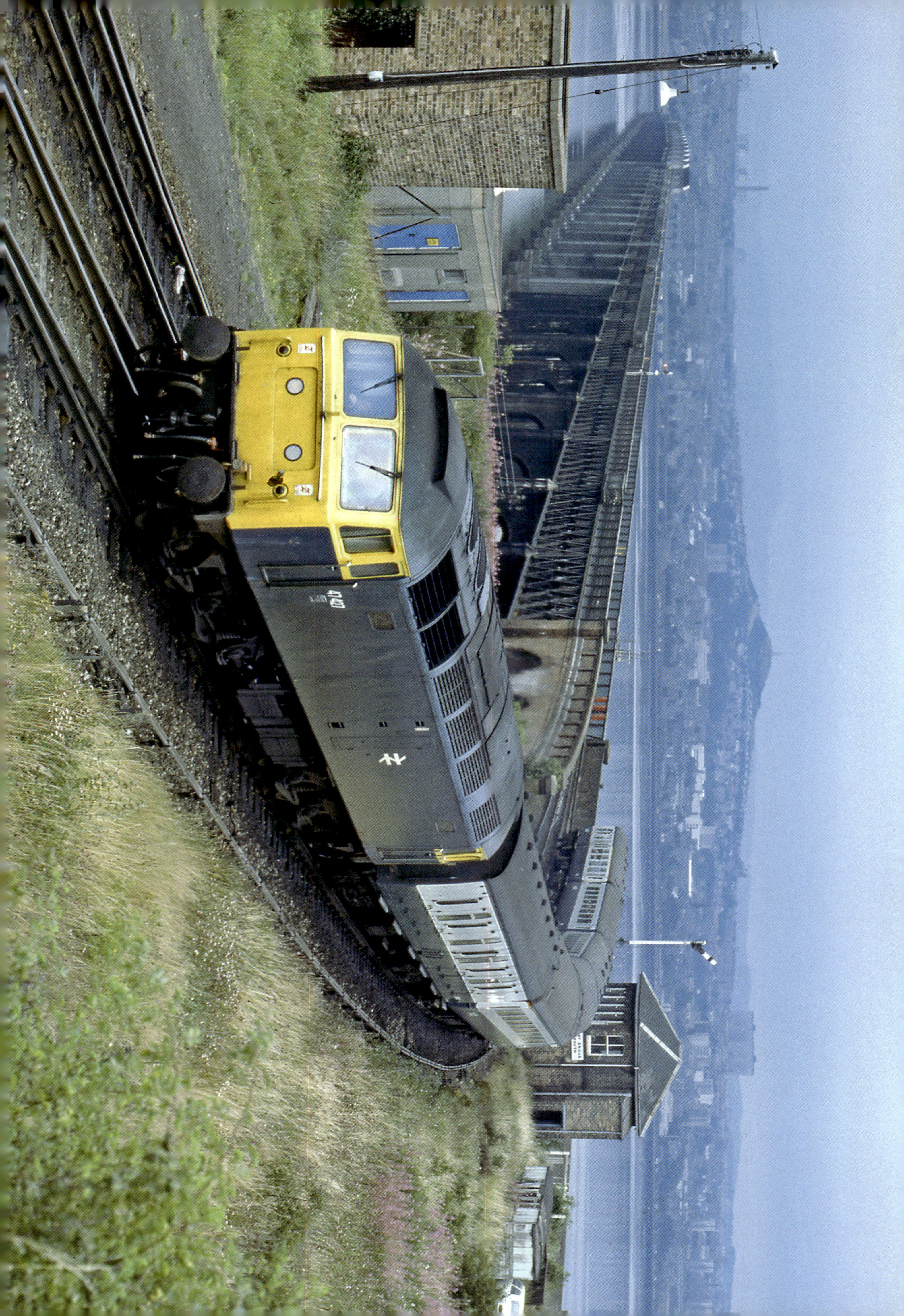

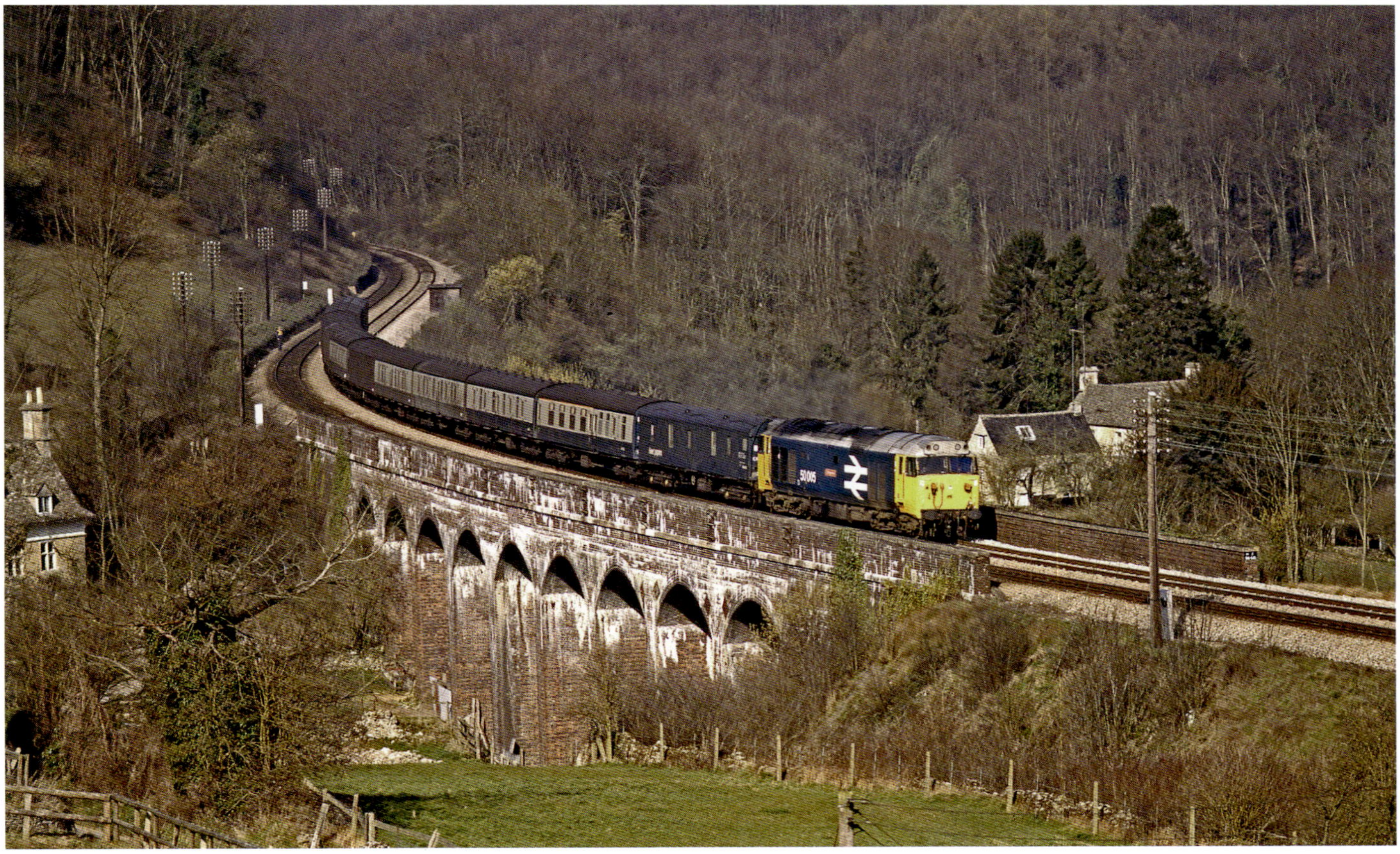

Frampton Mansell viaduct supports 50005 Collingwood as it climbs towards Sapperton with the morning Gloucester to Old Oak Common empty newspaper vans on 13 April 1984. ***Rail Photoprints/John Chalcroft***

Below: The equally impressive Slochd viaduct does likewise for 47615 Castell Caerffilli Caerphilly Castle as it heads south on 23 October 1985 with The Clansman which was the 10.30 Inverness to Euston. ***M Szczeblewski***

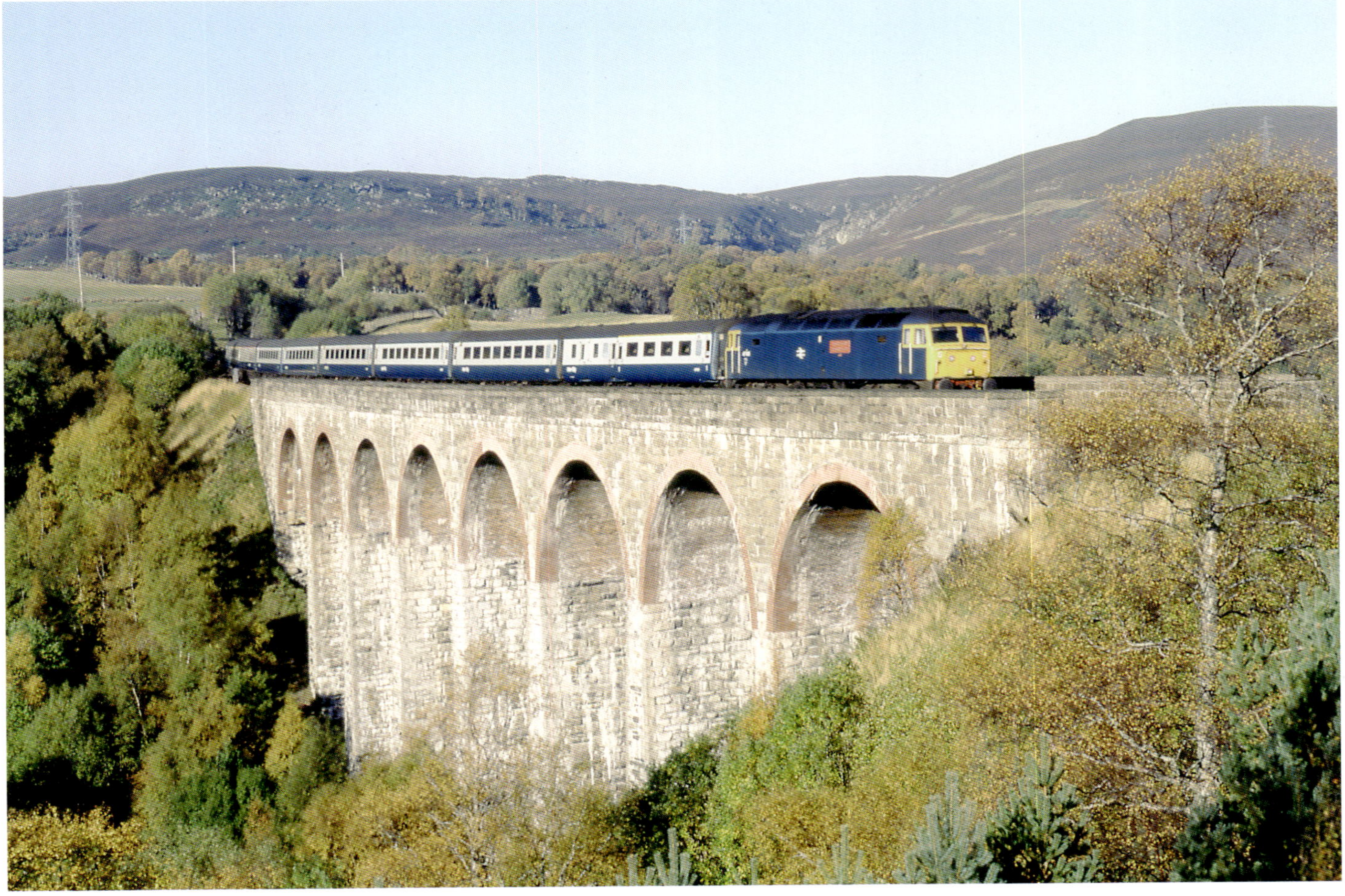

Page left: Entering the Kingdom of Fife from the north and off the Tay Bridge is 47427 with a through service from Aberdeen bound for Nottingham on 11 August 1982. ***Rail Photoprints/John Chalcroft***

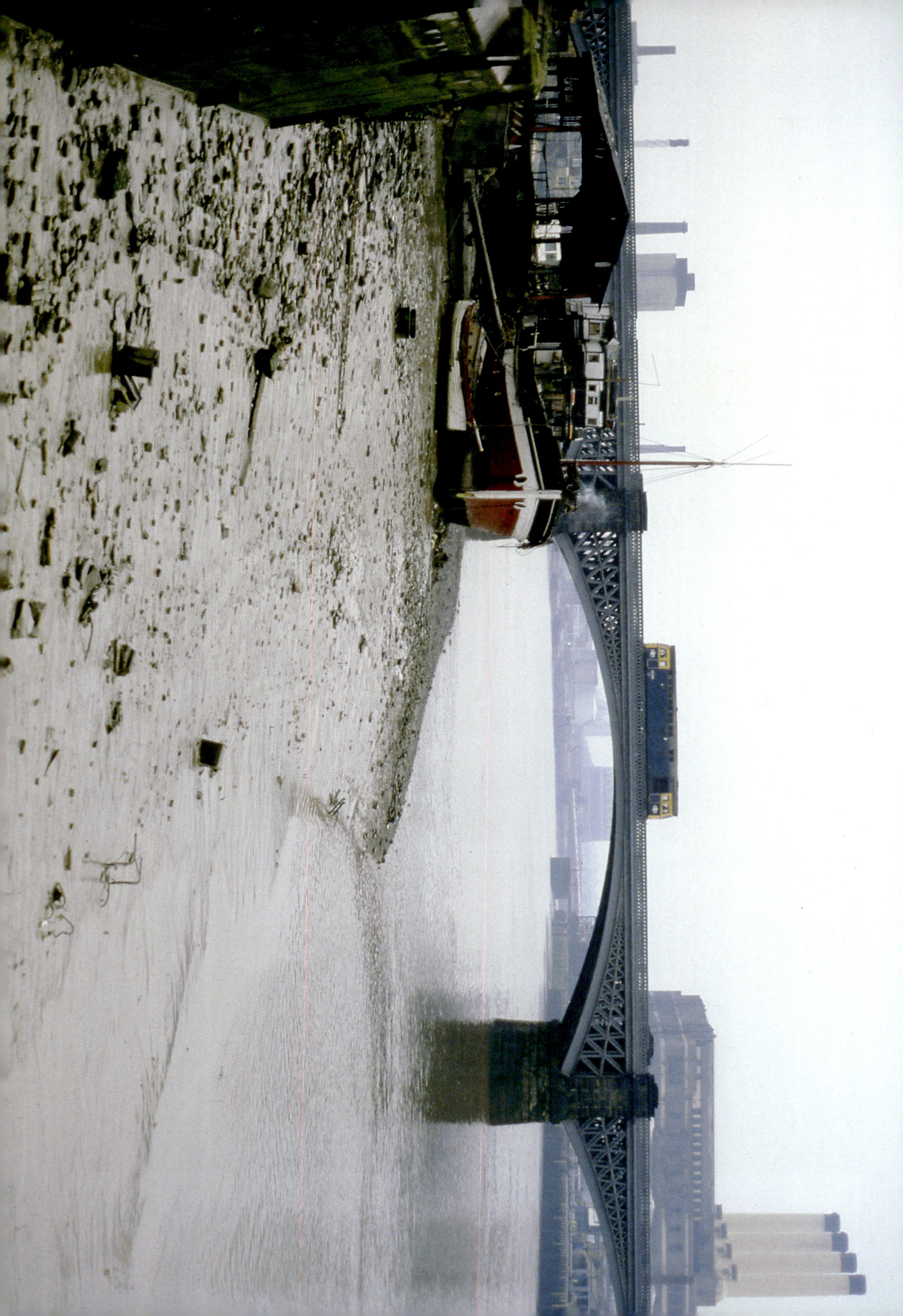

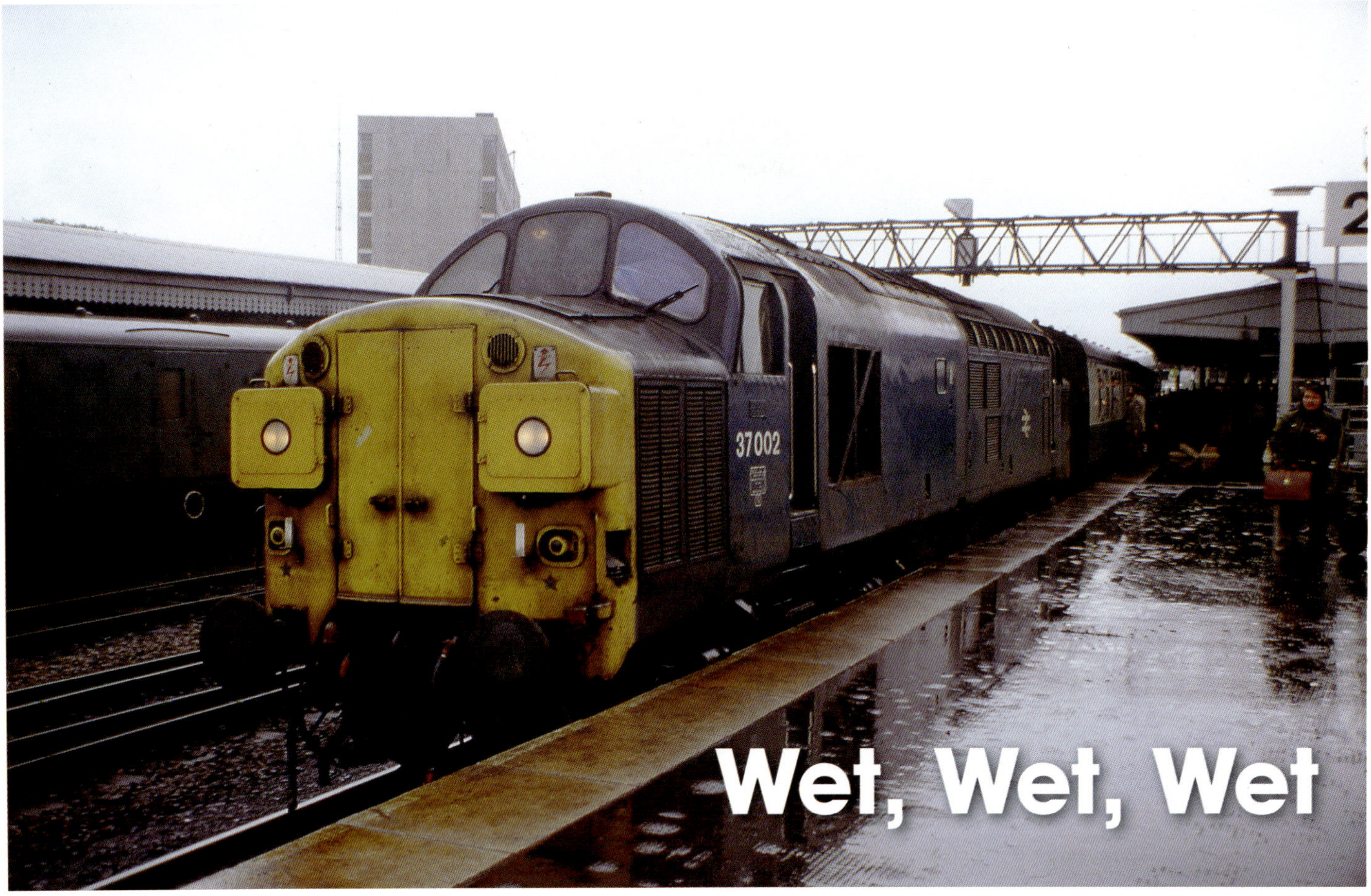

Our brave cameraman ventures out into a rain storm to record 37002 at Gloucester with the 08.23 Manchester to Swansea on 31 May 1980. The Scottish based band Wet, Wet, Wet would go on and become a big hit in the eighties. ***Gilroy A. Kerr***

Below: Sheltering from the rain in October 1987 under the cover of the carriage cleaning sheds at Clapham Junction was 73006. There is no missing locomotive numbers at speed with Large Logo livery! ***Richard Czyzewski***

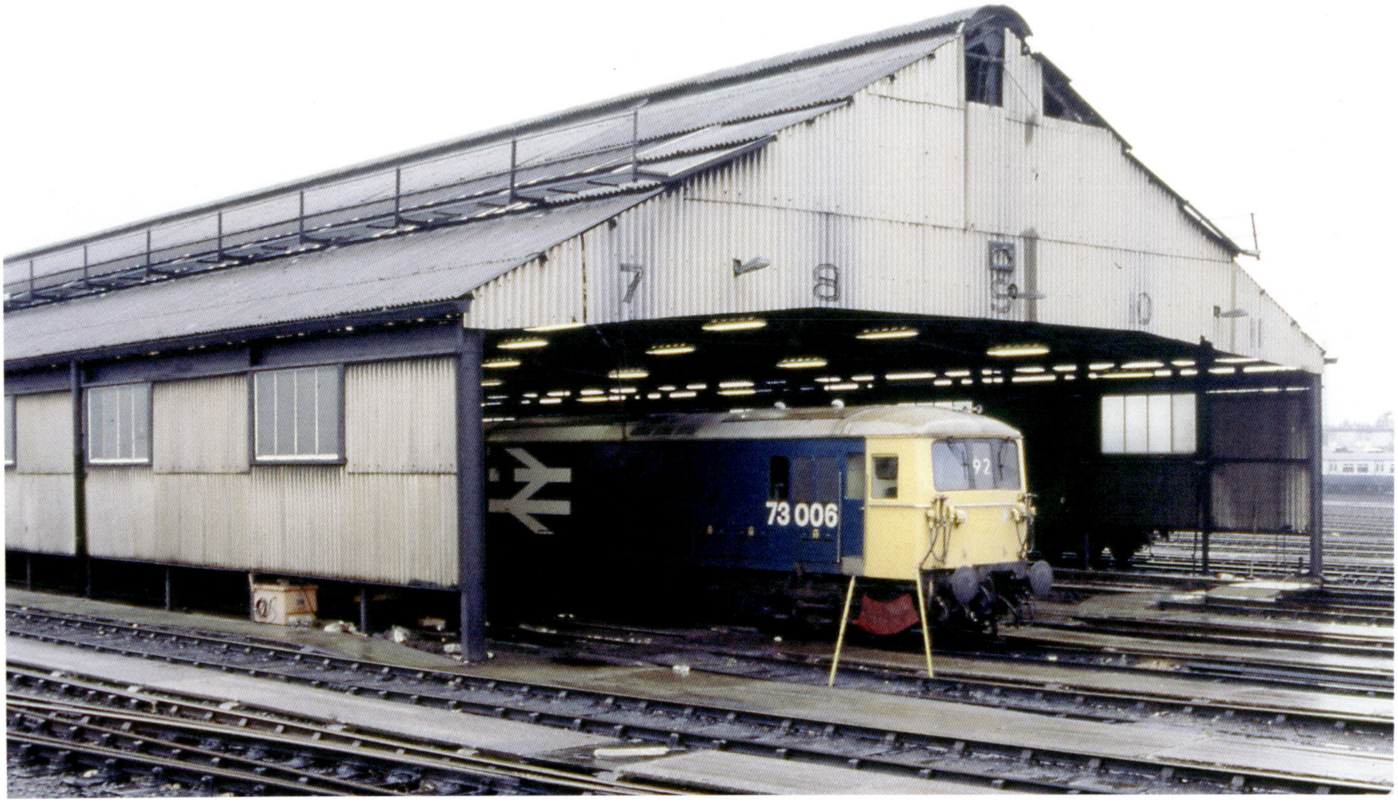

Page left: The River Thames is at low tide as this Class 33 heads light engine from Mitre Bridge to Hither Green as it crosses what is usually referred to as Chelsea Bridge on a very damp 17 October 1981. ***Colin Whitbread***

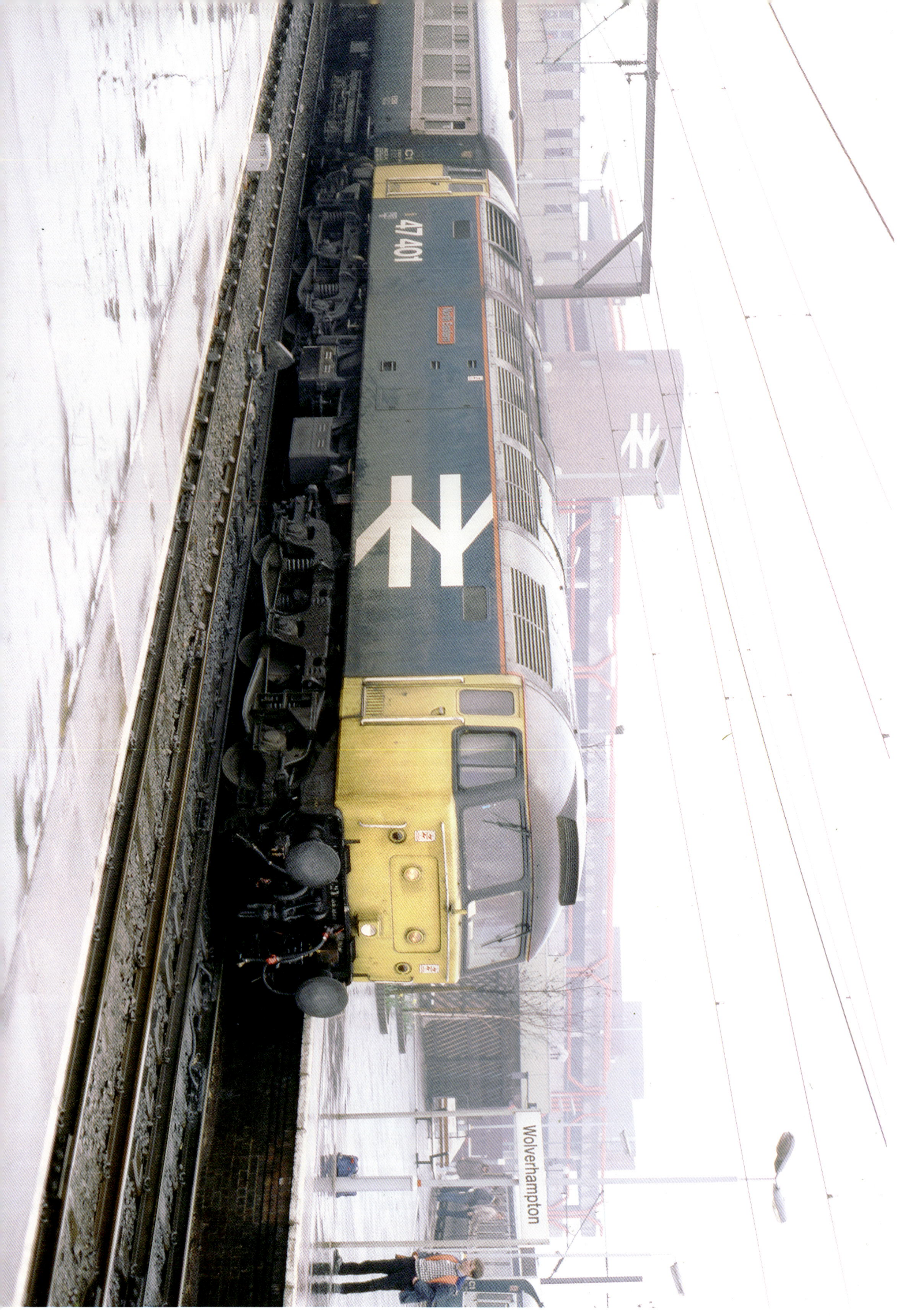
47 401
Wolverhampton

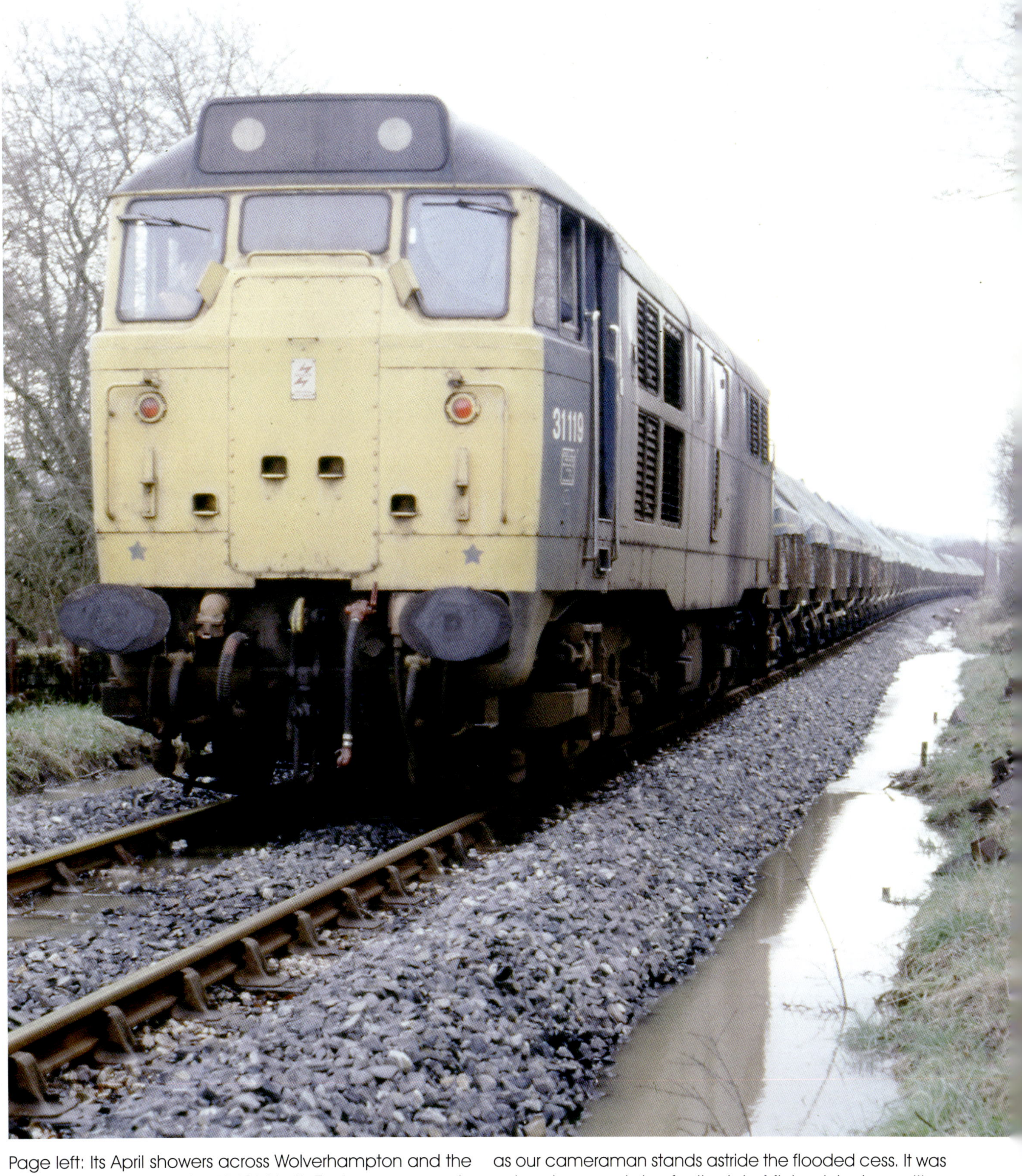

Page left: Its April showers across Wolverhampton and the Black Country in 1987 for 47401 North Eastern once again in Large Logo livery. ***David T. Williams***

Tiptoeing along the Heathfield branch on 27 January 1984 was 31119 which had to return to Exeter due to a washout, as our cameraman stands astride the flooded cess. It was not such a good day for the late Michael Jackson either as he managed to set fire to his hair whilst filming a Pepsi commercial... ***N P Cannon***

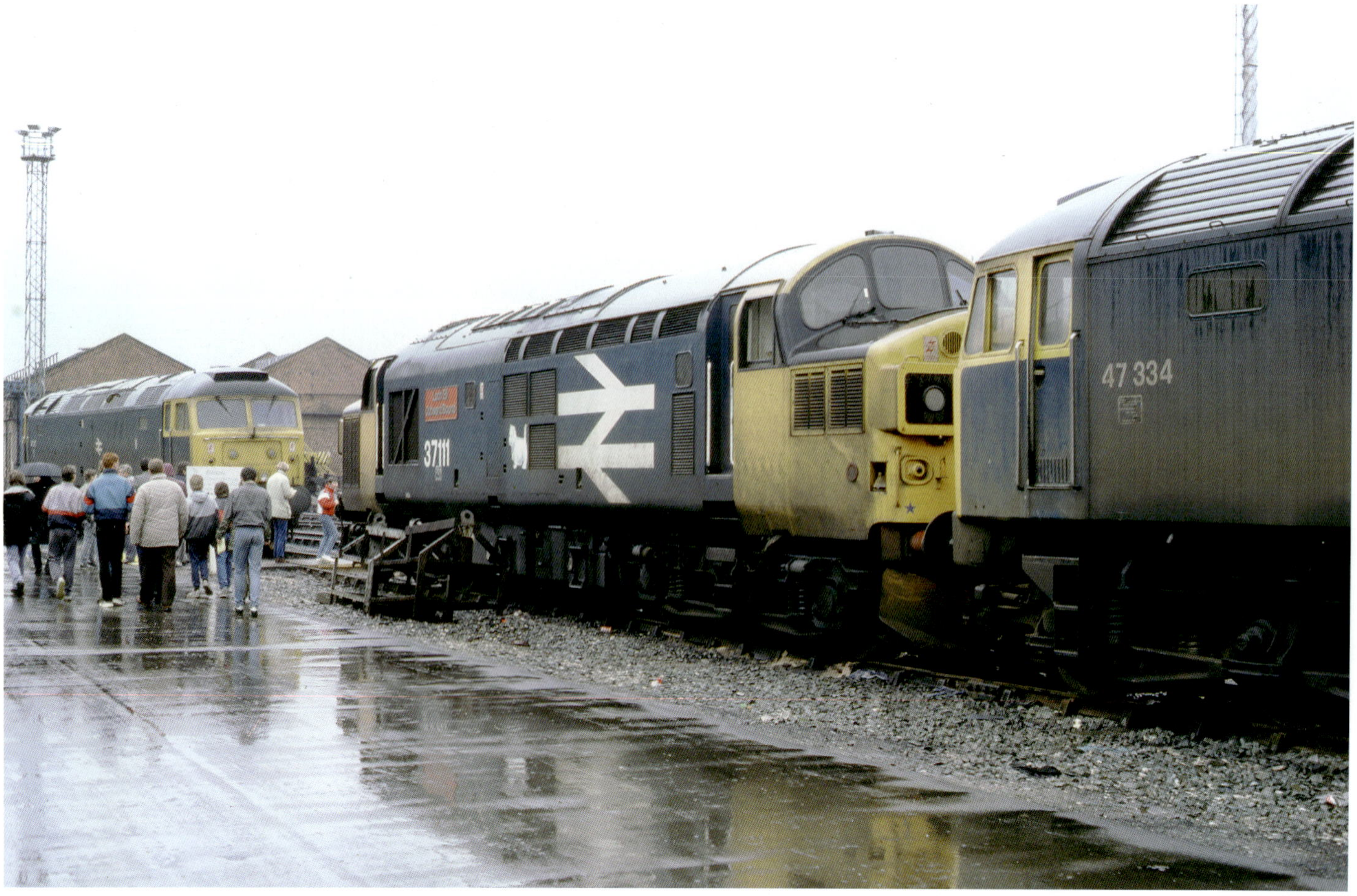

Recalling the fact that not all conducted visits to depots and works were in sunshine we explore Crewe Works in April 1988 which has 37111 Loch Eil Outward Bound in for repairs. Do you recall how hard it was to write numbers down on wet pages with a biro? ***David T. Williams***

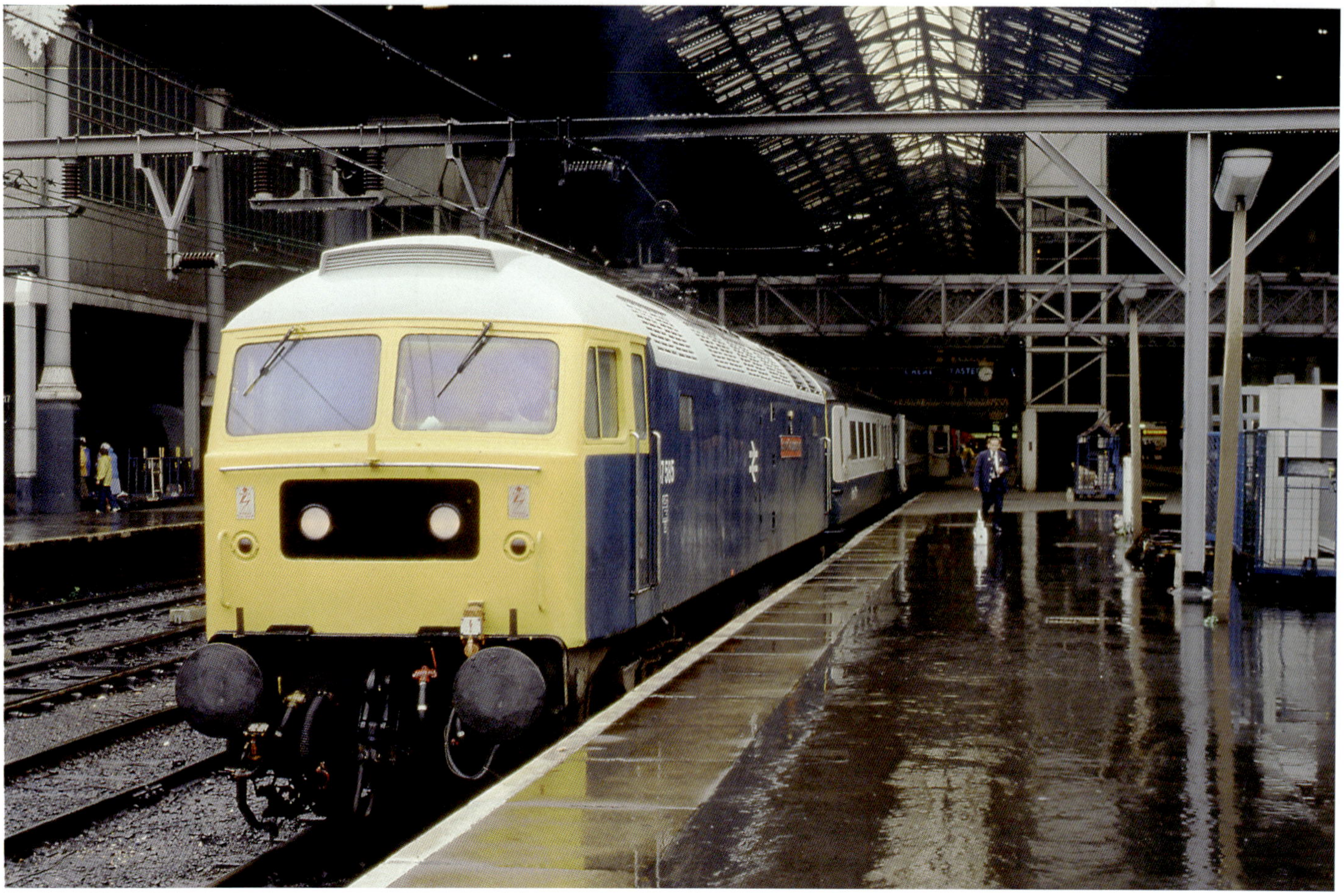

Its a heavy summer storm over London this time for 47585 County of Cambridgeshire which will take the 14.30 to Norwich out from Liverpool Street on 22 July 1981. ***Colin Whitbread***

On the Job

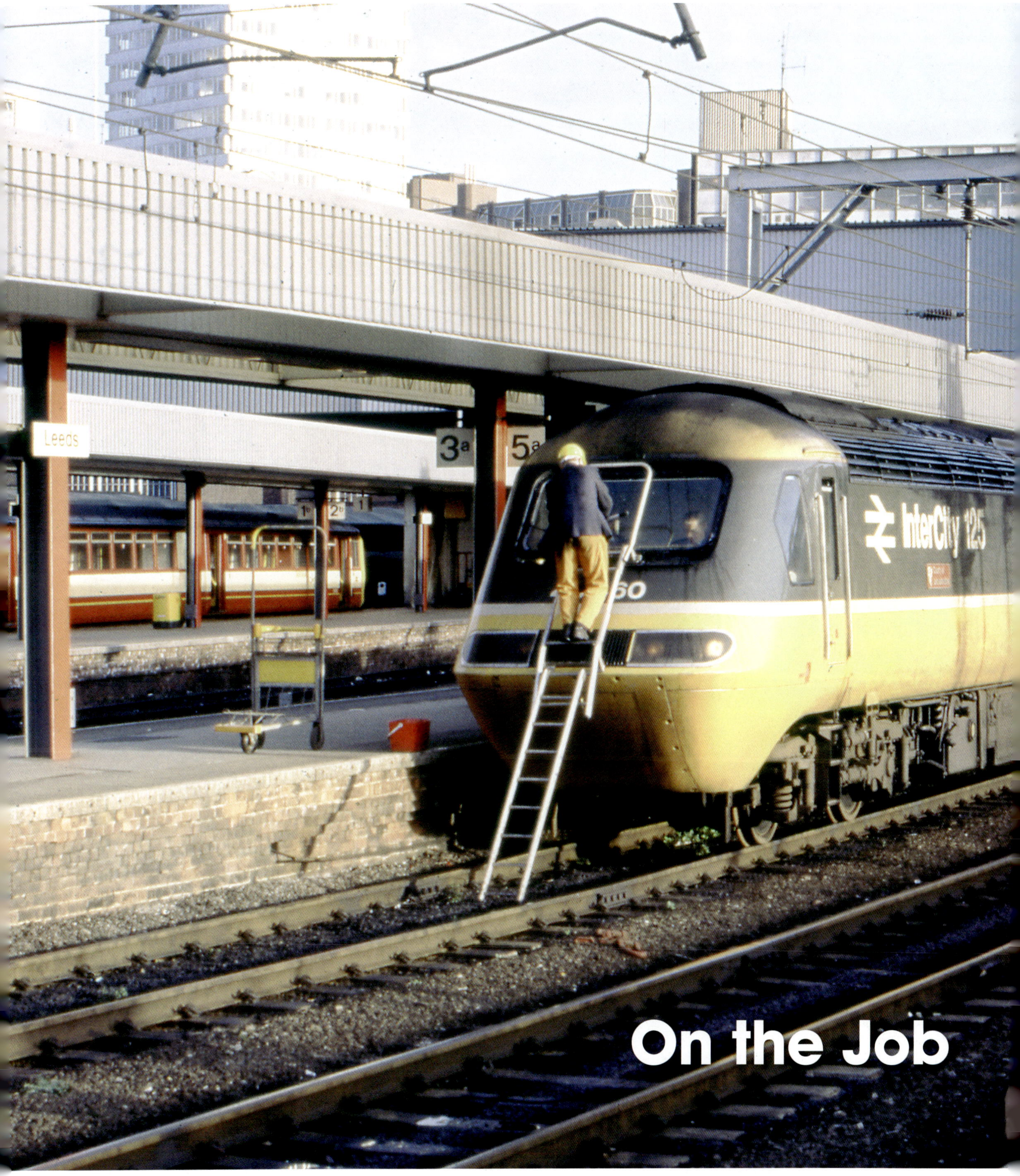

The driver of an HST service waits patiently for departure time as the front screen is cleaned for him at Leeds in January 1989. In the newspapers that month we unfortunately had to read about the Kegworth air diaster when a British Midland Boeing 737 tragically crashed into the embankment on the side of the M1 motorway on approach to East Midlands Airport, leaving 47 dead. ***Dave Southern***

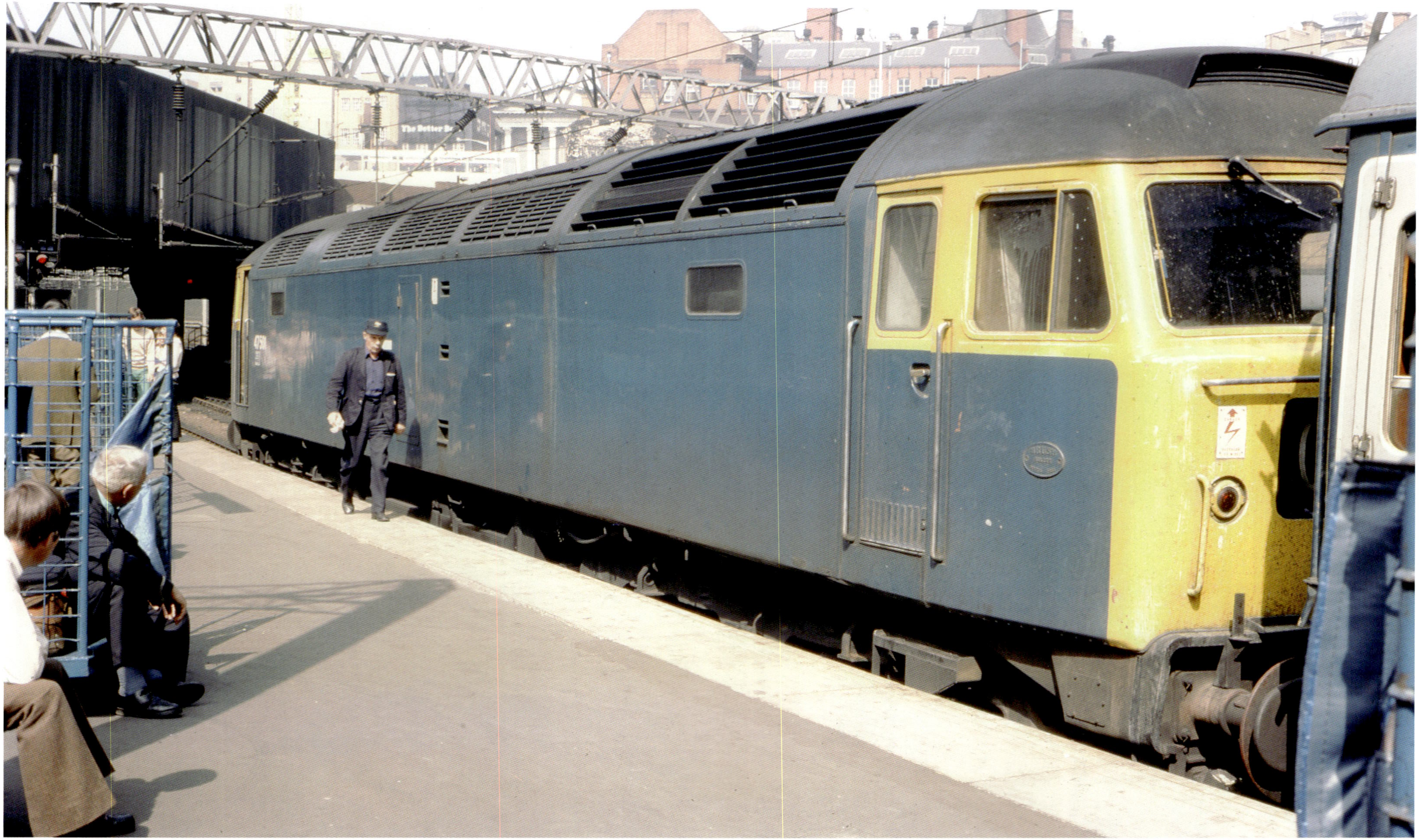

Those BRUTE trolleys were always popular as mobile seats for enthusiasts and passengers of all ages as we see at Birmingham New Street in the summer of 1980, as the driver of 47501 which was based at Landore at the time makes his way back to have a word with the guard before departure. Abba were at the top of the charts with The Winner Takes it All, and Moscow hosts the summer Olympics. The United States and a number of other countries boycotted the games because of the Soviet invasion of Afghanistan, though some athletes from some of the boycotting countries participated in the games, under the Olympic Flag. This prompted the Soviet-led boycott of the 1984 Summer Olympics. ***David T. Williams***

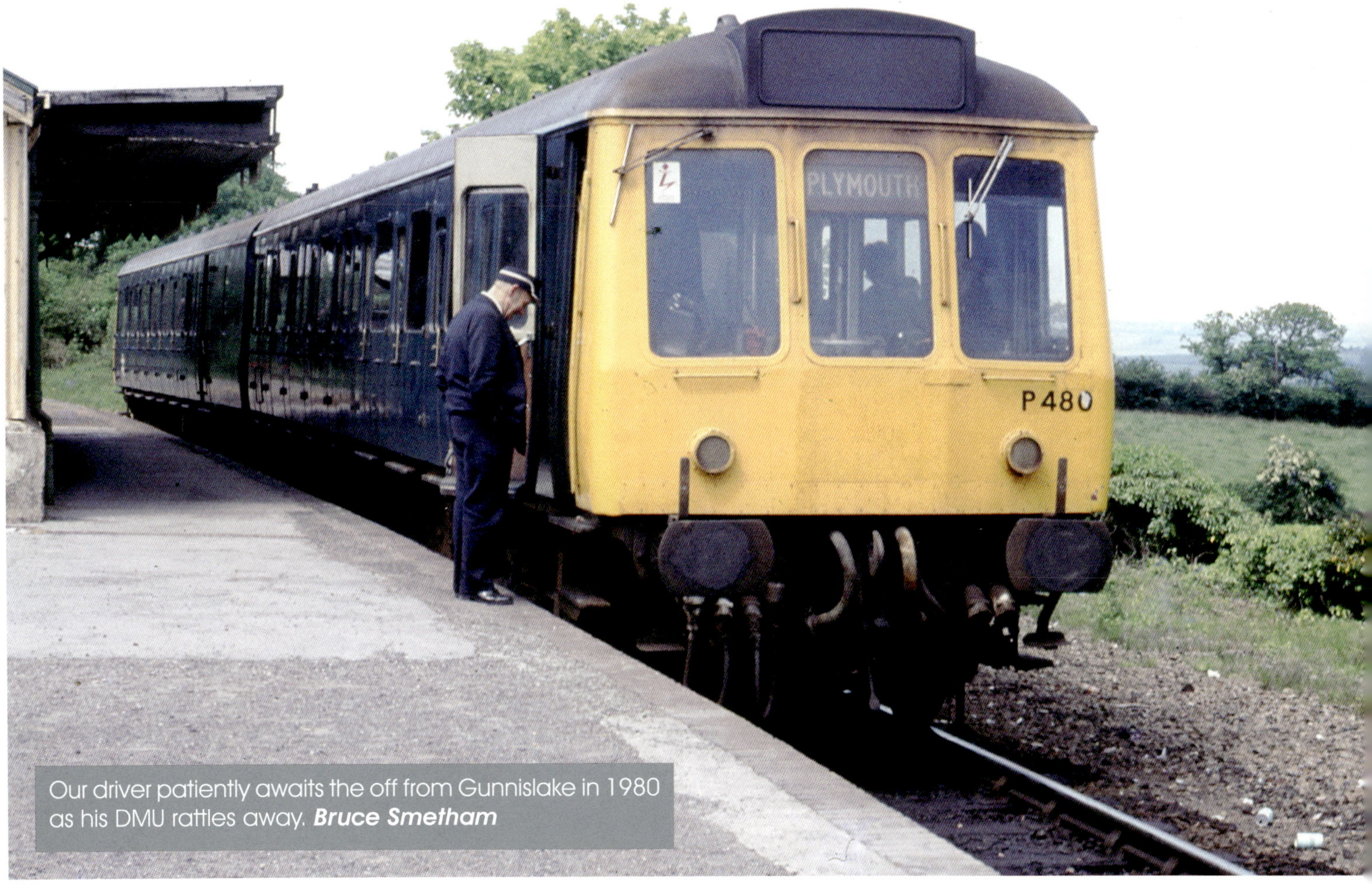

Our driver patiently awaits the off from Gunnislake in 1980 as his DMU rattles away. ***Bruce Smetham***

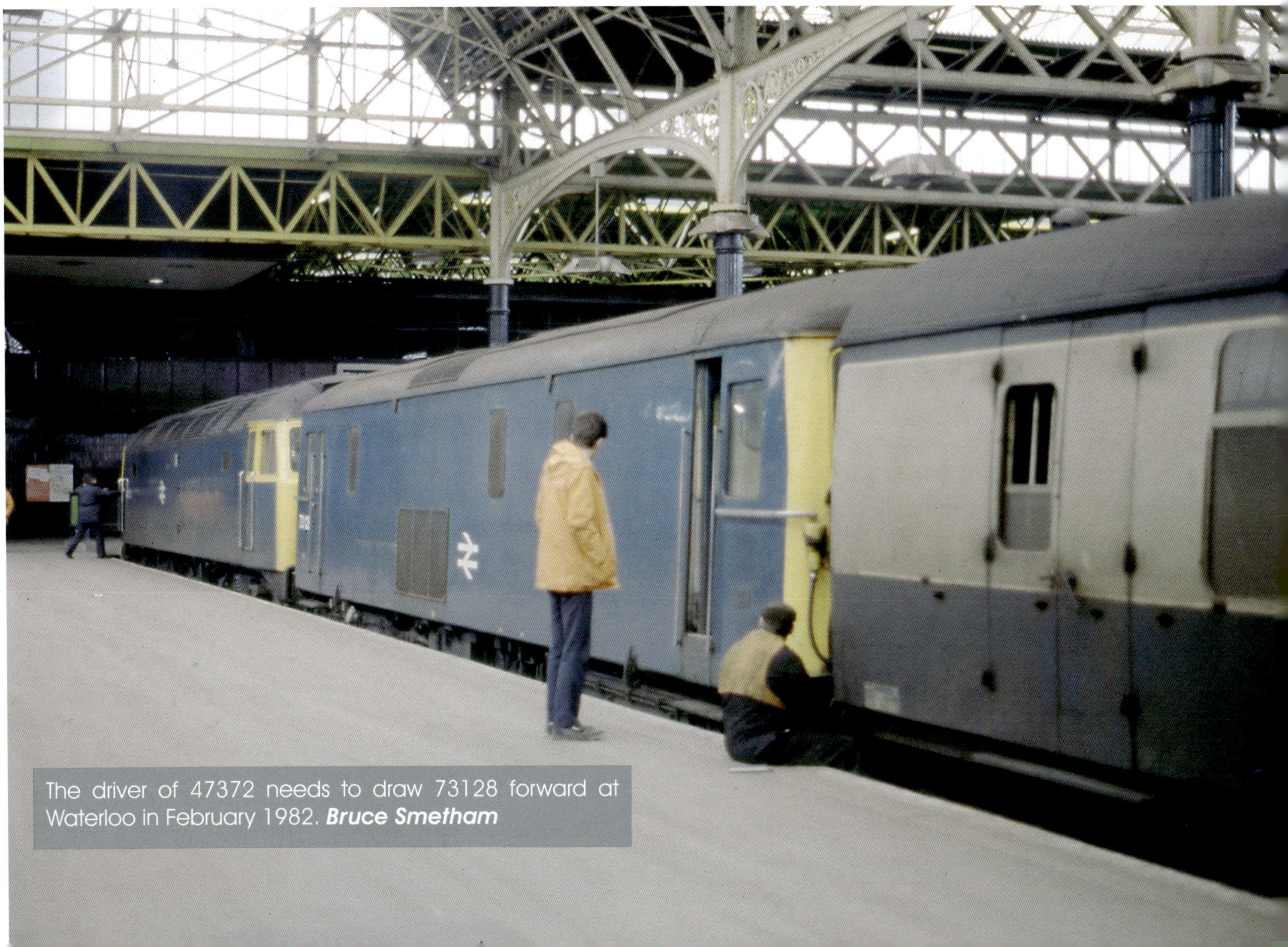

The driver of 47372 needs to draw 73128 forward at Waterloo in February 1982. ***Bruce Smetham***

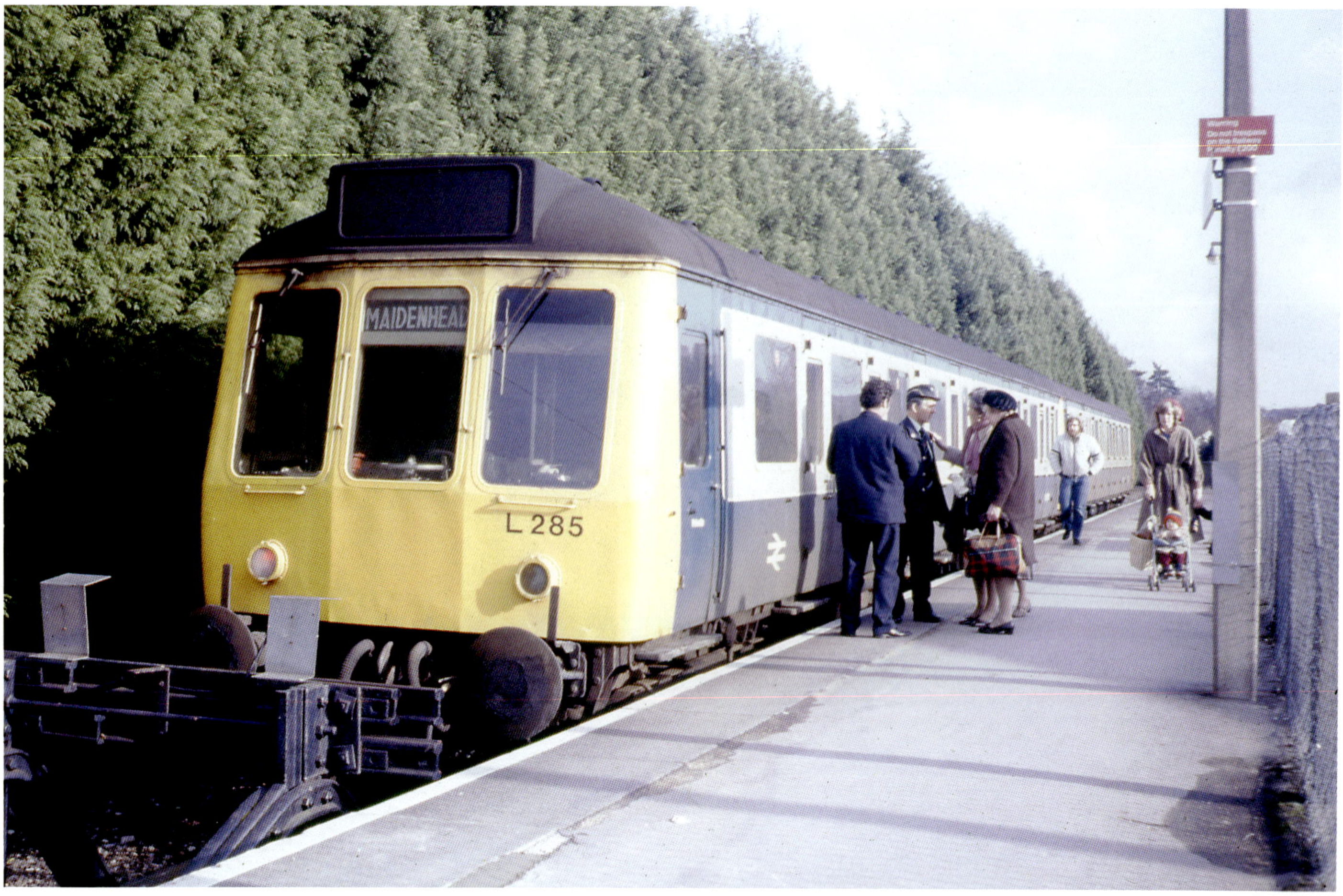

Friendly help from the train crew at Marlow at the end of the seven mile branch from Maidenhead whose service has long been nicknamed the Marlow Donkey. ***Strathwood Library Collection***

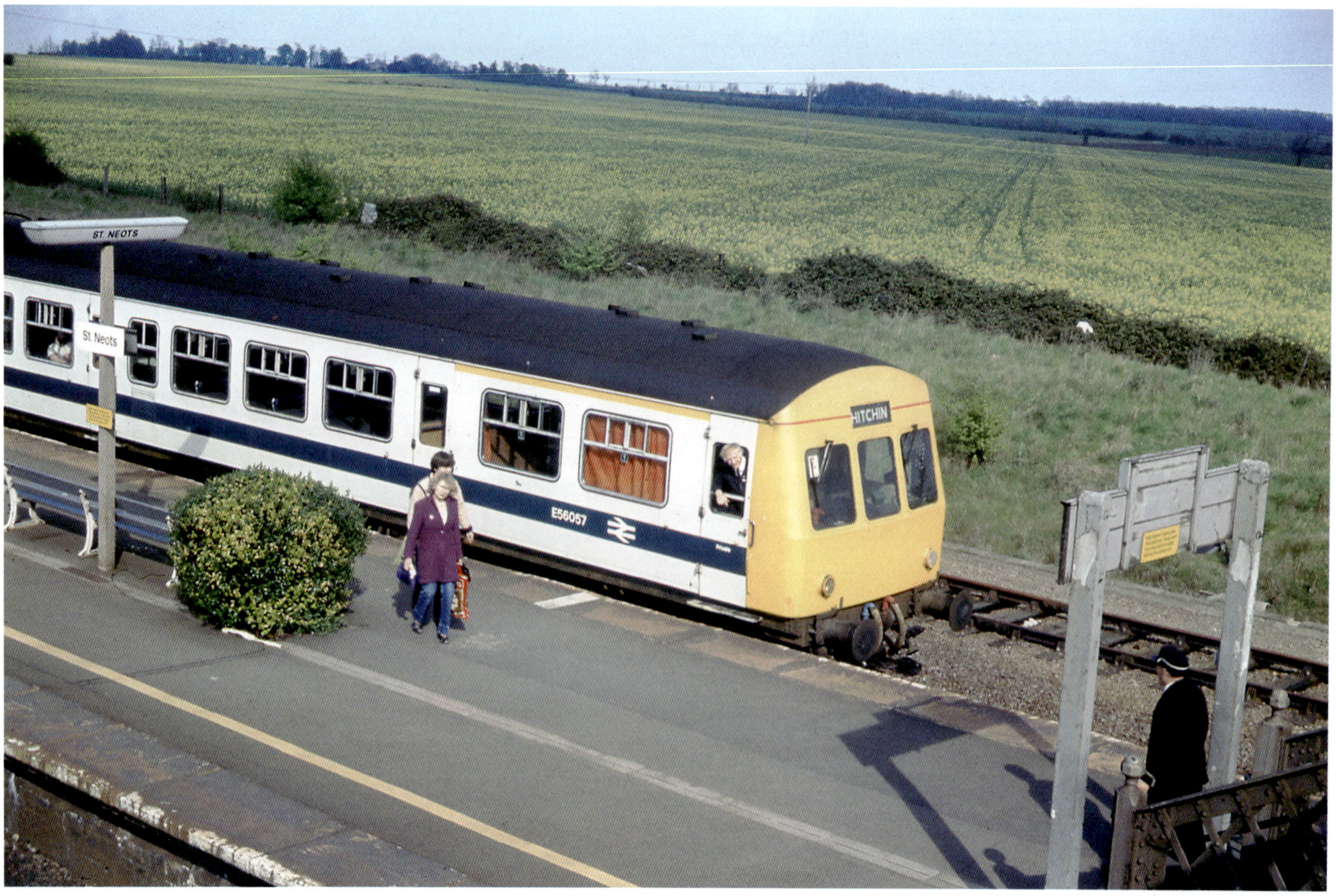

Tickets please at St. Neots, so much more personal and perhaps efficient than machines if one takes into account that staffed stations suffer less graffiti and vandalism. ***Strathwood Library Collection***

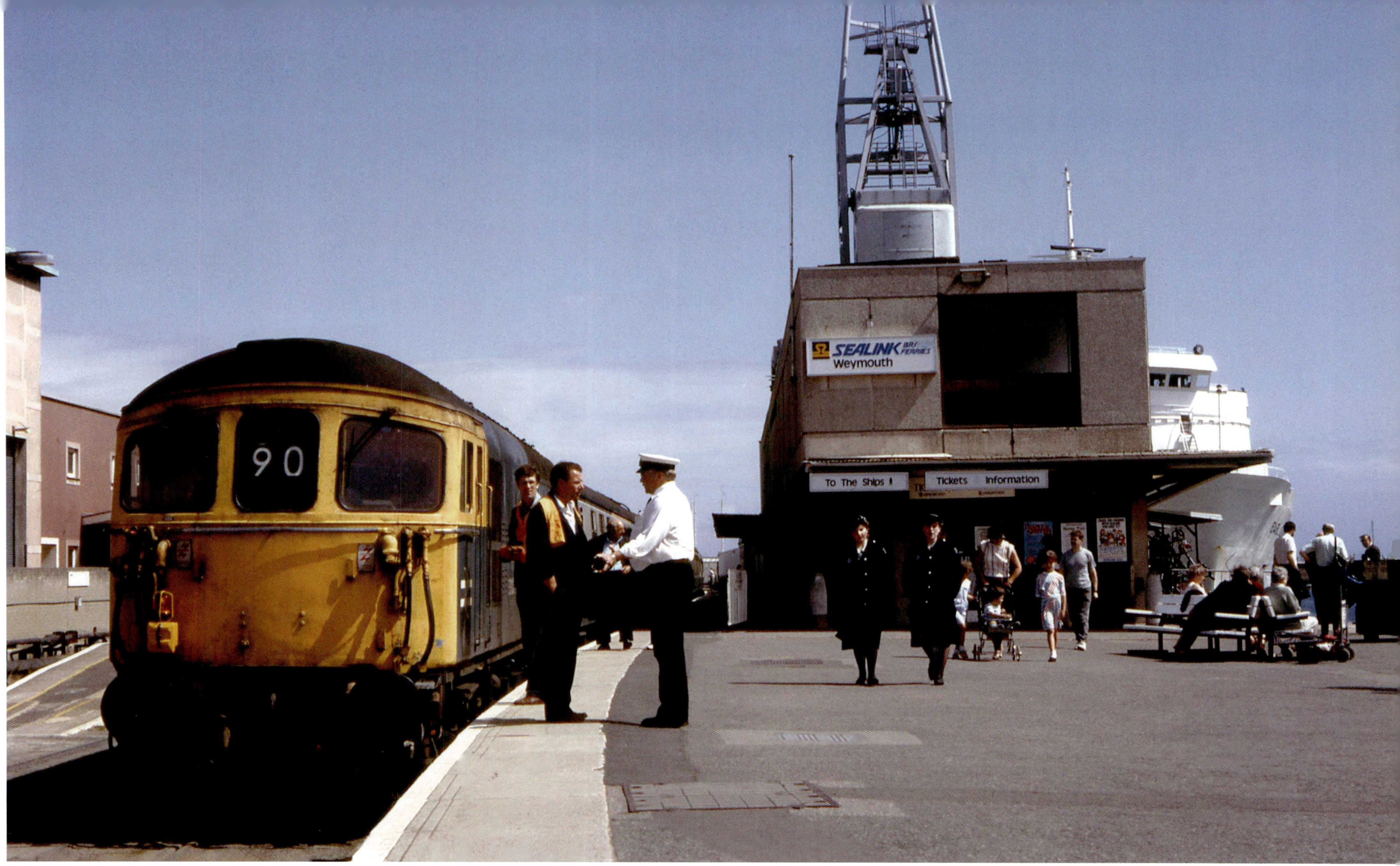

Whereas the presence of police and customs officials at Weymouth Quay would have been more than sufficient to deter miscreants. The staff who were compelled to walk in advance of the boat train today hauled by 33113 along the quayside tramway section discuss the departure arrangements, before fighting their way past the masses of parked cars along this section of line through the town. ***Richard Parkinson***

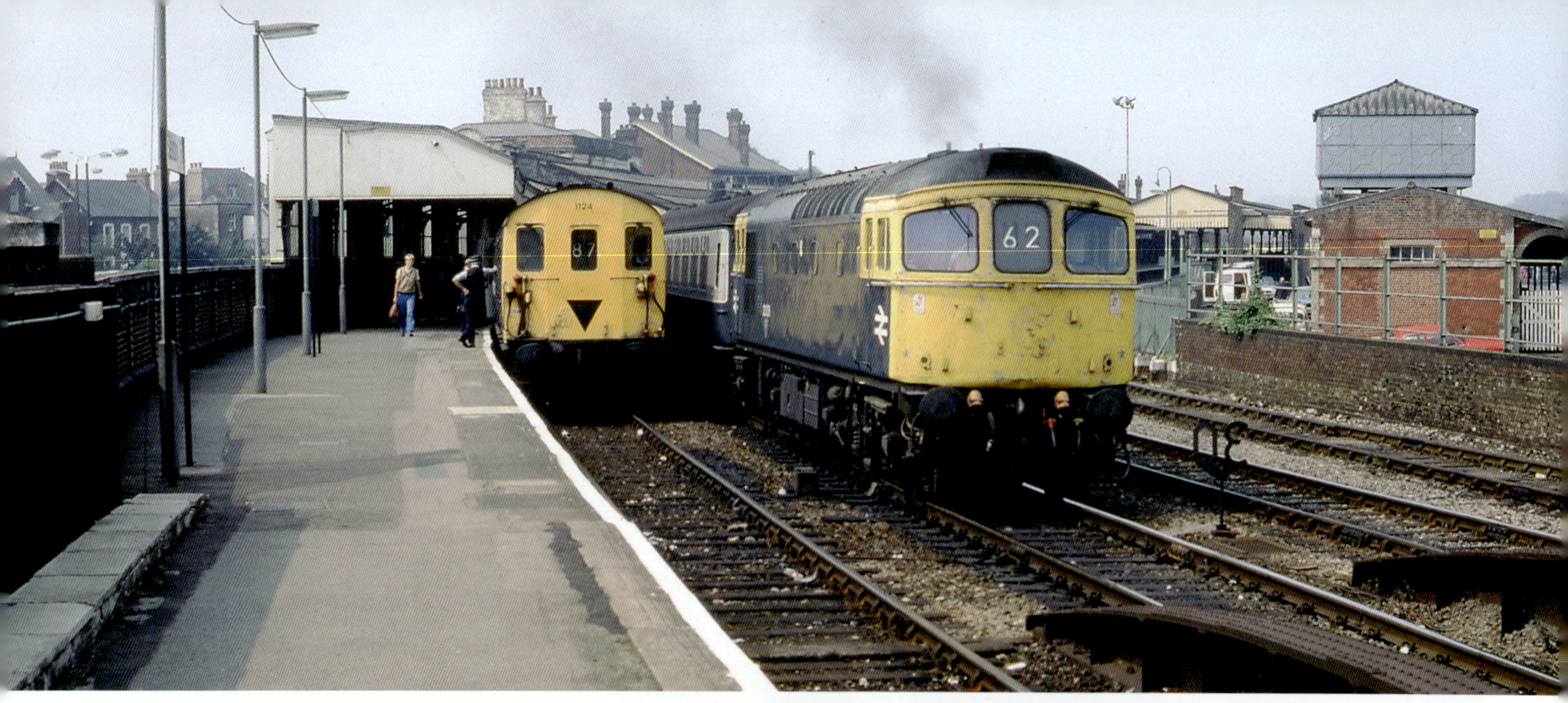
87
62

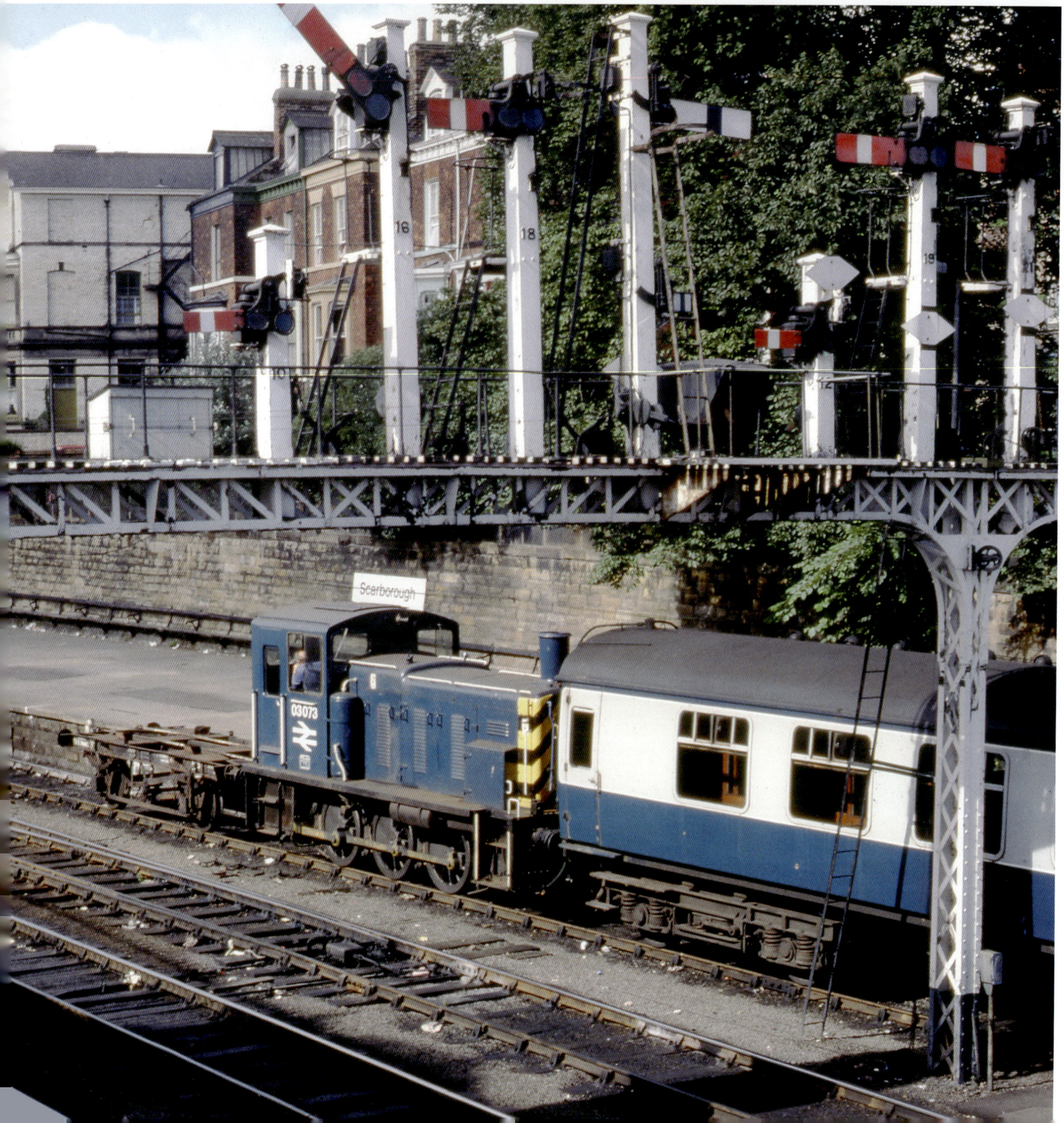
16
18
Scarborough
03073

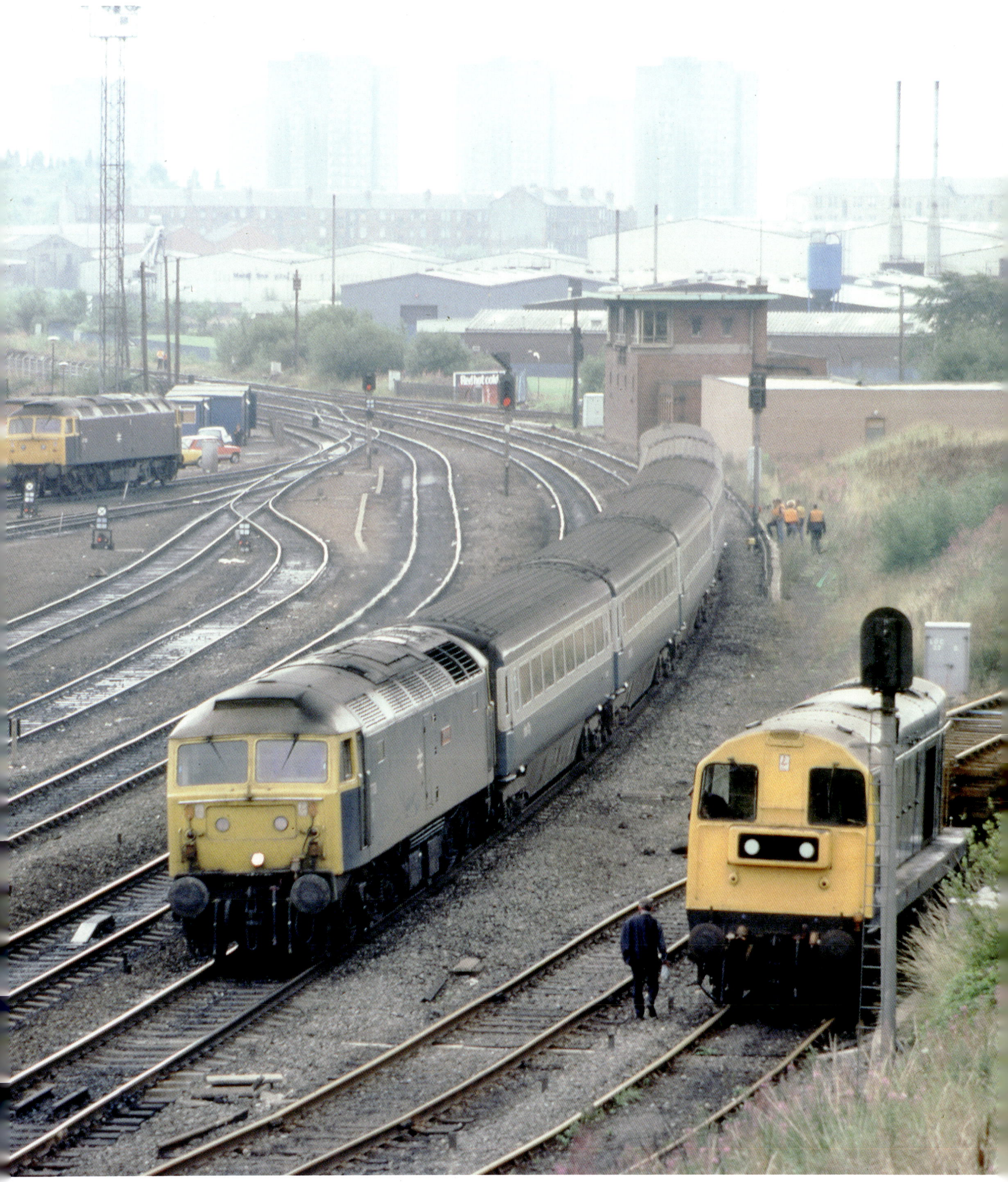

Page left: Blasting off from Salisbury on 8 August 1983 is 33026 whilst a local DEMU service waits to follow next. ***Ken Gambles***

Page left bottom: The work of a station pilot could be a leisurely one at times as 03073 tends to Scarborough's needs on 13 August 1983. ***Ken Gambles***

Lots of trackside activty opposite Eastfield depot on 24 August 1983 as 20149 waits with a permanent way train and 47708 Waverley ventures slowly past. ***Tom Bigley/Strathwood Library Collection***

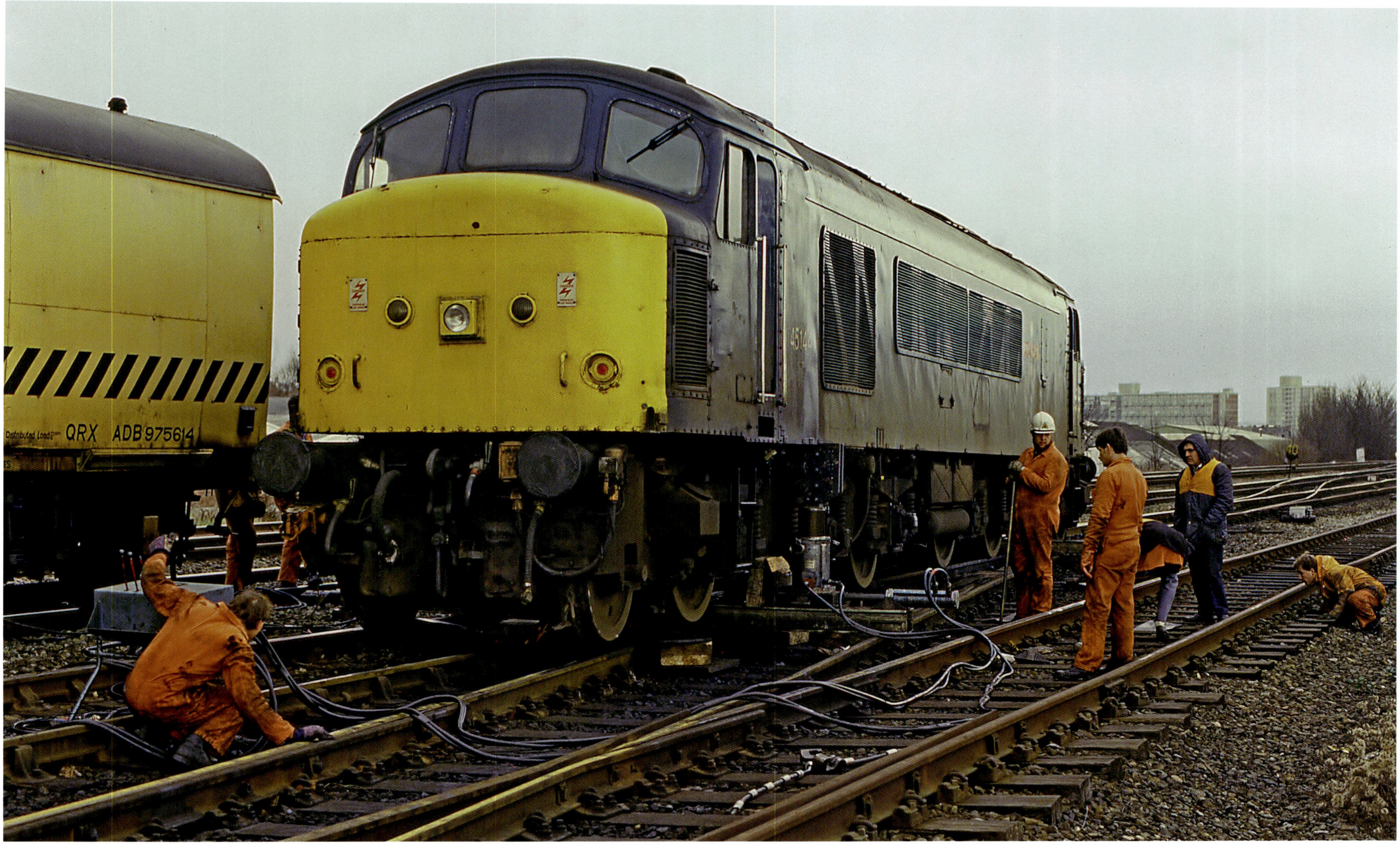

Whilst it looks to be a much more physical workout that may be required at Malago Vale in Bristol to get all 138 tons or so of 45144 back onto the track on 2 January 1988. It was this perhaps minor incident that led to the locomotive being withdrawn as the Peaks were being run down. Just coming to fame this year would be the French-Canadian singer Celine Dion, whilst representing Switzerland in the Eurovision Song Contest, held that year in Dublin, she won with the song "Ne partez pas sans moi". ***Rail Photoprints/John Chalcroft***

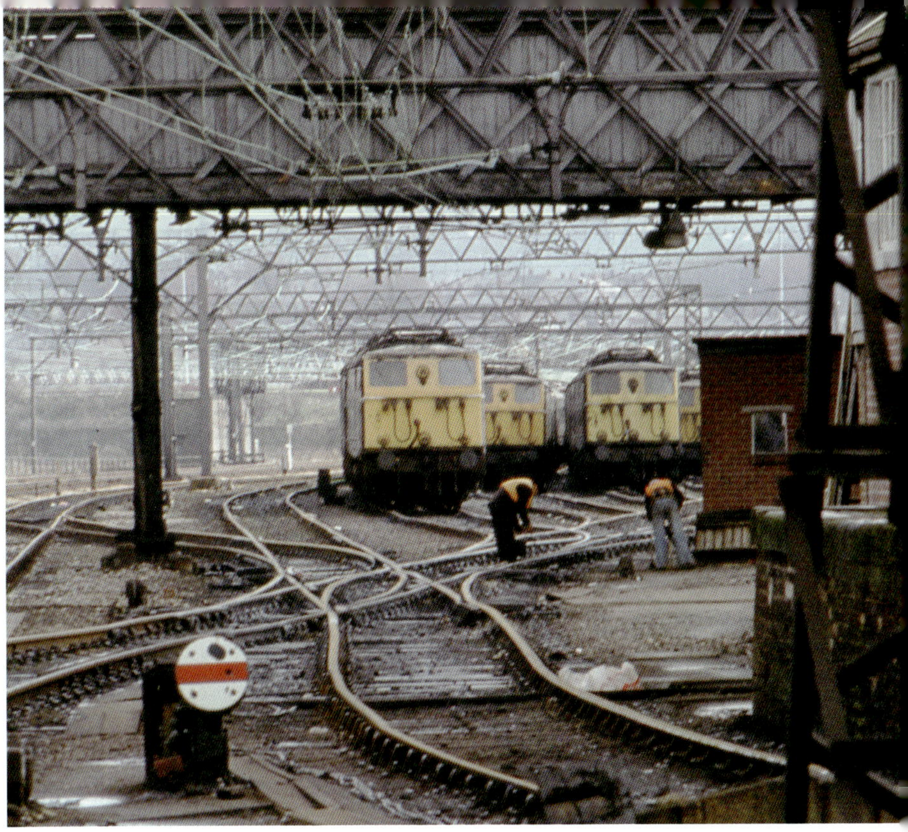

More hard work in the cold to maintain the pointwork at Guide Bridge as a batch of Class 76s hang on before closure of the Woodhead route. ***Bruce Smetham***

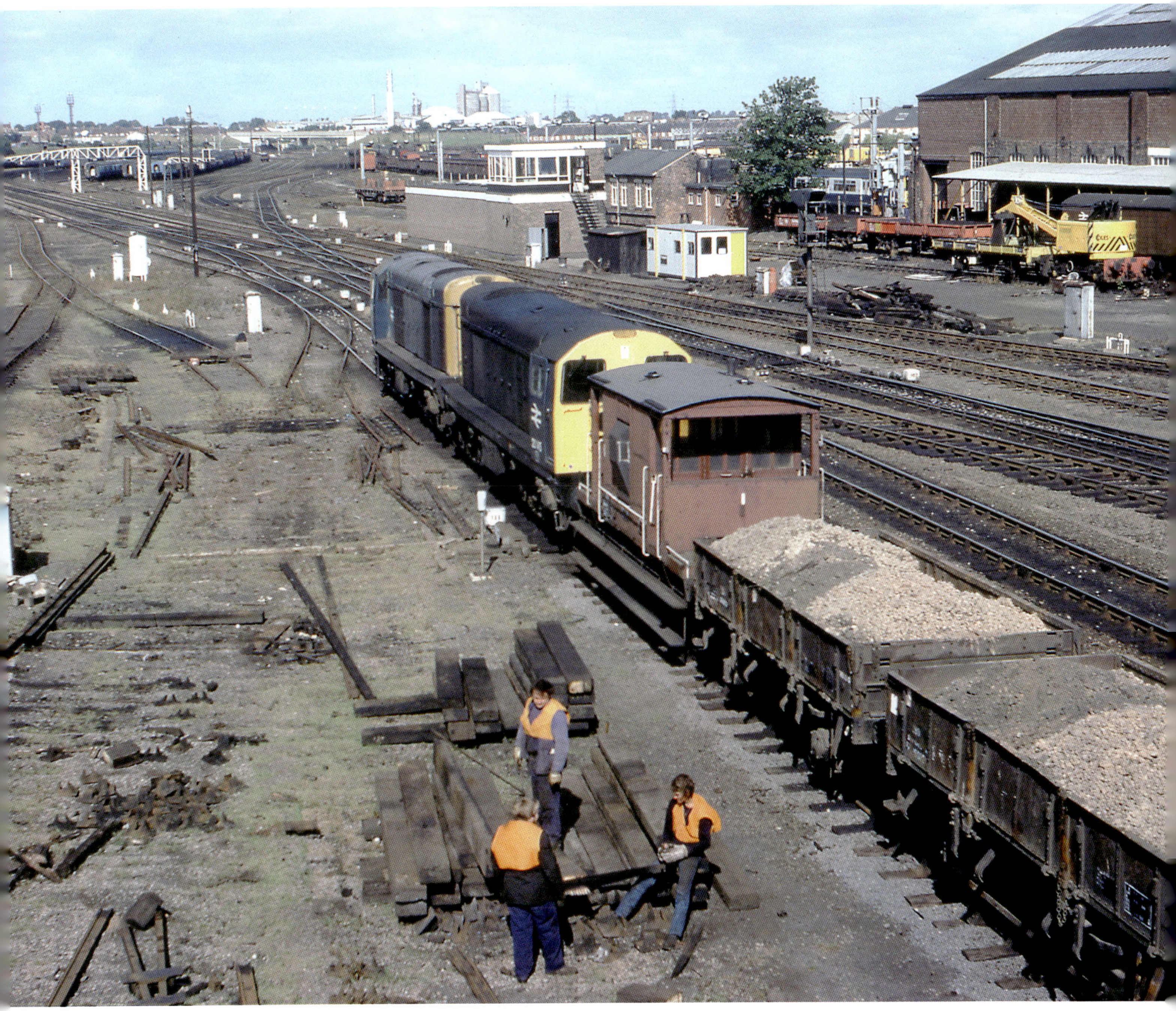

More trackwork being removed this time alongside the York avoiding line on 5 September 1983 as 20154 and 20145 find employment on the spoil clearance. ***Ken Gambles***

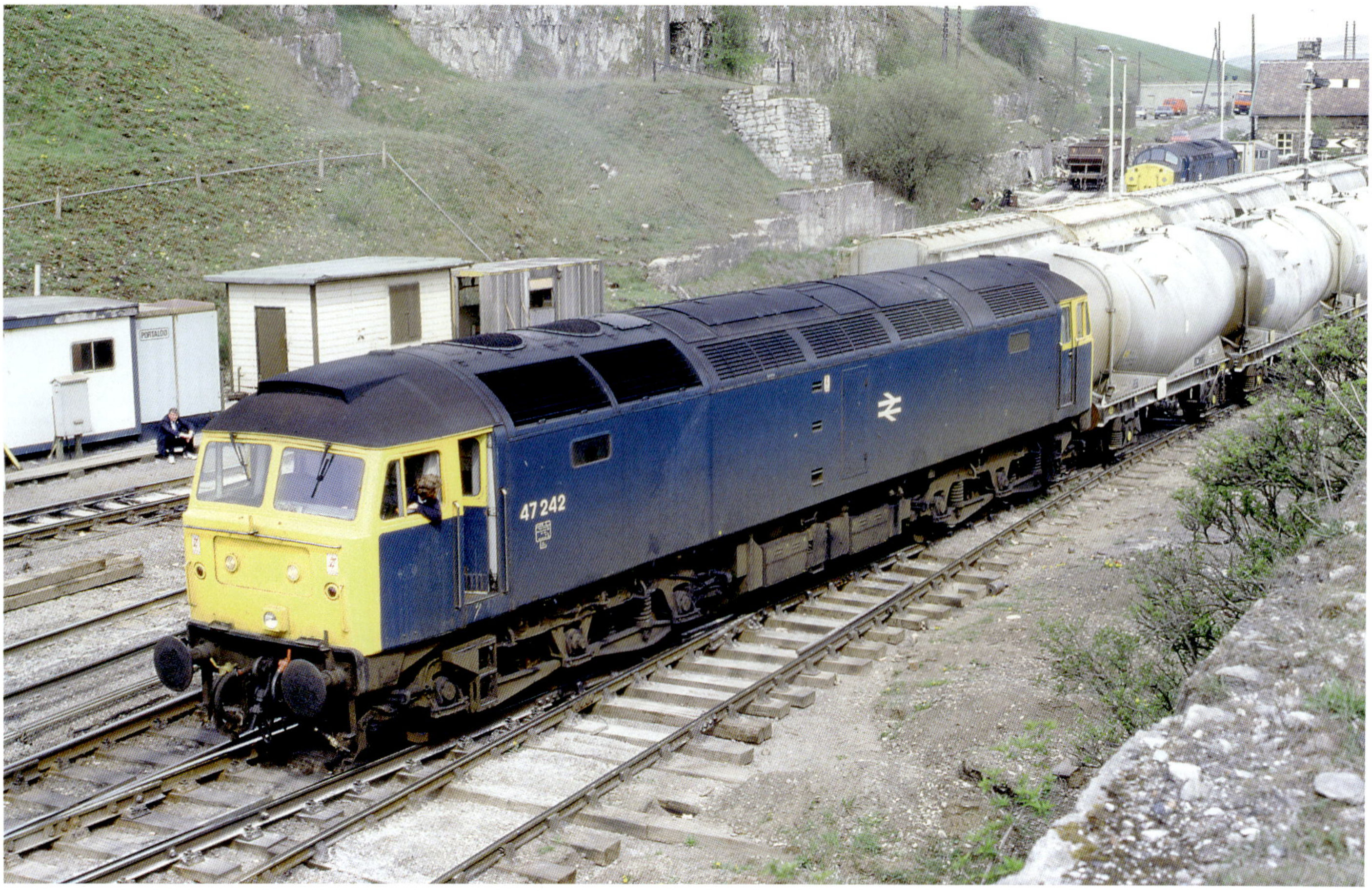

A glance back along his train for the driver of Cardiff based 47242 at Peak Forest on 15 May 1984, as someone relaxes on this warm day in front of the staff portakabins. ***Stuart Broughton***

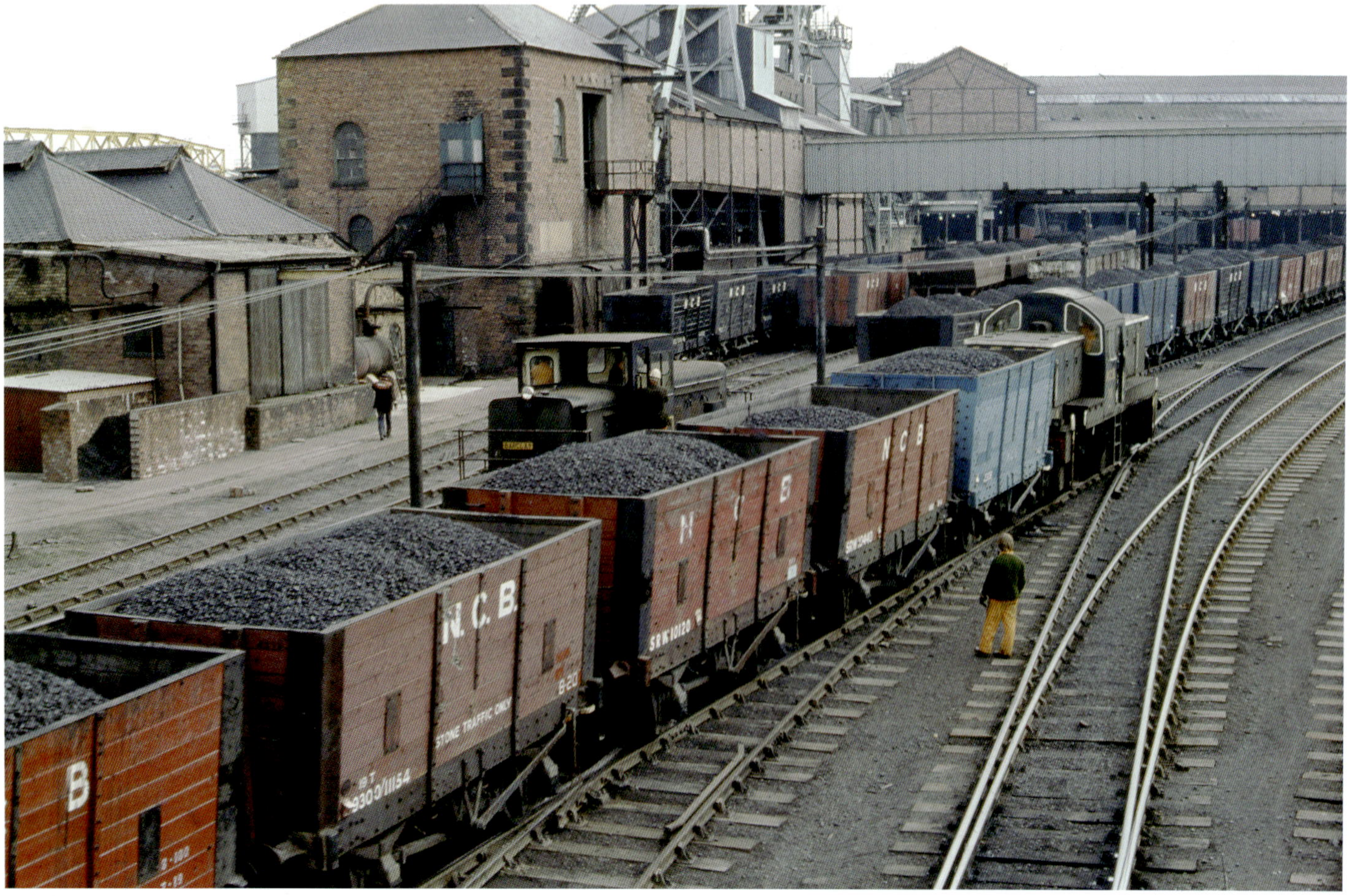

The once busy system at Ashington provides work for number 38 in May 1980, this Class 14 plied its trade as D9513 on Britsih Rail for just over three years before arriving here in late 1968. ***Alan Rintoul***

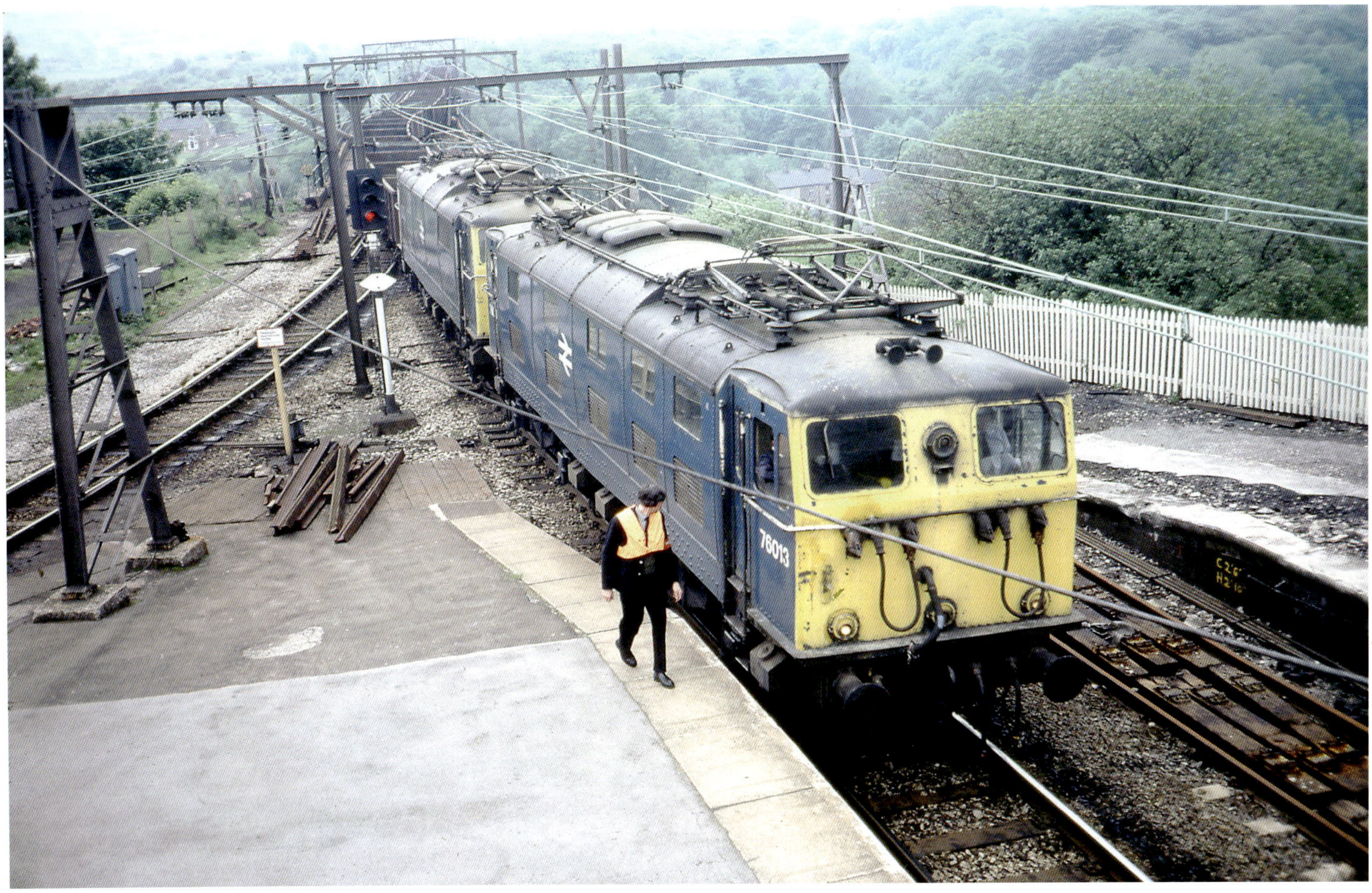

A pilot has just stepped off 76013 and 76026 as they work empties wrong line off Dinting viaduct on 29 May 1981, their pantographs are compressed to clear the footbridge that the photographer is perched upon. ***Ken Gambles***

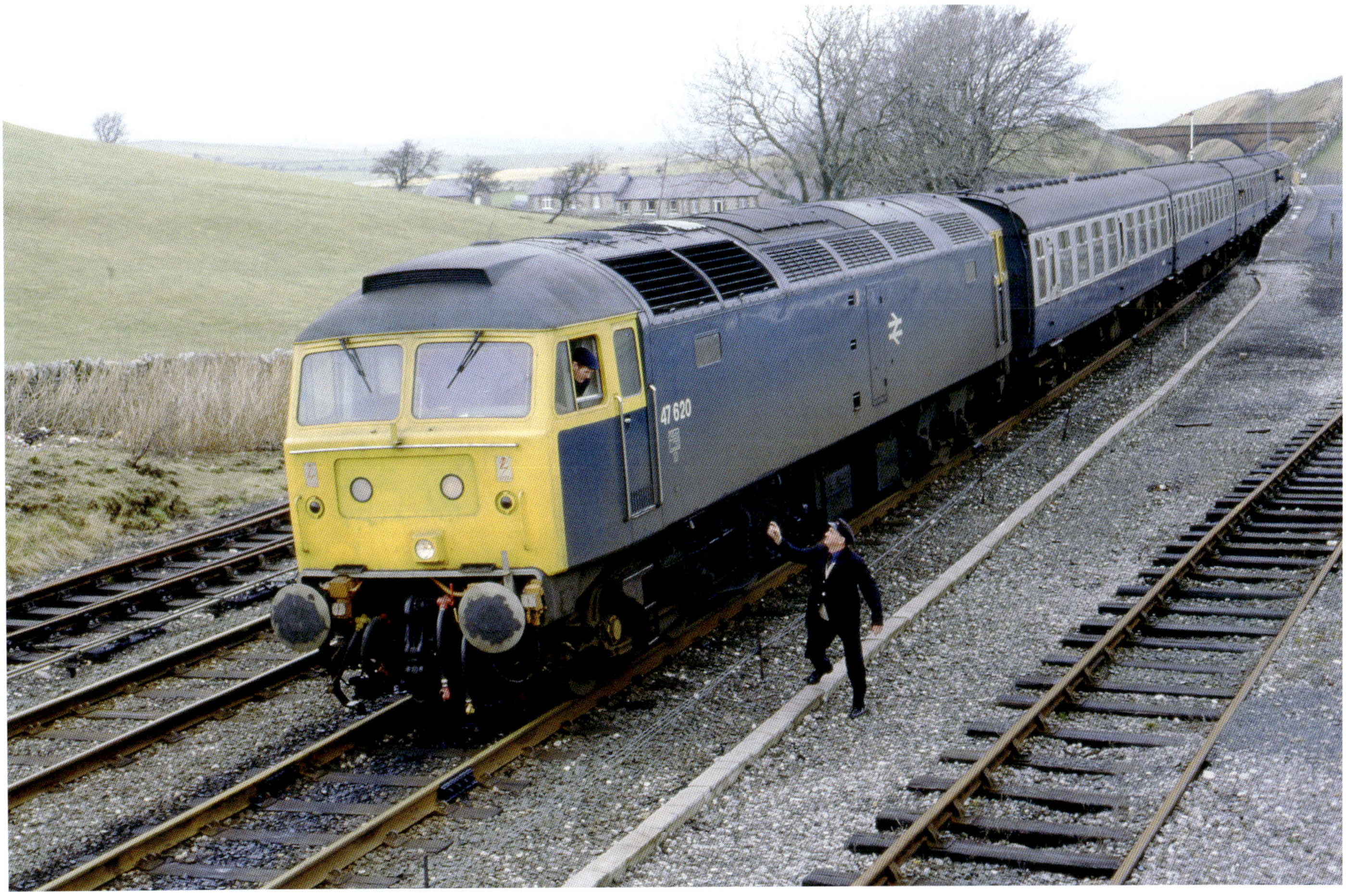

On 30 March 1985 the signalman at Kirkby Stephen passes on some news of sheep on the line to the driver of 47620 as he makes his way along the Settle & Carlisle. ***Late Pete Walton/Sid Steadman***

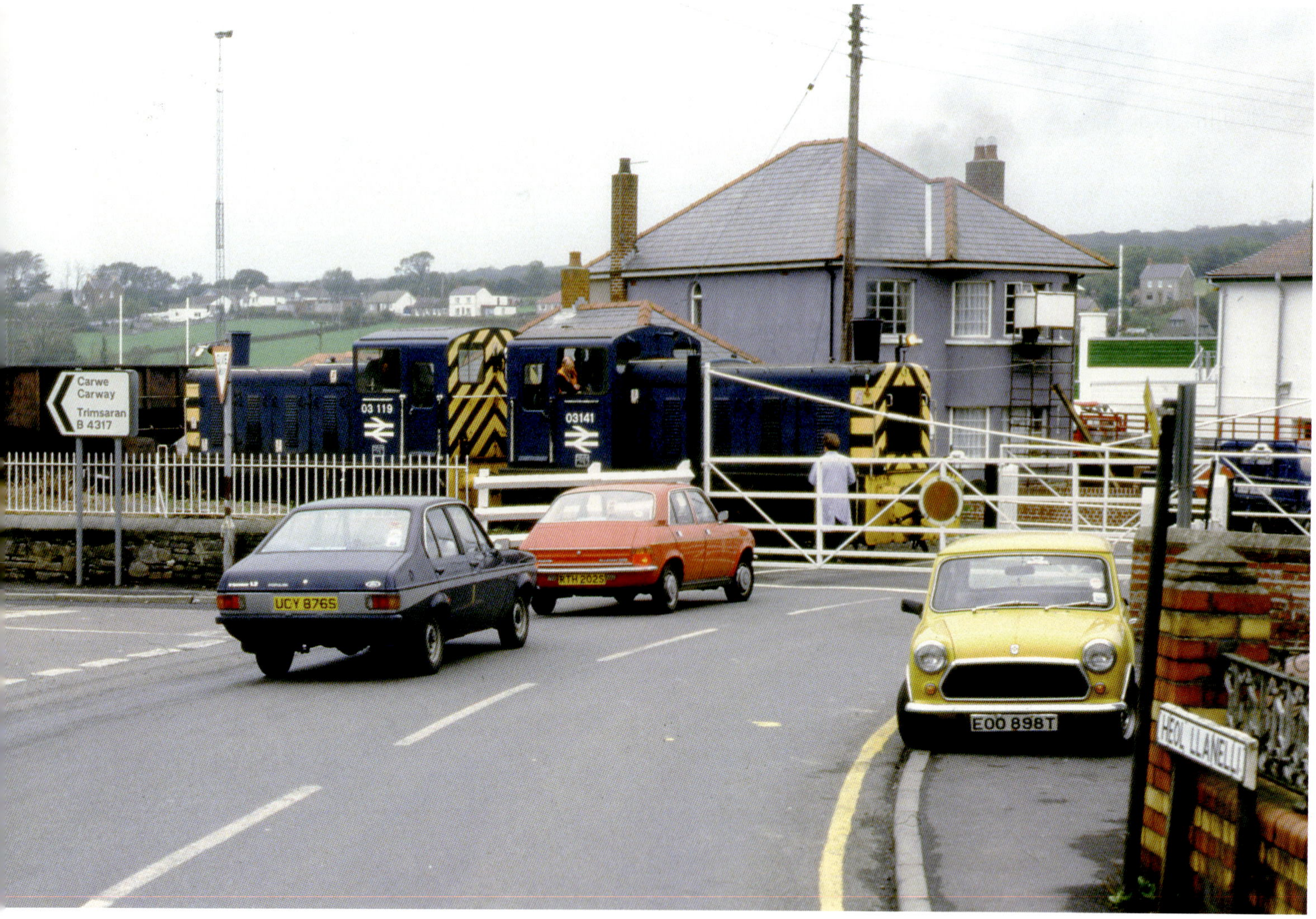

Its both the Class 03s and the period cars which catch the eye as 03141 and 03119 make their way through Pont-Yates with a rake of empties on 4 August 1983. ***Strathwood Library Collection***

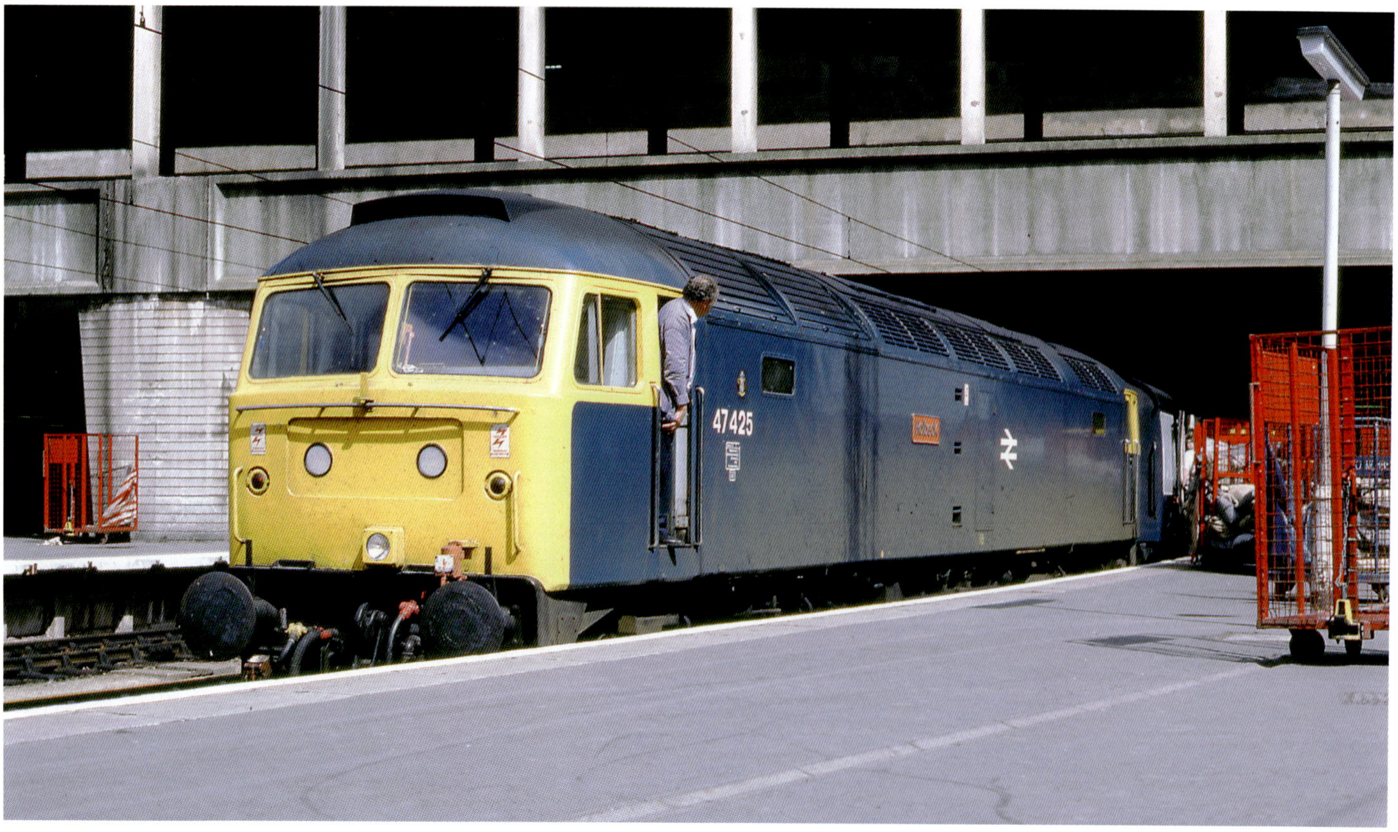

A long careful look back into the gloom of Birmingham's New Street station for the driver of 47425 Holbeck in August 1986 before making his departure. ***David T. Williams***

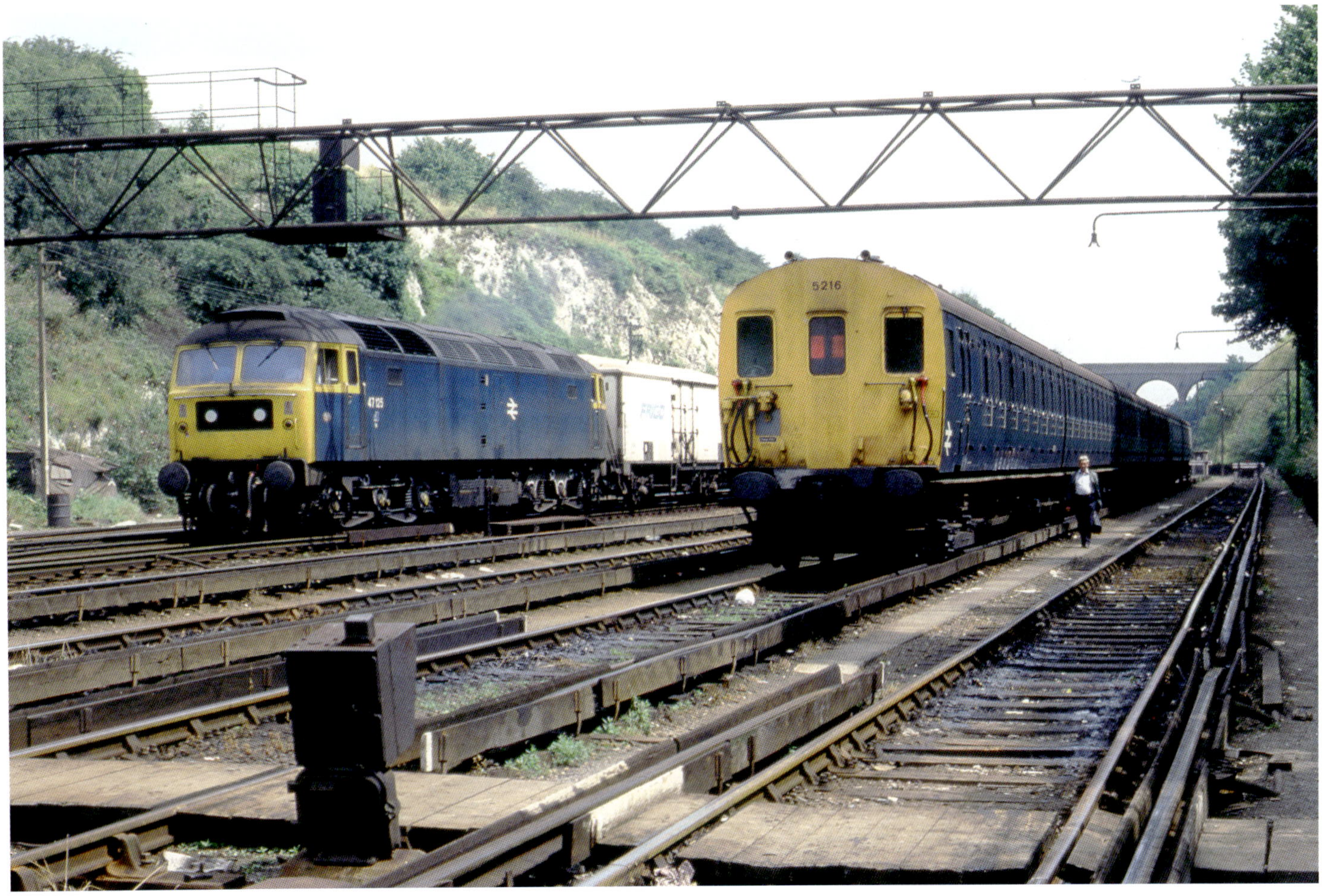

The off duty driver from the 4-EPB makes his way back along the kick protected third rail, whilst 47125 rolls by on 14 July 1981 at Dartford. ***Colin Whitbread***

More third rail vehicles as the celebrity Class 503 with a full cab of people makes its way past Birkenhead North depot with the Hertfordshire Railtours Mersey Punter on 5 April 1986. ***Rail Photoprints/the late Colin Whitfield***

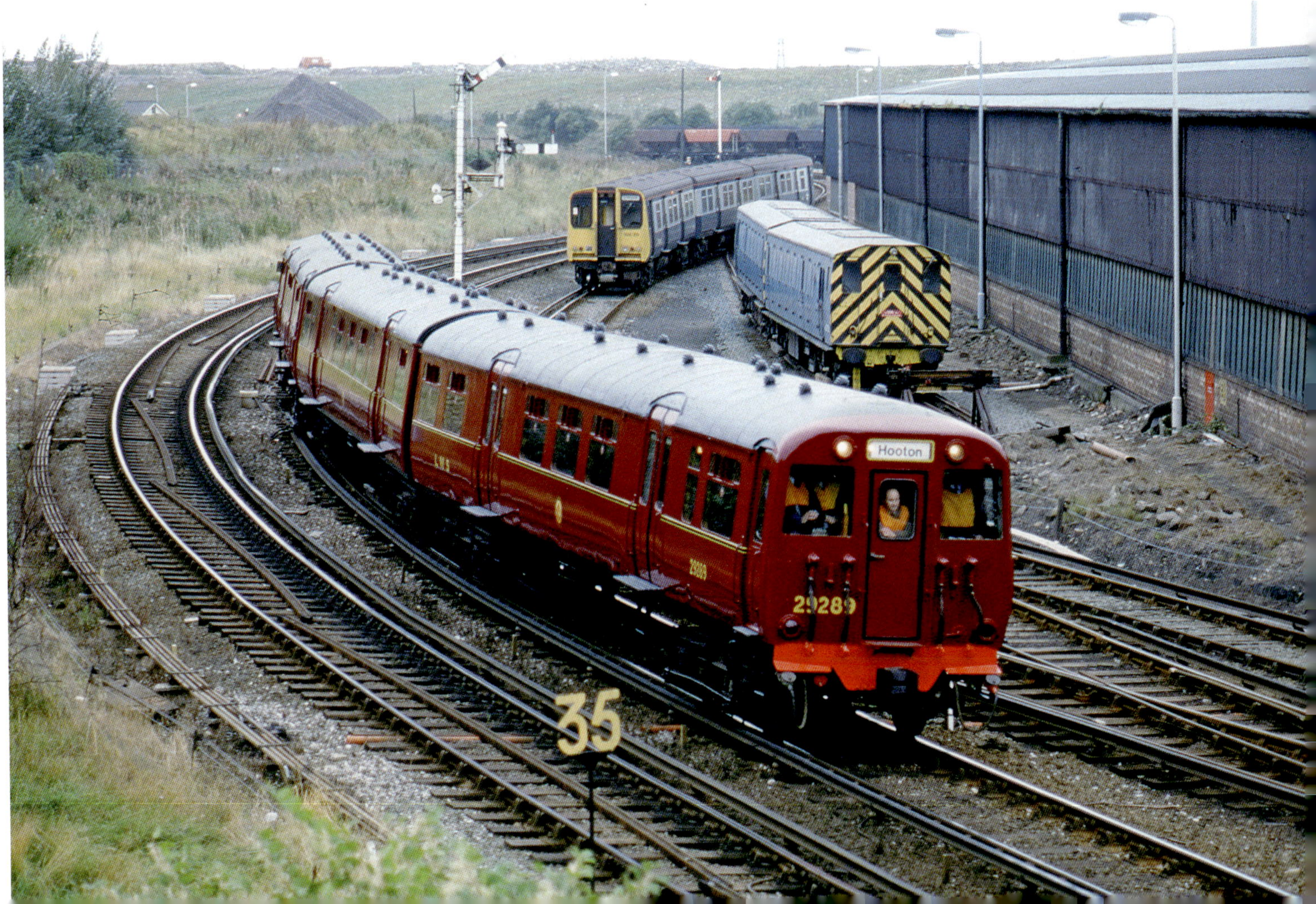

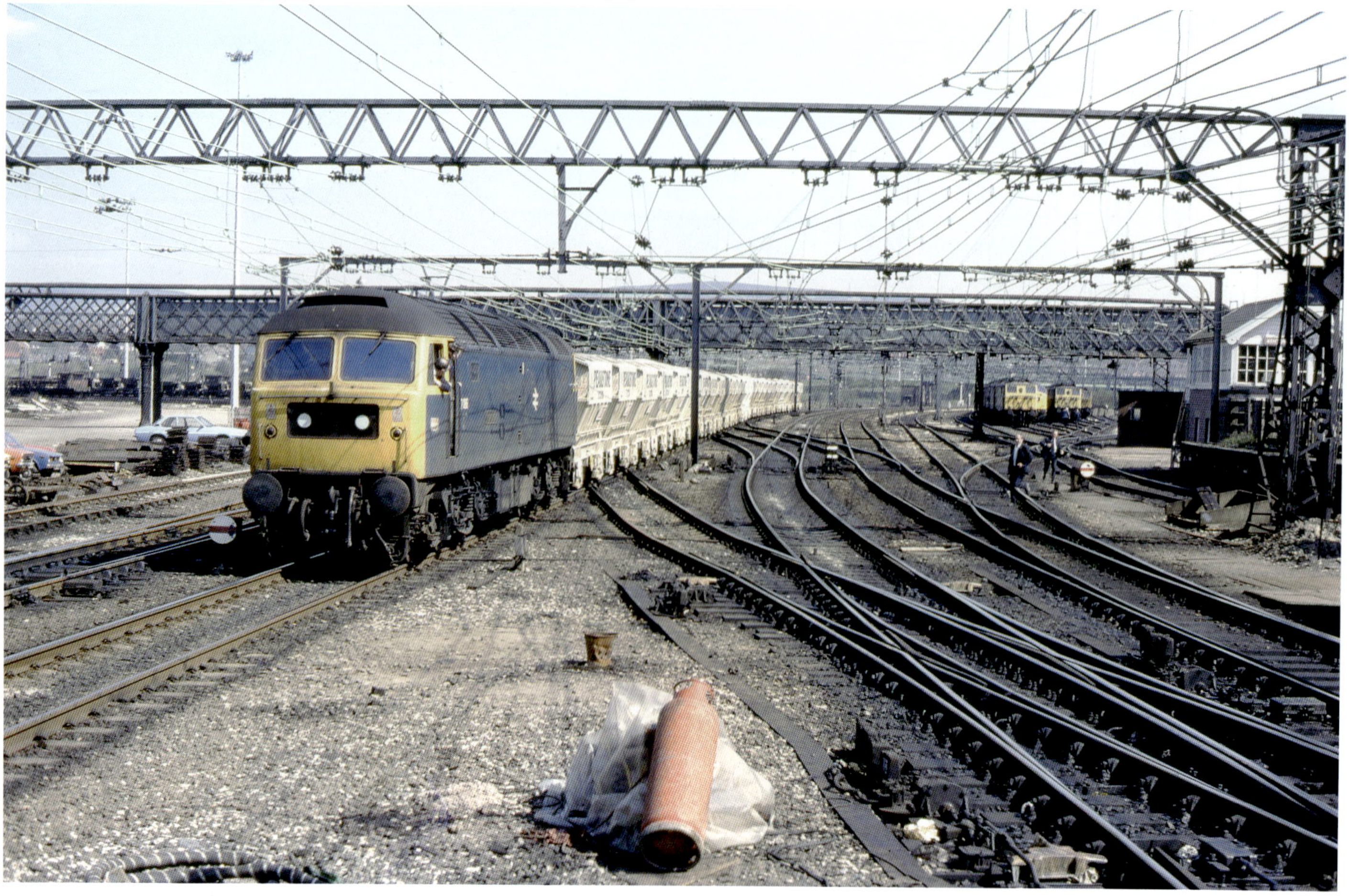

An exchange of words from the driver of 47086 Colossus with some colleagues as he passes Guide Bridge during April 1982, perhaps they were talking about the Falklands War which had just begun when Argentina invaded the Falkland Islands. ***Alan Rintoul***

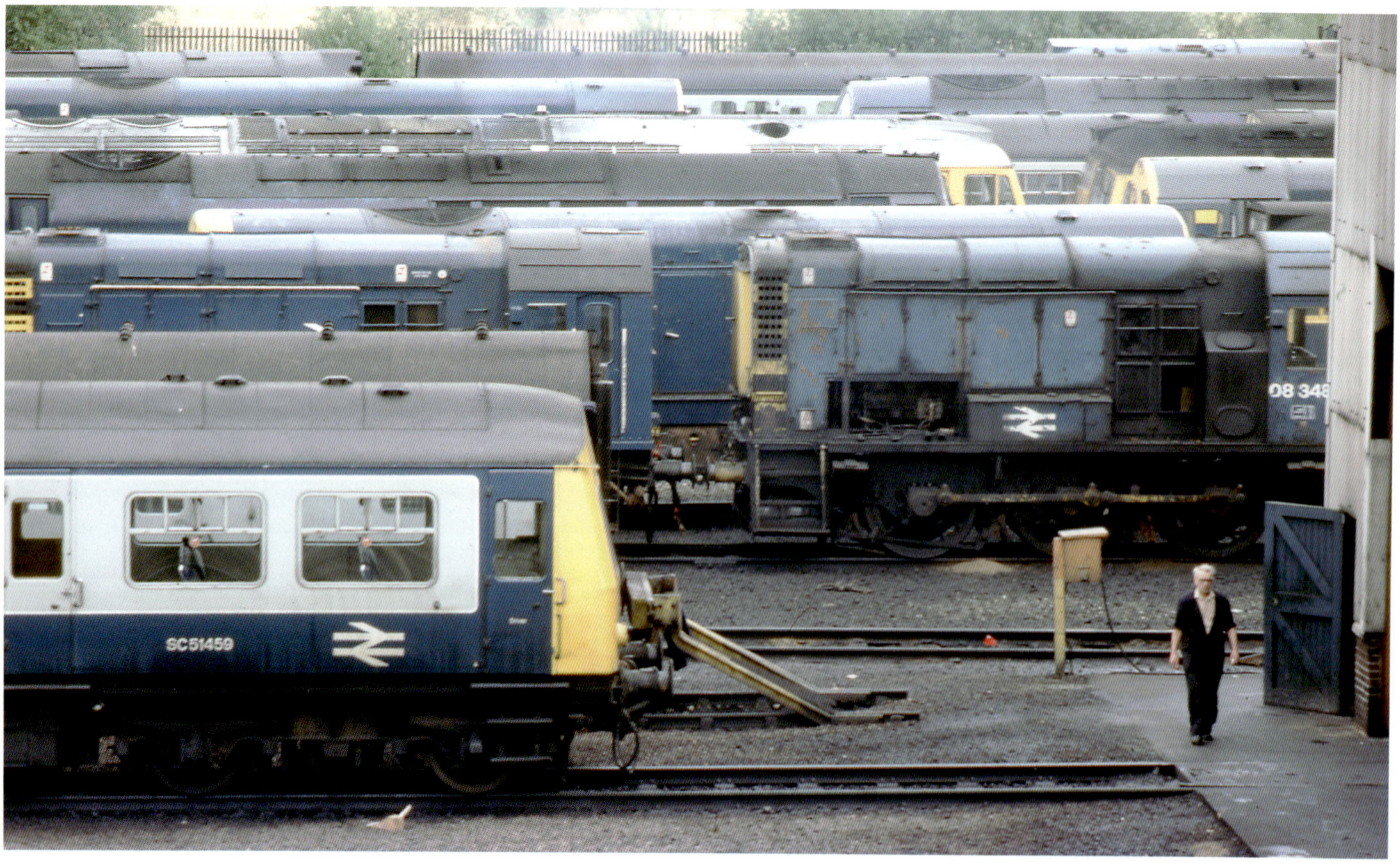

Its a full shed yard at Eastfield on 24 August 1983 as this fitter gets a gasp of fresh air during his day. On television at the time the series of Black Adder had begun on BBC One. Whilst ITV had broadcast Woodentop as part of its Storyboard series. this would later be turned into a series and re-titled The Bill as would Killer, which would also become a series as Taggart. ***Tom Bigley/Strathwood Library Collection***

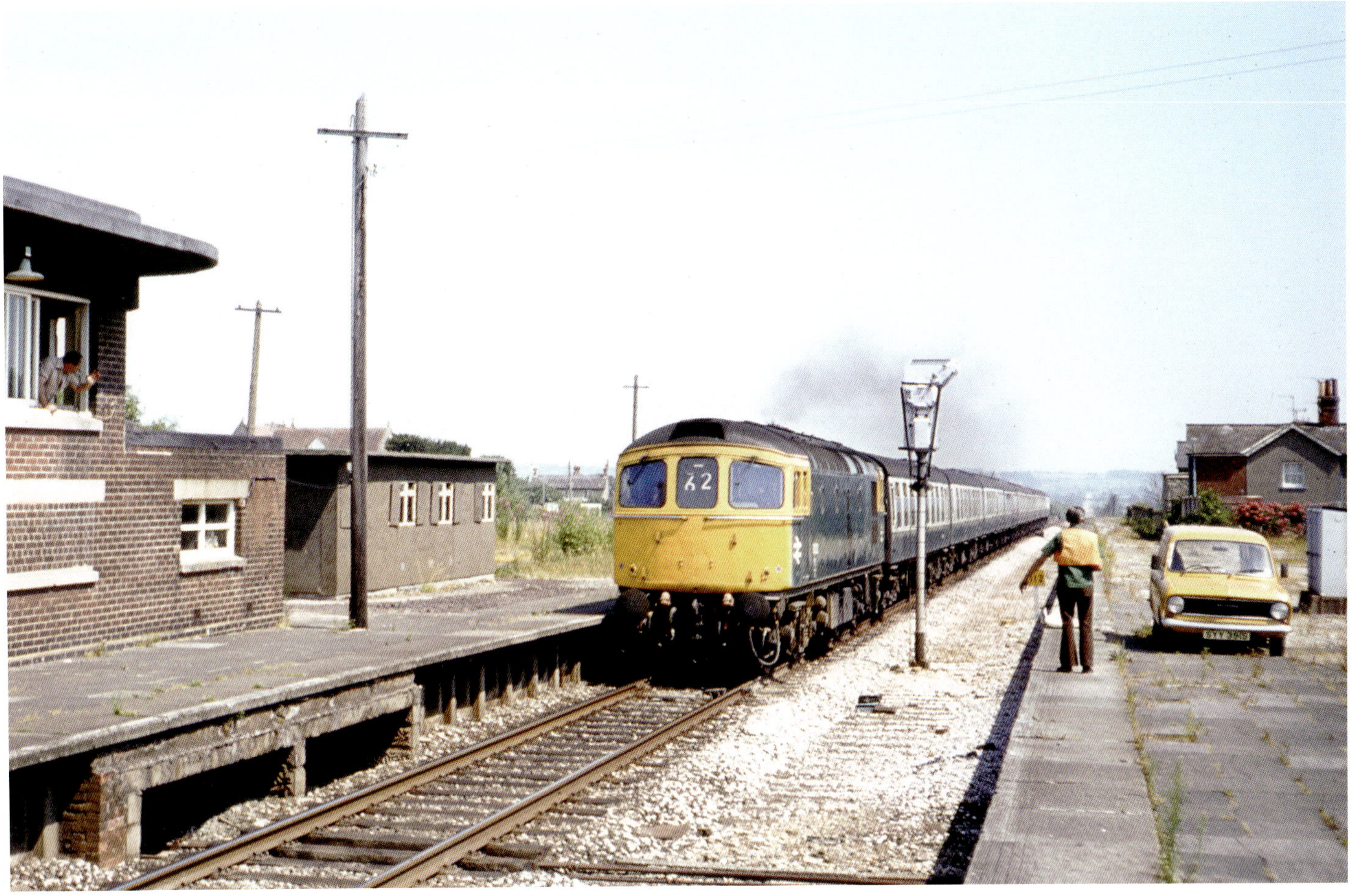

The signalman leans out from his classic Southern Railway built signal box to watch a colleague on the platform make a hand signal to the driver of 33021 as he approaches Templecombe at the start of the decade. ***Ken Gambles***

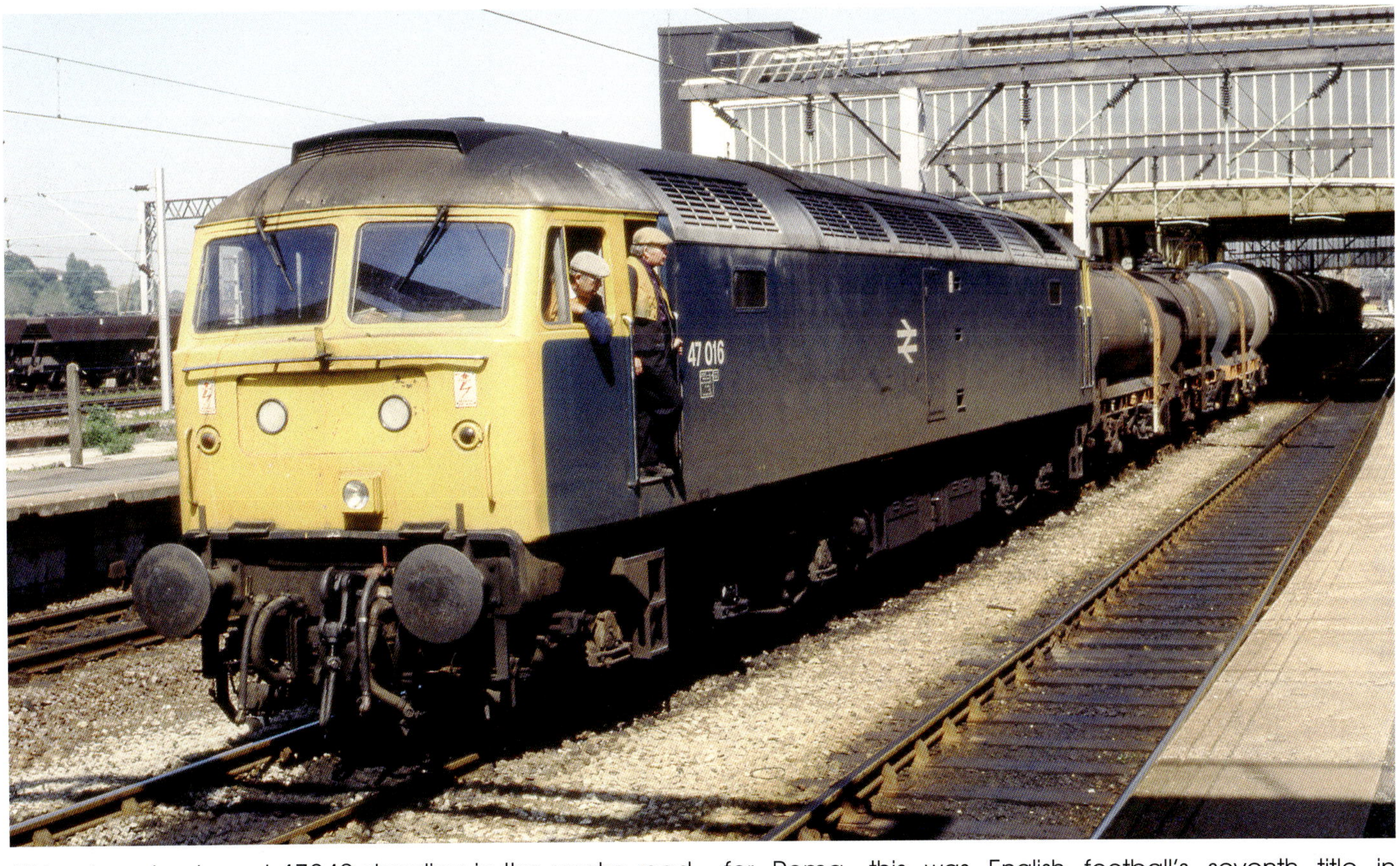

All is relaxed onboard 47242 standing in the centre road at Stoke-on-Trent on 8 June 1984. The European Cup was won for a fourth time by Liverpool in a penalty shootout in the final against Roma. The game had finished 1–1. Phil Neal had scored for Liverpool and Roberto Pruzzo for Roma. this was English football's seventh title in eight seasons. But is best remembered for the Liverpool goalkeeper Bruce Grobbelaar for making key saves and distracting his opponents during the penalty shootout with his leg-wobbling antics. ***Stuart Broughton***

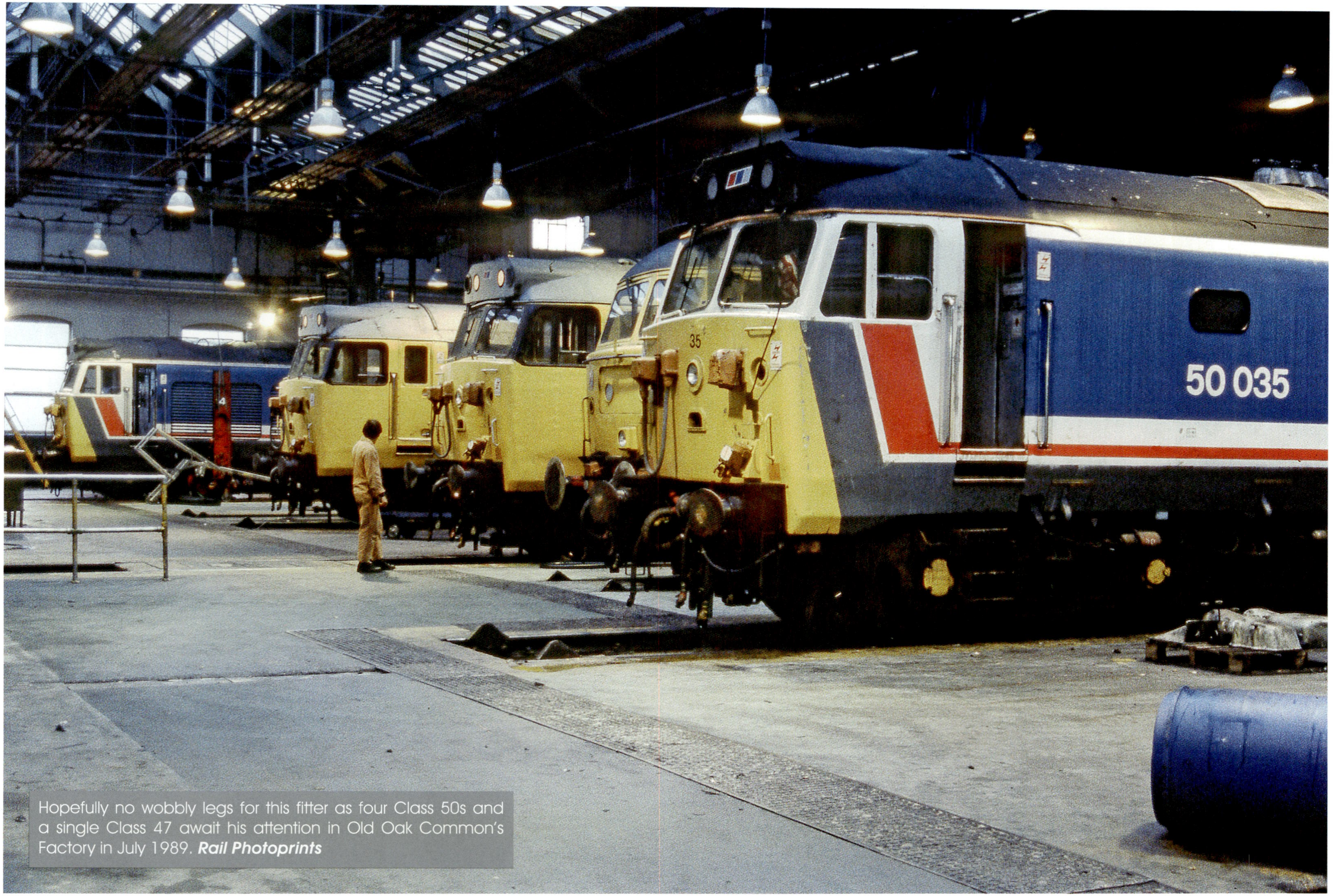

Hopefully no wobbly legs for this fitter as four Class 50s and a single Class 47 await his attention in Old Oak Common's Factory in July 1989. ***Rail Photoprints***

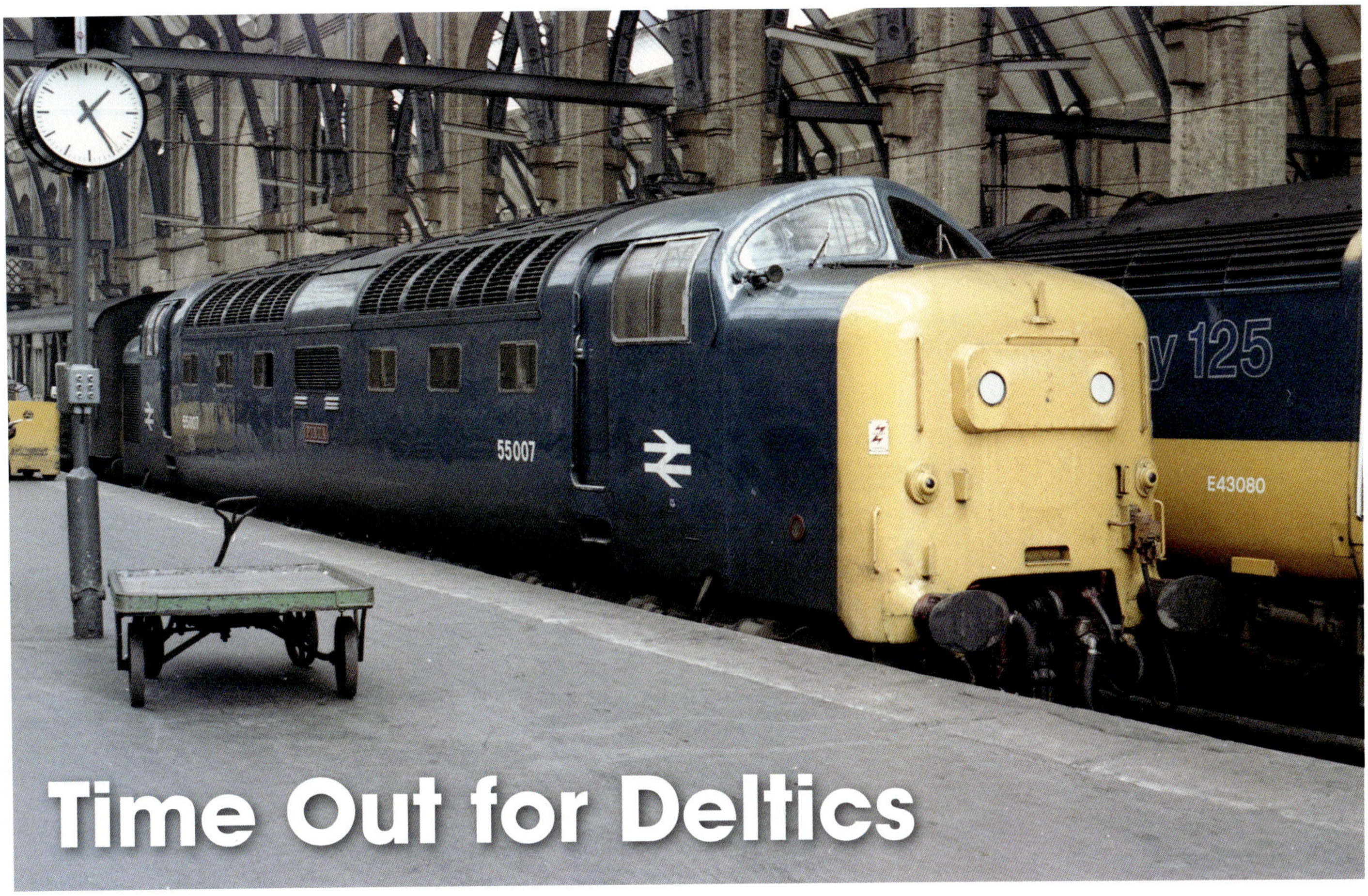

Time Out for Deltics

Having been shut down by its driver to keep the exhaust fumes down on the station concourse, 55007 Pinza awaits release from the bufferstops at Kings Cross in 1980. The Deltics had been very much an important part of the East Coast Main Line scene for almost twenty years at this point, however their reign was coming to an end as the eighties dawned. ***Strathwood Library Collection***

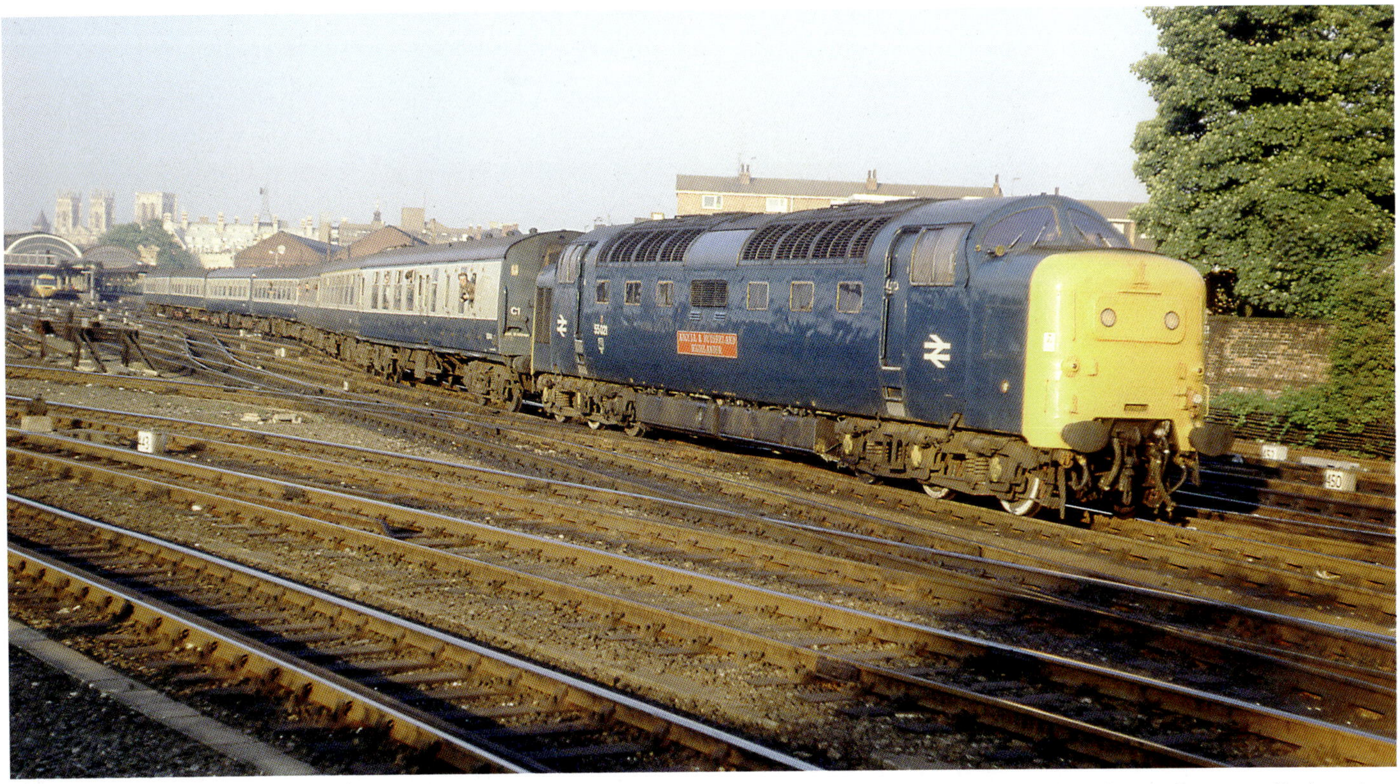

Although the southern end of this Anglo-Scottish route was already electrified the masts and gantries had yet to arrive at the historic city of York by September 1981. Views such as this one from under Holgate Bridge of 55021 Argyll & Sutherland Highlander were yet to be blemished by the wiring and all the extra security fencing that would arrive with it to keep tresspassers at a safe distance. ***Strathwood Library Collection***

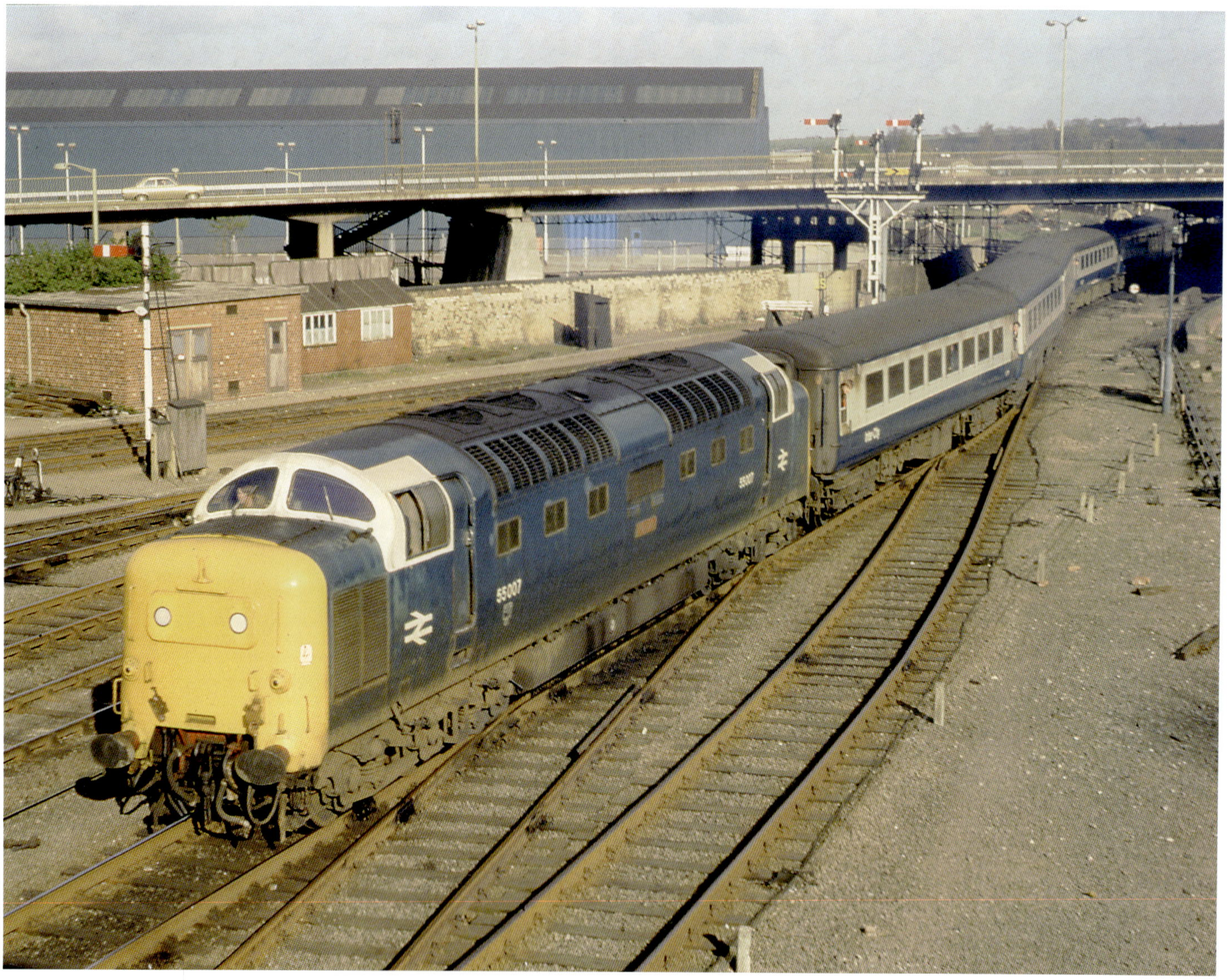

Finsbury Park's painters have customised 55007 Pinza in this next view of the Class 55 as it finds a diversion through Lincoln on Easter Sunday in 1981. ***Strathwood Library Collection***

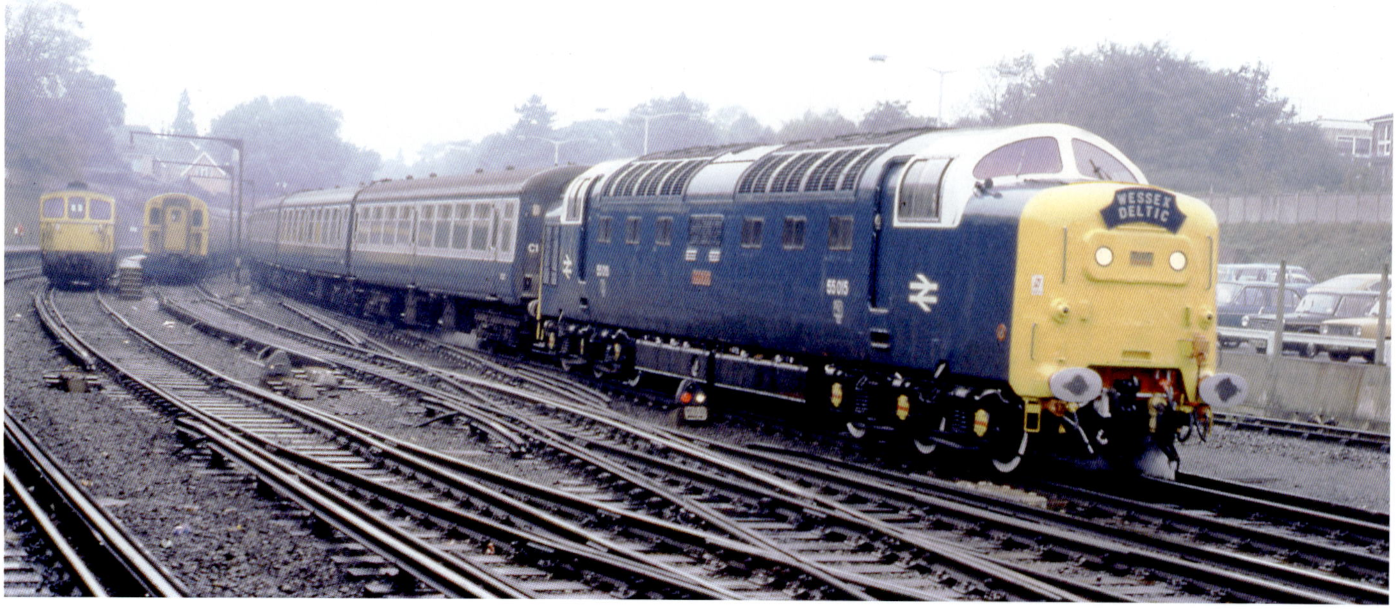

A much smarter turn out for 55015 Tulyar as it gets a workout on the Southern Region at Bournemouth on 17 October 1981, when it worked from Finsbury Park to the south coast and back. ***Strathwood Library Collection***

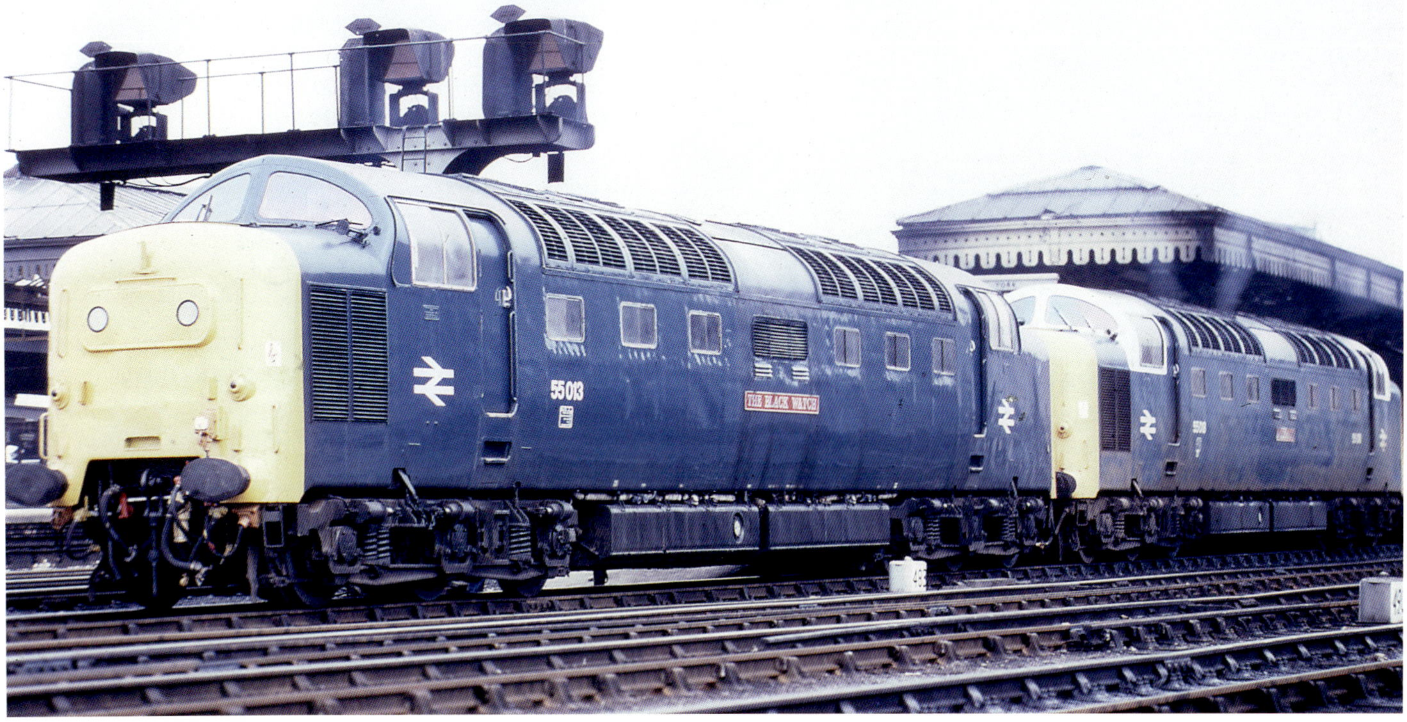

Both 55013 The Black Watch and 55018 Ballymoss prepare the 14.10 York to Kings Cross at York in November 1981 as almost all Deltic movements attracted enthusiasts wherever they went at this late stage of their careers. ***Strathwood Library Collection***

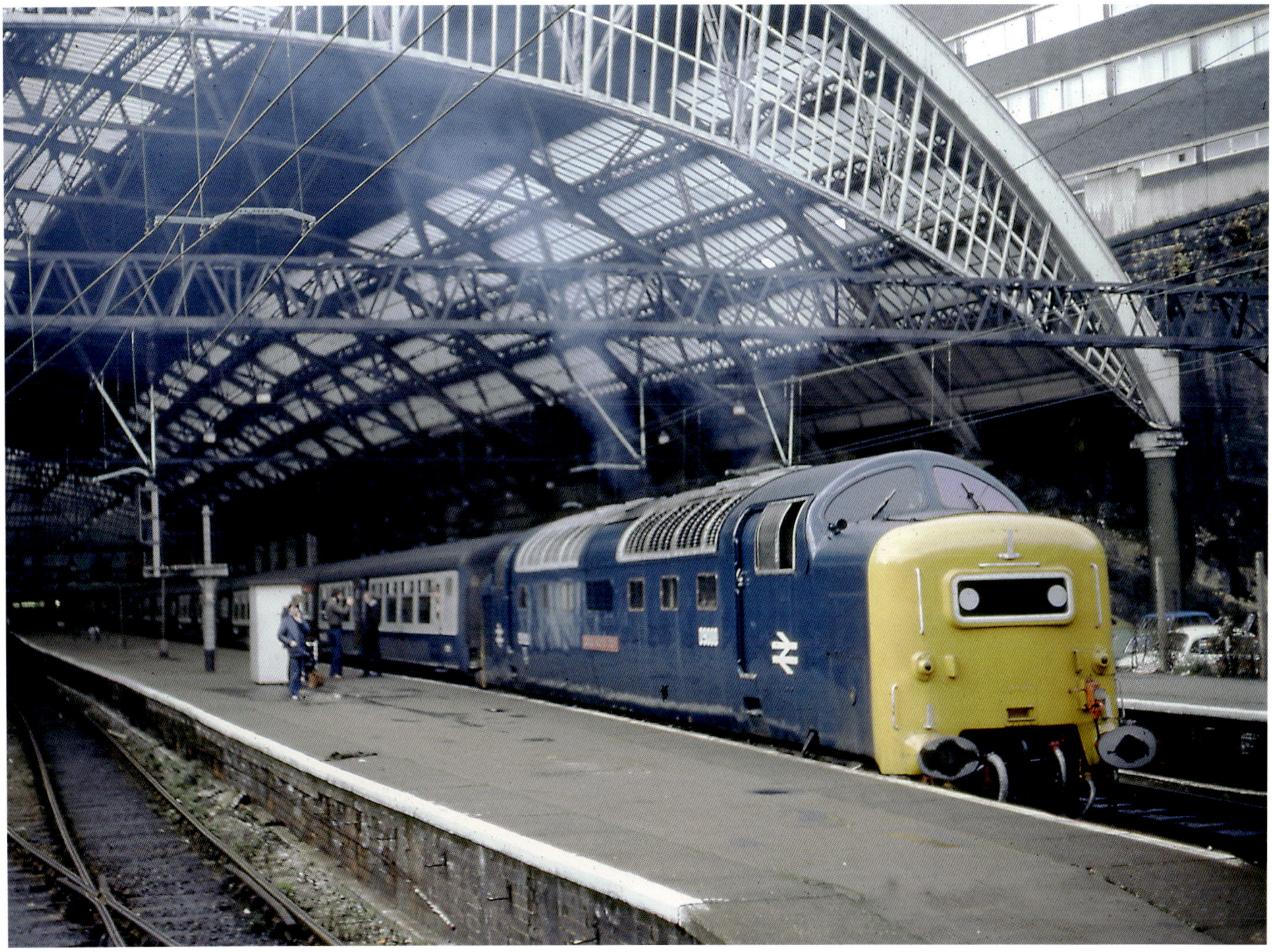

Their use on Trans-Pennine services out of Liverpool Lime Street such as here with 55022 Royal Scots Grey on 4 November 1981 proved immensely popular with enthusiasts. ***Strathwood Library Collection***

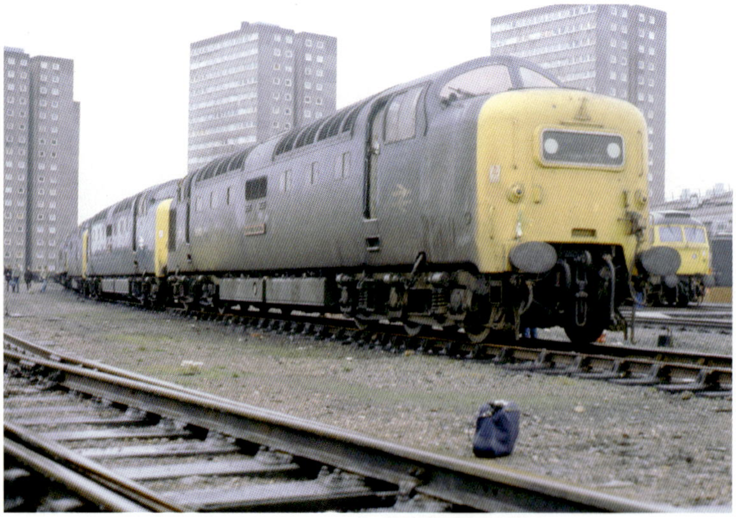

By the end of 1981 it was all over and Deltics were laid up wherever they were stopped for a brief spell before they were concentrated on Doncaster for scrapping, this was the scene at Finsbury Park with 55008 The Green Howards leading the parade. ***Strathwood Library Collection***

A full train with not a spare window to be found as 55022 Royal Scots Grey charges out of Waverley on 2 January 1982, for the last time, or so we thought in the gloom of Edinburgh that day. ***Alan Rintoul***

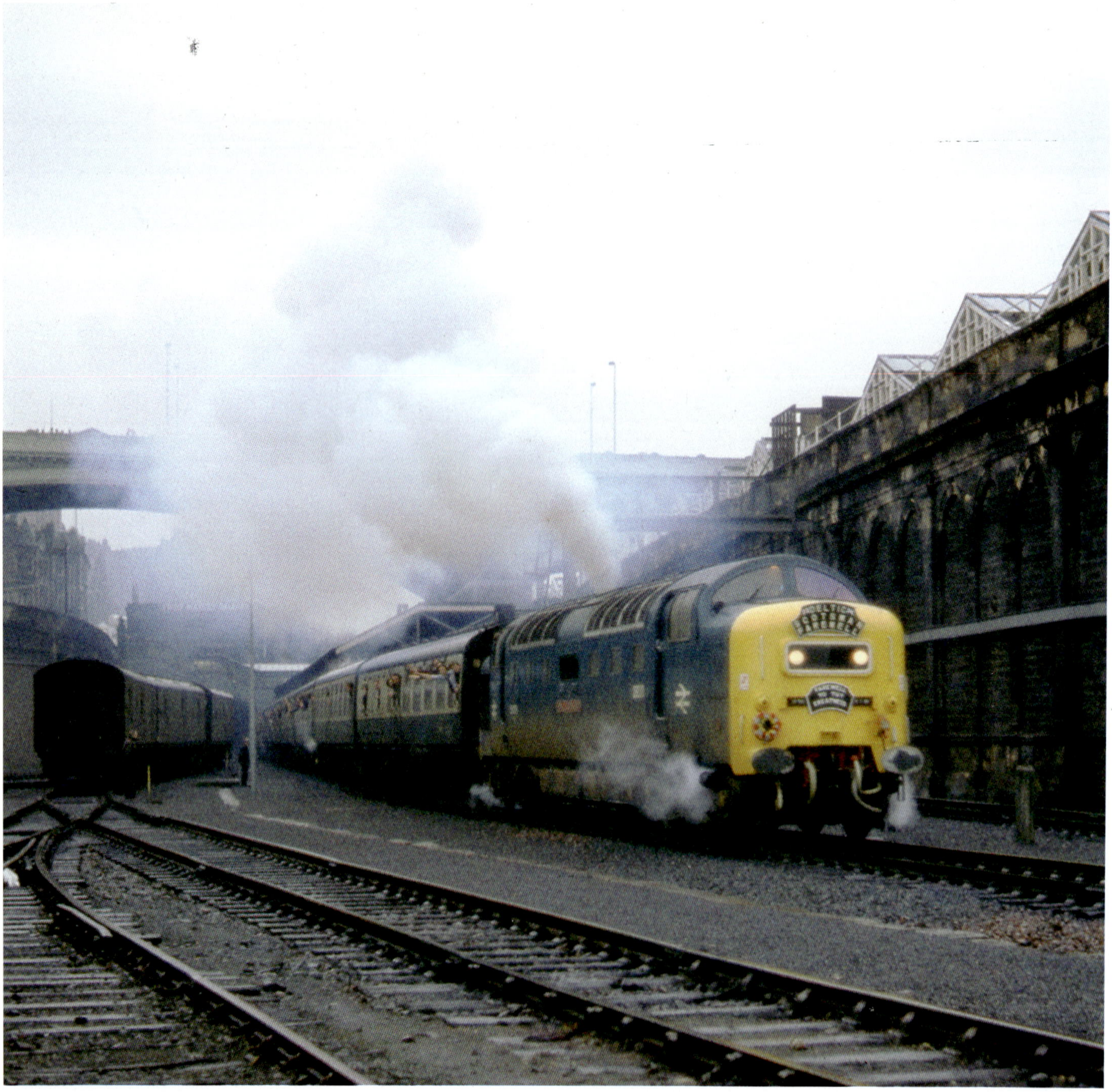

Opposite: Finally one last time in the parade ring for 55007 Pinza as the locomotive was displayed at Doncaster for the specially arranged Deltic Open Day at the works on 27 February 1982. As August began that year Pinza would be no more, the cutters having completed their task. ***Stuart Broughton***

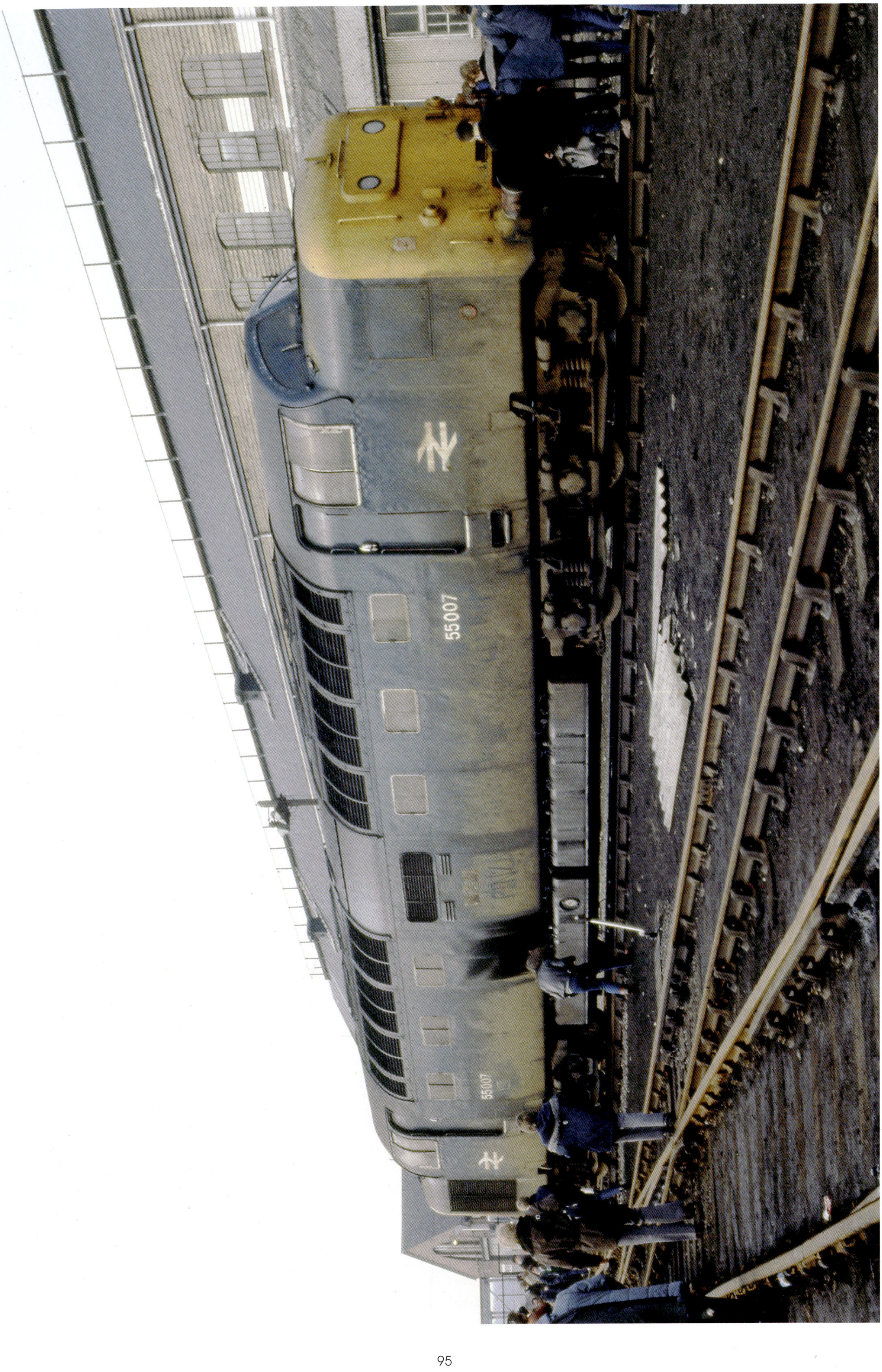
55007
55007

Help To Preserve Our Railway Heritage

Strathwood not only publish books on our railway heritage but have also set up the Railway Photographic Preservation Association as a Charitable Trust to house an archive of images comprising over 200,000 photographic negatives and slides.

The archive was established to not only preserve the collections of over one hundred photographers both living and deceased, but to also make their work available to a younger audience for the future. To achieve this aim, we have begun an energetic programme to publish a considerable number of books. Allied to this we are making as many as possible of the photographs and slides we hold, available as copies to interested enthusiasts, individuals, societies and other publishers.

Many photographers have chosen Strathwood to care for their collections and to publish the best examples of their work for posterity.

If you have negatives or colour slides of transport subjects then we would like to hear from you. We purchase, accept on loan, or welcome donations of material to the archive. Photographers always receive recognition for their work when it is used by publishers (A N Other/Strathwood Library). To answer why so many images are just credited as Strathwood Library Collection in this volume, the reason is we do not know who the original photographer was. This is usually because their collection gets split up via auctions or collectors upon their death with no record of the late photographer for us to credit. Please do not let this happen to your collection. Make contact with us today to discuss what can be done to ensure you work is fully credited and recognised for both today and the future.

Please call us today if you would like to see your work in print, perhaps in a similar fashion to this publication. We also undertake publications to benefit charities and societies on behalf of our contributors. In addition we can store, and catalogue collections on behalf of clubs and societies by way of loan, thereby releasing such groups to concentrate on other aspects of their activities.

Strathwood Ltd,
Glenavon House,
Kinchurdy Road,
Boat of Garten,
Inverness-shire,
PH24 3BP.

Telephone 01479 831139

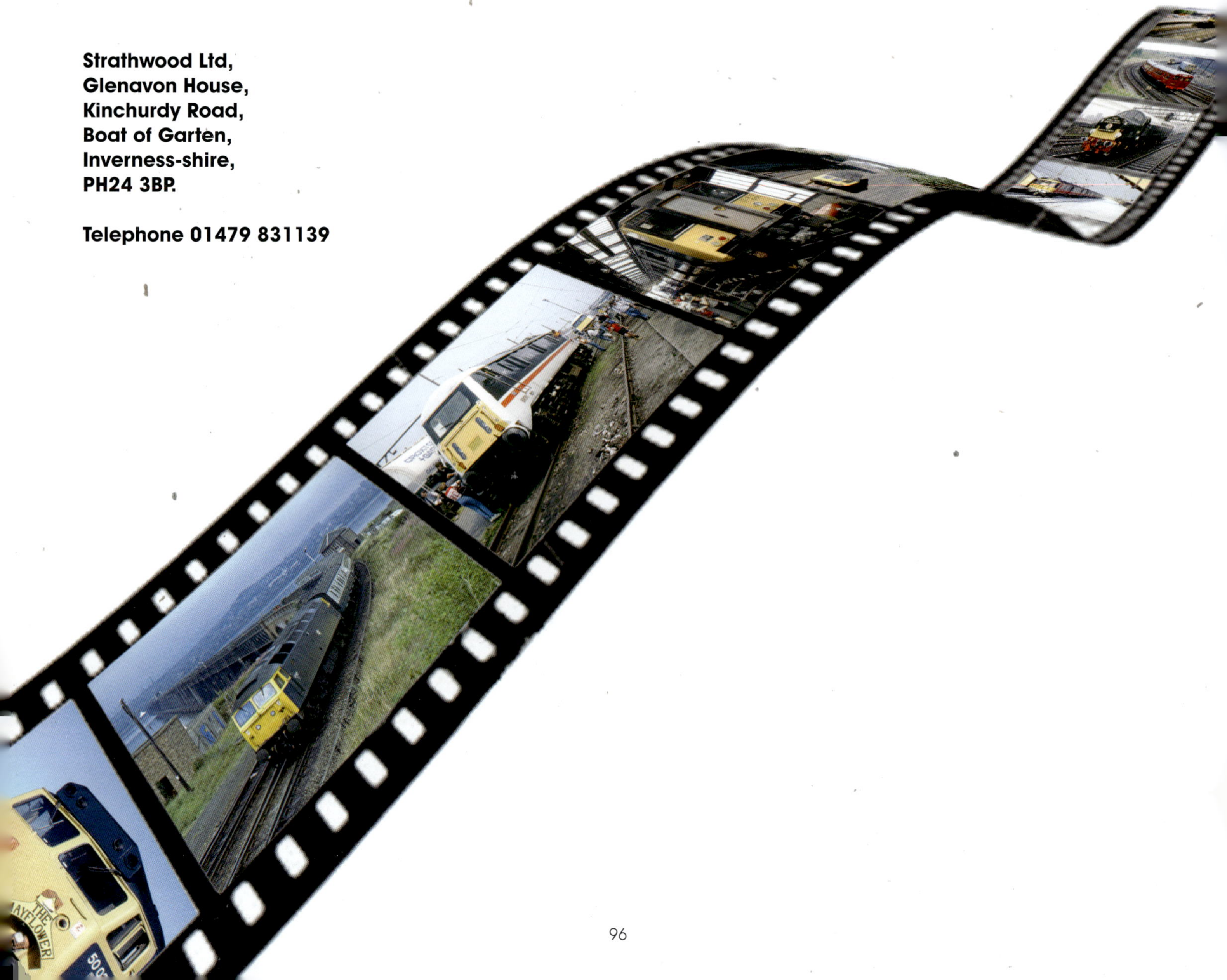